DATE DUE

**A FINE WILL BE CHARGED
FOR EACH OVERDUE BOOK**

HERMAN MELVILLE

LITERATURE AND LIFE: AMERICAN WRITERS
Select list of titles in the series:

LOUIS AUCHINCLOSS	*Christopher C. Dahl*
SAUL BELLOW	*Robert F. Kiernan*
TRUMAN CAPOTE	*Helen S. Garson*
WILLA CATHER	*Edward Wagenknecht*
JAMES FENIMORE COOPER	*Robert Emmet Long*
STEPHEN CRANE	*Bettina L. Knapp*
EMILY DICKINSON	*Bettina L. Knapp*
E. L. DOCTOROW	*John G. Parks*
THEODORE DREISER	*James Lundquist*
ROBERT FROST	*Elaine Barry*
NATHANIEL HAWTHORNE	*Edward Wagenknecht*
JOSEPH HELLER	*Judith Ruderman*
ERNEST HEMINGWAY	*Peter L. Hays*
THE NOVELS OF HENRY JAMES	*Edward Wagenknecht*
THE TALES OF HENRY JAMES	*Edward Wagenknecht*
JACK LONDON	*James Lundquist*
HENRY WADSWORTH LONGFELLOW	*Edward Wagenknecht*
MARY MCCARTHY	*Willene Schaefer Hardy*
H. L. MENCKEN	*Vincent Fitzpatrick*
JAMES A. MICHENER	*George J. Becker*
ARTHUR MILLER	*June Schlueter and James K. Flanagan*
HENRY MILLER	*J. D. Brown*
ANAÏS NIN	*Bettina L. Knapp*
CLIFFORD ODETS	*Gabriel Miller*
JOHN O'HARA	*Robert Emmet Long*
THE PLAYS OF EUGENE O'NEILL	*Virginia Floyd*
EDGAR ALLAN POE	*Bettina L. Knapp*
J. D. SALINGER	*James Lundquist*
SAM SHEPARD	*Martin Tucker*
GERTRUDE STEIN	*Bettina L. Knapp*
JOHN STEINBECK	*Paul McCarthy*
WILLIAM STYRON	*Judith Ruderman*
JAMES THURBER	*Robert Emmet Long*
MARK TWAIN	*Robert Keith Miller*
NATHANAEL WEST	*Robert Emmet Long*
WALT WHITMAN	*Bettina L. Knapp*
THORNTON WILDER	*David Castronovo*
EDMUND WILSON	*David Castronovo*

Complete list of titles in the series available from the publisher on request.

HERMAN MELVILLE

David Kirby

A Frederick Ungar Book
CONTINUUM • NEW YORK

1993

The Continuum Publishing Company
370 Lexington Avenue
New York, NY 10017

Printed in the United States of America

Library of Congress Cataloging-in-Publication Data

Kirby, David K.
    Herman Melville / David Kirby.
        p.   cm. — (Literature and life series)
    "A Frederick Ungar Book"
    ISBN 0–8264–0608–4 (acid-free)
    1. Melville, Herman, 1819–1891. 2. Novelists, American—19th
century—Biography. I. Title. II. Series.
PS2386.K57 1993
813'.3—dc20
[B]   93–12946
                                                      CIP

This book is dedicated with thanks to those who joined me as we discovered more about Melville than either they or I knew: Tommy Allen; the students of ENG 6939–05, especially Doug Burgess, Al Glover, Valerie Jephson, Tom O'Donnell, and Ann Turkle; and of course my friend and colleague R. Bruce Bickley, Jr.

Why then do you try to "enlarge" your mind?
Subtilize it.

— *Moby-Dick*, Chapter 74

Contents

Introduction

Contained within each book is an entire library, and the present undertaking is no exception. It is impossible for me to look at these pages without seeing in them the myriad books about and by Herman Melville, notably the nearly complete Northwestern-Newberry edition of his collected works.

But other, stranger books are at the heart of this volume as well. In many ways, the catalyst for this study is Matteo Guarnaccia's *Taipi,* a seventy-two-page cartoon rendering of Melville's *Typee,* which I discovered a few years ago as I was browsing through the books of an outdoor stall in Venice.[1] As I fumbled with my liras (and my Italian), I wondered what readerly interest would impel an Italian artist and his publisher to produce a detailed and handsomely illustrated edition of an American author's little-known first work.

I had taught Melville for many years and published on "Bartleby" and other works, but when I held *Taipi* in my hands, I experienced literally the extensive spread of Melville's reputation in this century. An author who died in obscurity and who is known primarily for *Moby-Dick,* a work that did not receive significant recognition until long after his death, has, in less than a hundred years, become so venerated internationally that even his relatively minor work is now not only translated but also popularized in comic-book form.

Though Melville did not visit Venice during the Italian tour of 1857, it is diverting to think that his shade watched me as I thumbed my copy of *Taipi* in that sunny Venetian piazza and began thinking my way toward the writing of this book; if so, that spirit might have laughed, albeit sourly. Melville's life does not appear to have been a happy one, in the main; the adjective *resigned* describes his mature outlook more accurately than any other. As a youth, he was something of a drifter (he called one of his autobiographical books

Omoo, which means "rover" in an island dialect) or, to use a literary term, a picaro, one who wandered from place to place and from job to job — from identity to identity, even.

Given the influence of formative years, it is hardly surprising that the preponderance of Melville's writing centers on the figure of the drifter whose goal is survival more than anything else. Tommo, Typee, Mardi, Redburn, White-Jacket, Ishmael, Pierre, Israel Potter, Bartleby, Billy Budd: all of these protagonists are, despite their surface differences, groundless searchers for a standpoint, a position, a place in life and all that goes with it. There are rare moments in Melville's writing when one of those rootless wanderers discovers the security for which he has been searching. But it is a philosophical security rather than an experiential one; moreover, it is a security that includes the apprehension that nothing in life is secure, that, in the words of Amy Clampitt's poem "Nothing Stays Put," "The world is a wheel. / All that we know, that we're / made of, is motion."[2]

Discovering in Venice how far Melville's reputation had traveled, I read him with new eyes and saw how much a traveler he really was. In literary history, the picaro is a person of dubious parentage, no particular occupation, and flexible morals. Though the picaro appears originally in such sixteenth-century Spanish novels as the anonymously authored *Lazarillo de Tormes,* he has come to be an important character in many later novels, possibly because he reflects a basic human character type: for every Huckleberry Finn, there are countless youngsters engaged in solitary battles, and against daunting odds, for identity and personhood.[3] Pitchforked into an uncaring cosmos at an early age, the picaro learns that the world is full of deviltry, often subtly disguised. His youth, poverty, and lack of social standing arrayed against him, the picaro is forced to serve different masters, don various masks, and play whatever roles are required of him, which means that sooner or later he will find himself involved in activities that are distasteful or even repugnant. Such was the life of the young Melville, and such are the lives of his chief protagonists.

In a seminal article on the difference between the European and the American picaro, Pierre-Yves Petillon observes that in the Old World the picaro moves through a vertical hierarchy of class differences, whereas in the New World he moves through a horizontal one marked by different stages of civilization.[4] The result is a paradox: whereas too much mobility is seen as a stigma, the picaro can nonetheless be perceived as a protean figure with unlimited potential.

As chapter 1 of this study demonstrates, there is a sound biographical basis for the presence in Melville's work of both a fondness for and a suspicion of rootlessness — and, one may as well say, a fondness for and a suspicion of permanence, too. Descended from prosperity, Melville had to exchange the stability of home and family for a life among some of humanity's most desperate characters. The suffering he saw and experienced as a young sailor repelled him, yet it was his maritime adventures that gave him his first — in his lifetime, his only — literary success. Even after he had published widely, married, and, by starting his own family, meticulously reclaimed his bourgeois birthright, Melville seemed often to feel the constraints of conventional life; twice in later life he made sea voyages that mimicked the days of his penniless yet carefree youth.

No wonder Melville's work is shot through with ambivalence and outright contradiction. This does not mean that his career defies description; to the contrary, Melville's career poses a singular challenge that this book attempts to meet. In attempting to view Melville as individual, citizen, and artist, I have tried to write neither the biography of an author nor a critical study of the works produced throughout his career; instead, my goal has been to write a biography of that career. The notes to each chapter will guide the reader to the many worthwhile books and essays on Melville's personal history and on his writings, but this book will focus on the life of his most intense self, that is, the writer self: how it developed, how it worked, how it reacted to success and failure.

This is the fourth and, unless circumstances argue otherwise, the last in a series of books I have written, books that, though very different in subject manner, nonetheless are of quite similar construction. They deal with Reconstruction writer Grace King, with novelist par excellence Henry James, and with contemporary poet Mark Strand.[5] Like this book on Melville, each of the others is also the biography of a career. A career as a writer is highly inadvisable; like actors and musicians, most writers do not succeed, and the ones who do have to cope as much with failure as success — and even success can be problematic, as the headlines tell us.

What I have learned from my four subjects, though, and from Melville most definitively — so definitively that, as I say, I see no need to write another book of this sort — is that real writers have two traits in common, no matter how different they may be otherwise. The first is that they never give up. The second trait, and it is closely related to the first, is that they adapt. Even more than the other three writers I have studied, Melville demonstrated throughout his career an aggressive resistance to discouragement; when he found one door closed to him, he looked around until he found another that was open. Even during the decades of public silence that followed the realization that his fictions were no longer marketable, he wrote the poems that alone would have guaranteed him a permanent if minor position in United States literature. And as he lay on his deathbed, he wrote one of the finest short fictions of his or of any time.

The story of Melville's career begins earlier than many readers may think: not with the cannibal tales that made him famous as a young man and that he would later regard ruefully as the primitive works of youth, but with two brief "Fragments from a Writing Desk" that appeared in a small-town newspaper when he was still in his teens. As discussed in chapter 1, the fragments feature two very different styles, one rhetorical and windy, the other plotty and linear. Throughout his career, Melville alternated between the two styles; in his best work, he combined the two in fictions that are both philosophical and adventurous. In other words, the largely rhetorical Melville wrote most of *Mardi* and nearly all of *Pierre* and *The Confidence-Man;* the largely plotty one wrote *Typee, Omoo,* and *Redburn.* The Melville who combined the two styles is, of course, the one who wrote *Moby-Dick* and the timeless short fiction: "Bartleby the Scrivener," "Benito Cereno," and "Billy Budd."

One way of organizing Melville's prodigious, uneven output is to divide it into three groups: (1) the early and lesser-known novels, which are largely fact-based but which include the otherworldly *Mardi;* (2) *Moby-Dick,* the masterpiece equaled in celebrity only by Leonardo's *Mona Lisa* and thus a work known to virtually every literate person in the world, if only through some cartoon or advertisement; and (3) the later work, slightly better known than that of the first period even though it includes the masterful short fiction. From our point of view, Melville seems to tack through the stormy seascape of his life and art like the sailor he was, alternating boredom and risk, success and failure. Not merely a wanderer but a searcher as well, Melville was looking for answers with an earnestness lacked by most authors; his letters and journals make it clear that the questing in his novels is no mere literary device.

If one asks whether or not Melville found (or even knew) what he was looking for, the answer would probably have to be a negative one. Isaiah Berlin divides thinkers into two classes, hedgehogs and foxes; while hedgehogs "relate everything to a single central vision," foxes "pursue many ends, often unrelated and even contradictory, connected, if at all, only in some *de facto* way, for some psychological or physiological cause, related by no moral or aesthetic principle."[6] Berlin suggests that Tolstoy was a fox by nature yet thought he should have been a hedgehog, and the same can be said of Melville. However, whereas Berlin thinks Tolstoy misinterpreted his own achievement and misled others as well, Melville gave up his quest for a "single central vision" in midlife. While he is often and wrongly made to represent the stereotype of the failed artist, Melville has been praised by his fellow novelist John Updike for his dignified withdrawal from a search that could have only ended in futility.[7]

But there are moments in Melville's writing when he seems very close to understanding the world as he describes it, a place of infinite variety whose parts make a coherent whole without losing their individual characters. The most significant of these passages occurs in *White-Jacket;* it is discussed in detail in chapter 2, and again when it is echoed in Melville's later works.

In addition to Melville's own writings, many fine works of biography and literary criticism stand behind this book — so many, indeed, that one is justified in asking if another comprehensive study is even needed. However, of the available introductory texts, each excellent in its way, Leon Howard's study is too brief for anyone other than the most basic student, while those by John Freeman and Newton Arvin are well written but dated.[8]

The revised edition of Tyrus Hillway's Twayne volume has deservedly been the introductory volume of choice in recent times, though it is nearly fourteen years old now.[9] Thus Hillway's viewpoint is somewhat outdated; he makes Melville out to be a kind of writing machine programmed for a brilliant career, whereas readers in the nineties will see him more as a tentative, doubtful, would-be constructor of his own identity. And whereas early studies often treat such works as *Mardi* and *Pierre* as puzzling botches, the present one reflects the more current tendency to see all of Melville's writing as worthy in some way and to view even the seeming anomalies as meaningful parts of the author's total production. For all the strife attending the so-called theory wars that make academe especially exciting these days, current readers are lucky to live in a time when literary texts can be taken on their own terms. Without abandoning traditional hermeneutical readings of literary texts, today English departments benefit from the breadth that comes with such reading strategies as deconstruction and New Historicism. That is to say, poems and stories can now be seen not as mere instructional works that succeed or fail on the basis of simple clarity but as the intricate artifacts of complicated, even contradictory individuals and of particular sets of sociocultural circumstances as well.

Of course, this is the first general book on Melville based on the authoritative Northwestern-Newberry edition with its invaluable notes, whose editors are thanked daily if silently by Melvilleans the world over, as are the officers of the Melville Society of America, publishers of the indispensable quarterly *Extracts*. Academic societies are noted for their savage competitiveness; in the experience of this writer, however, the members of the Melville Society are, as an Ahab-less crew of the *Pequod,* harmonious in their diversity.

This study is respectfully dedicated to those who assisted immeasurably in its formulation. They alone know the sentiments that prompt the agonized howl that concludes chapter 32 of *Moby-Dick* — "Oh, Time, Strength, Cash, and Patience!"

Chronology

1819   August 1: Herman Melville born, New York City.

1830   Family moves to Albany, N.Y.

1832   Father dies.

1839   First professional work, "Fragments from a Writing Desk," appears in a newspaper in Lansingburgh, New York, to which the family had moved the previous year. First voyage (to Liverpool); later Melville will base his novel *Redburn* on this trip. Employed as schoolteacher at the Greenbush Academy in Greenbush, New York.

1840   Travels in the Midwest; later he will use this experience in *The Confidence-Man*.

1841   Sails to the Pacific on the whaler *Acushnet*, where he hears stories of the killer whale Mocha Dick.

1842   Deserts and lives among the natives of Nukuheva. Rescued by the whaler *Lucy Ann,* whose crew later mutinies. Ships out of Eimeo on a third whaler, the *Charles and Henry.* These experiences will form the basis of *Typee, Omoo,* and *Mardi.*

1843   Ships for Boston aboard the naval vessel *United States;* later will base *White-Jacket* on this voyage.

1846   Publishes *Typee,* the first book of his Polynesian trilogy.

1847   Publishes *Omoo.* Marries Elizabeth Shaw on August 4; a New York newspaper heralds the marriage of "MR. HERMAN TYPEE OMOO MELVILLE."

1849   February 16: Malcolm Melville is born. Polynesian trilogy completed with publication of *Mardi*. Publishes *Redburn*.

1850   Publishes *White-Jacket*. Moves family to Arrowhead farm in Pittsfield, Massachusetts. Befriends Hawthorne and publishes "Hawthorne and His Mosses."

1851   Publishes *Moby-Dick*. October 22: Stanwix Melville is born.

1852   Publishes *Pierre*, which prompts one newspaper to run the headline "HERMAN MELVILLE CRAZY."

1853   May 22: Elizabeth Melville is born.

1855   March 2: Frances Melville is born. Publishes *Israel Potter*.

1856   Publishes *The Piazza Tales*, which includes "Bartleby" and "Benito Cereno."

1856–57 Sails to Europe and the Holy Land, where he gathers materials for lectures and the long poem *Clarel*.

1857   Publishes *The Confidence-Man*.

1857–60 Lectures in the North and Midwest.

1863   The Melvilles move from Massachusetts to New York City.

1864   Visits the front in Virginia and gathers material for Civil War poems.

1866   Publishes *Battle-Pieces*. Is appointed deputy inspector of customs in New York.

1867   Malcolm Melville dies of self-inflicted gunshot.

1876   Publishes *Clarel*.

1885   Retires from customs post.

1886   Stanwix Melville dies after a long illness.

1888   Publishes *John Marr and Other Sailors* in a private edition of twenty-five copies.

1891   Publishes *Timoleon* in a private edition of twenty-five copies. Completes draft of "Billy Budd," which will not be published until 1924. September 28: dies, forgotten by the public; one newspaper reporter notes the death of "Henry Melville."

1924   "Billy Budd" is published, and the Melville renaissance begins in earnest.

1

The Life

Loomings

It is a fundamental paradox of biography that the better known someone becomes, the harder he or she is to know. Melville's own granddaughter wrote that "the core of the man remains incommunicable: suggestion of his quality is all that is possible."[1] This book will treat Herman Melville as an extraordinary individual, as a citizen of mid-nineteenth-century America, and as an artist. But the emphasis here will be on the formation of Herman Melville's mind and art; this study is, as I have suggested in the introduction, neither a critical analysis nor a biography per se but the biography of a career.

Yet in order to ask ourselves, "What made it possible for Melville to write *Moby-Dick* as well as the other books so different from his masterpiece?" we must first ask ourselves, "How did such a person emerge from such a period in our culture?" For very different reasons, Melville's times often seem much like our own. When social structures are uncertain, when old institutions crumble before new ones can be erected in their stead, at least one can say that, if one is describing a time of uncertainty, one is describing an epoch of immense opportunity as well. In Melville's day and ours, there is much to fear, much to hope for — above all, much to learn from.

The twin themes of uncertainty and potential must have been doubly evident amidst the chaos of a large, chronically penniless yet ambitious family. One of eight children, Herman Melville was born in New York City on August 1, 1819.[2] Consistent with the times and the Melvilles' desperate attempts at gentility, the five women of the family were economically dependent on the five men. Of these, the father, Allan Melvill, a debt-ridden failure of a businessman, died when Herman was twelve, thus pitchforking him and his brothers into an early and reluctant maturity (after his death, Maria Gansevoort Melvill added the final *e* to the family name). Herman's formal schooling ended at fifteen, and if, according to Eleanor Melville Metcalf, "it was not all child labor during the next five years," still "it was five years of varying fortunes" (13). The Widow Melville led her brood from one house to another and trimmed expenses as best she could while the future author worked variously as teacher, clerk, farmer, and storekeeper.

If Melville became a wage earner at an unripe age, however, he had an early start in the writing profession as well. He had written some letters to the Albany *Microscope* in 1838, but his first professional writings appeared in a newspaper published in a nearby small town. On May 4, 1839, and then again on May 18, the *Democratic Press and Lansingburgh Advertiser* printed "Fragments from a Writing Desk," evidently the first of what might have been a regular column had its author not had to turn his hand to more profitable pursuits. The first of these "Fragments" is a preening letter to a fictional friend in which the author describes three attractive young women in overblown terms; a jocular yet learned piece, liberally sprinkled with quotes from and allusions to classical authors, this "Fragment" is very much in the tradition of letters written throughout history by young men eager to let their friends know that they are connoisseurs of feminine pulchritude, yes, but even more of their own rhetoric.

The second "Fragment" is more substantive. A genuine mystery, it is the story of a man who gets a summons to a clandestine rendezvous; entering a grove, he approaches a villa and is drawn up into it via a basket. Inside, he enters an exquisitely appointed apartment, where he encounters a silent and melancholy beauty before whom he prostrates himself. While the first fragment is largely an expression of a speaker's self-love, the second treats themes that will figure largely in Melville's writing, namely the pursuit of an ideal and the failure to achieve it. Merton M. Sealts, Jr., notes that the second fragment also deals with muteness, a theme central to such later works as "Bartleby the Scrivener," "Benito Cereno," *The Confidence-Man,* and "Billy Budd."[3]

With their common theme of romantic love, these two fragments illustrate the extremes of Melville's writing. The first is a largely empty piece driven more by self-enchantment than anything else, whereas the second is a tensely written and masterful (if incomplete) approach to some important themes. Throughout the rest of his career, Melville vacillated between these two positions: on the one hand, high-blown and self-regarding rhetoric; on the other, careful craft and significant themes.

For the moment, however, the Melville family was in no position to tolerate a belle-lettristic trifler in its midst. Thus, before Melville was to write his great picaresque narratives, he was obliged to live the picaro's life. Herman's older brother Gansevoort was able to arrange a berth for his sibling on the *St. Lawrence,* a medium-sized merchant ship bound for Liverpool with a cargo of cotton and now, among its crew of sixteen, an inexperienced deckhand whose name would nonetheless become synonymous with the seafaring life. Melville's first voyage was not an easy one; indeed, none of them was, given the rude technology of the day, the cramped, often noisome conditions of life below decks, and the authoritarian rule of the ship's hierarchy. But his day-to-day experiences on the *St. Lawrence* not only provided him with material for his novel *Redburn* but may also have taught him something about the management of his own energies, a lesson that would serve him well once he entered full-time the demanding, uncertain profession of authorship.

There was always something to do on the *St. Lawrence:* decks to be scrubbed and then "holystoned," or rubbed with a soft sandstone, rust to be chipped, surfaces to be painted, rigging to be adjusted, and a dozen trades — carpentry, sail making, blacksmithing, cookery, even housekeeping — to be practiced as professionally as possible even though one's time, space, and resources were severely constrained. For fourteen hours a day, every man aboard the *St. Lawrence* was, to a greater or lesser degree, a jack-of-all-trades, and none more so than the menials who did the dirty work, one of whom, at least, was able to exchange eventually the cunning skill mastery of the sailor for the writer's shrewd command of artifice.

Another aspect of his maiden voyage made a lasting impression on Melville, who had not turned twenty yet, and that was his discovery of the slums of Liverpool. The port city had received thousands of immigrants from Ireland, Wales, and the cities of the English Midlands; with unemployment at a high, tens of thousands of Liverpudlians lived in cellars as dank as, yet filthier than, the forecastle of the well-scrubbed *St. Lawrence,* and twice as many more occupied aboveground dwellings that were nearly as bad. Fifteen hundred vessels visited the port each year, and the sailors who manned them found that their every desire could be satisfied in the gin mills and public houses that were pervasive in the dingier districts. Melville dramatizes the suffering of the Liverpudlians by having the eponymous hero of *Redburn* stumble across a starving mother and three children, one of them dead; Redburn busies himself for days, trying to help them, to no avail. The city had recently replaced a feudal system of warring authorities with a more efficient central administration, but reform moves slowly, and it would be nine years before a public health officer was appointed who might have helped the little family. On shipboard, Melville must have at least occasionally congratulated himself on his escape from the poverty of his own family life; now, however, he saw that poverty could, for a widow and her fatherless children, be not only confining but fatal. That such an injustice could transpire not in developing America but in the more established motherland was a strong suggestion that "civilization" had its lethal aspects as well.

Back in New York, Herman took a position as schoolteacher at Greenbush Academy. That a sailor whose own schooling had stopped at age fifteen could become a teacher is another reminder of the unsettled state of Melville's America, particularly with regard to the laxity with which the professions were viewed. Nations as well as individuals mature at their own rates, however, and if the national identity was as yet still uncertain, so was Melville's own. Though his experiences on board the *St. Lawrence* and in the slums of Liverpool would mark his work forever, he was still far from making good on the promise of his early journalistic efforts. For a while, at least, the "Fragments" from his writing desk seemed as though they might be the sum total of Melville's literary output.

Polynesia

Following the closure of his school and a spate of travel-cum-job-hunting, Melville returned to the one trade he was certain of, and in the last days of December 1840 he signed the articles as an ordinary seaman aboard a whaler, the *Acushnet,* which set sail in January for the Pacific via Cape Horn. Melville comments on this transition in the first chapter of *Moby-Dick,* where Ishmael notes that his being made to "jump from spar to spar, like a grasshopper in a May meadow ... is unpleasant enough ... if just previous to putting your hand into the tar-pot, you have been lording it as a country schoolmaster, making the tallest boys stand in awe of you."[4]

But the young Melville was learning a lesson that the mature Melville articulated thus: "Who aint [*sic*] a slave?... however the old sea-captains may order me about — however they may punch and thump me about, I have the satisfaction of knowing that it is all right; that everybody else is one way or other served in much the same way and so the universal thump is passed around, and all hands should rub each other's shoulder blades, and be content" (6). Perhaps Melville was a lifelong champion of democracy and foe of tyranny in part because he was fortunate enough to live in a time and place where one could be a giver of thumps one day and a receiver of them the next.

There were other lessons to be learned on his second voyage. If Melville had absorbed the rudiments of seamanship on board the *St. Lawrence,* on the *Acushnet* he not only mastered the specific techniques of whaling that would make up so much of his masterpiece but also assimilated the lore of the old salts. One of the stories he encountered was a widely published tale about a white-humped sperm whale named Mocha Dick who had stove and sunk the whaler *Essex* in 1819 to avenge the deaths of three of his comrades.

This kernel of fact would grow into a mighty fiction, but the immediate appeal of the Mocha Dick story should not overshadow another important aspect, namely, Melville's evident enthusiasm for the story's author and for the wider possibility of authorship as a profession. The first mate of the *Essex,* Owen Chase, had published an account of the attack that had been widely reprinted; Melville not only met Chase's son (who was serving on another vessel) and questioned him about his father but also convinced himself that the captain of another ship was Owen Chase himself, a point on which Melville's biographers are inconclusive. Melville's lowly place in the maritime hierarchy kept him from questioning the "father" as he had the son, but perhaps that was best, since he could admire the whaler-writer from a distance and perhaps imagine himself in that worthy's shoes. Before Melville could make *Moby-Dick* out of Owen Chase's story, first he had to create the prospect of "Herman Melville, author" from the lineaments of Chase himself.

Life aboard the *Acushnet* provided material for later literary usage, but otherwise the voyage yielded less than Melville expected. A poor catch and a quarrelsome captain (one made doubly quarrelsome, no doubt, by the prospect of scanty profits) were reasons enough to make Melville jump ship on the island of Nukuheva (sometimes spelled "Nuku Hiva" on modern maps) in the Marquesas. In this he was joined by a watchmate, one "Toby," and together the two tars made their way into a valley occupied, they hoped, by the hospitable Happars rather than the reputedly cannibalistic Typees. Of course, their hopes were thwarted, and Melville and Toby ended up in the midst of the islanders they wanted most to avoid. Yet if, as he reports in *Typee,* Melville was concerned enough to keep a careful eye on the meal preparation of his hosts, apparently there was never any real danger that the Typees might make a tasty dinner of the two Americans. Melville and Toby lived among the Typees for nearly a month, a stay whose tone might be said to be one of hospitable detainment.

Besides, the future author suffered from a mysterious ailment of the leg that made it possible for him to do little more than make the anthropological observations that would comprise much of the narrative he would write a few years later. This infection was also the key to Melville's eventual escape from the Typees; when it was clear that more sophisticated medical treatment was required, the islanders let Toby seek help. His first effort was a failure — ironically, Toby was wounded and rebuffed by the very Happars the sailors had sought earlier — but following his second and successful attempt to leave the village, apparently Toby was able to spread the word that a white man was living among the Typees against his will. Good hands being in short supply in these parts, the captain of the Australian whaling barque *Lucy Ann* arranged for Melville's rescue. The account of his escape in *Typee* is melodramatic and almost certainly overdone; for all that is known about the incident, the Typees may have released their "captive" gladly.

On board the *Lucy Ann,* Melville discovered that, following a sojourn among the Polynesians, he had merely gone from a bad ship to a worse one. A number of the crew had deserted rather than put up with the ship's crowded cabins, ineffectual captain, and drunken mate, and two had been sent back to the mainland in chains to be tried for mutiny. When the *Lucy Ann* landed in Tahiti, then, members of the crew mutinied again, this time joined by Melville. The penalties for mutiny were severe, but the captain, realizing how his own position would have been compromised by another report of failure to control his sailors, reacted with disgust more than vengefulness, and the mutineers underwent an imprisonment that does not appear to have been much more onerous than Melville's stay among the Typees.

At Papeete, Melville made the further acquaintance of John B. Troy, the former steward of the *Lucy Ann,* certainly a mutineer, and, if the ship's officers are to be believed, an embezzler as well. For Melville, the attraction was that Troy was reckless, witty, and, most important, well-read. He became friends with the tall, thin blond whose looks accounted for the nickname of "Long Ghost" and who was to become a central character in *Omoo,* where he was also promoted to ship's doctor (as custodian and dispenser of the very medical stores he was accused of stealing, Troy would have been called "doctor" by the crew, though he was far from being a medical man). Together the two slipped away to the nearby island of Imeeo or Eimeo (now Moorea); here, having escaped their unsavory reputations, they meant to make a new start.

The plan worked, and before long Melville had signed up for his third whaling voyage, this time on the *Charles and Henry* (which becomes the *Leviathan* in *Omoo* and the *Arcturion* in *Mardi*). His new captain was just as luckless as that of the *Acushnet* had been, but this time the journey itself, which lasted nearly three months, was not only leisurely but pleasant, as Melville was to recall in *Mardi.* When the *Charles and Henry* put in at Lahaina on Maui, one of the Sandwich Islands (now Hawai'i), Melville actually received an honorable discharge that contrasts markedly with his departures in disgrace from the two previous whalers. Making his way to Honolulu in search of commercial opportunities nonexistent in Lahaina, he worked as a pinsetter in a bowling alley briefly before taking on more remunerative work as a clerk and bookkeeper at a general store. If one compares the image of Melville as pinsetter to the more familiar image of Melville the bearded demigod of American literature, one senses the reality of that peculiarly American lack of identity at this time that was as much a problem for an individual as it was for the larger culture.

In Honolulu, Melville once again saw shocking evidence of a disparity he had noticed elsewhere in the Pacific, namely, the difference between the prosperous lives of the colonists and the picturesque yet wretched existences of the natives. The European powers were bad enough — the French elsewhere, the British here — but even worse were the missionaries, singled out for special animus by Melville in *Typee* and *Omoo*. Repelled by these conditions, perhaps eager for a taste of the sea life again, and certainly impatient for the familiar sights and sounds of home, Melville enlisted in the Navy on August 17, 1843, and shipped out as an ordinary seaman on the frigate *United States,* bound for Boston.

Gatherings

Even though Melville had seen a fair amount of human unpleasantness on his three previous voyages, nothing had quite prepared him for the institutionalized brutality of life aboard the *United States.* After all, the whaling captains had been interested only in such disciplinary measures as would result in shipboard efficiency and therefore the greatest profits. In the navy, however, the stakes were perceived as higher — if battles were to be not only fought but won, then the men needed to have instilled in them the prideful yet obedient character necessary to their patriotic calling. And if the men lacked that character, then it was beaten into them.

When the frigate was barely under way, all hands were called on deck to see two sailors lashed with a cat-o'-nine-tails for striking a sentry and smuggling liquor on board and two apprentices whipped with a lighter "kitten" for fighting and the use of abusive language. Melville was to witness an astonishing number of floggings — in all, 163 seamen and apprentices were thrashed publicly during the time it took the *United States* to make its way from Honolulu to Boston. While it is safe to say, as his writings certainly attest, that he learned a harsh lesson about institutionalized cruelty, one must also wonder if he did not puzzle over human nature and ask himself what made so many men risk such pain and disgrace over such petty gains.

Nor was flogging the most severe penalty that awaited the derelict sailor. In accordance with naval regulations, the articles of war were read to the assembled men on the first Sunday of every month, and the men of the *United States,* including a nervous future author who had recently deserted and then joined a mutiny, were reminded that death was a likelihood for those who breached the laws of the sea and that a man might die for an infraction that would be regarded much less harshly on shore. This was a new of way of looking at things for the Melville who earlier took a rather flexible approach to maritime law and who would argue in both *Typee* and *Omoo* that the wronged sailor was justified in desertion and mutiny. Previously his supple morals allowed him to do as he thought best, but his experiences aboard the *United States* taught him that there was more to morality than well-reasoned (if self-serving) argument: whaling captains might shrug off insubordination, but the state would kill you for it.

Melville's final work of fiction, "Billy Budd," would deal with just such a paradox, and it would have a real-life basis. Not long before, three men had been summarily hanged aboard the USS *Somers* following a brief and little-understood "mutiny"; according to maritime gossip, one of them, a great favorite with the crew, had died shouting, "God bless the flag!" If this were not enough to contemplate, Melville's own cousin, Guert Gansevoort, whom he had idolized as a boy and was now a lieutenant in the navy, had been in charge of the mutineers' court-martial and was now vilified by the sailors of the fleet as the bloodiest of murderers.

The future author had plenty of time to think about such matters during his watches on the main-royal yard, nearly two hundred feet above the deck. The roll of the ship sent him out over the water and then back, and he was so far from the officers who would have otherwise assigned him to busywork that he could only have been hailed down by megaphone. Melville sometimes stayed on the main-royal yard even when off duty, in part, no doubt, to roll over his experiences in his mind but also to escape the peskiness of his superiors.

Melville did look up to some of his shipmates, but not to those who had been put over him by naval command. He addressed his identity problem in part by associating with fellows much like himself or, more accurately, like the self that was developing, that is to say, a menial though an independent-minded and unschooled scholar. His closest companion on the *United States* was Jack Chase, a bookish chap and a linguist as well. Chase discussed with Melville the works of Shakespeare and Homer and Walter Scott, and he recited in Portuguese Camoëns's epic of sea life, the *Lusiad*. There were other literary friends as well: Ephraim Curtiss Hine, an aficionado of sentimental verse; Griffith Williams, a raconteur who spouted original tales of mirth and good humor; and "Edward Norton," a penetrating analyst of literature who later settled down under his real name of Oliver Russ, married, and named his son Herman after the most promising member of this shipboard literary circle.

Authorship

His days as a sailor over, Melville returned to the writing desk from which his earlier "Fragments" had issued. The time was right, certainly; public interest in travel literature was high, and publishers were eager to exploit their readerships' interest in cannibalism, the hardships of the sailor's lot, and other exotica. Encouraged by family and friends, Melville set to work, cheerfully borrowing from such books as Charles S. Stewart's *A Visit to the South Seas, in the United States' Ship Vincennes* whenever memory or invention failed him. The resulting manuscript was turned down by the Harpers but was published in England by John Murray as the *Narrative of a Four Months' Residence among the Natives of a Valley of the Marquesas Islands* and finally in the US by Wiley and Putnam as *Typee: A Peep at Polynesian Life.*

The book was a success; copies sold briskly, and complimentary if anonymous reviews appeared from such figures as Nathaniel Hawthorne, Margaret Fuller, and Walt Whitman. His publishers were concerned over the book's risqué descriptions of island mores, its criticism of the missionaries, and the assertion by some reviewers that the account was less than factual — John Murray was later joined by several reviewers who thought the writing too good to be the work of an ordinary jack-tar. (This explains why the title of the British edition is more literal than that of the American.) At least this latter charge was laid to rest with the sudden appearance of Richard Tobias Greene, the "Toby" of Melville's adventures, who wrote a letter to the Buffalo *Commercial Advertiser* reporting that he would be happy to testify to the accuracy of the entire work.

Thus the writer who was to become one of the most inventive American novelists was put in the odd position of insisting on the truthfulness of his writing — even as he was deeply into the writing of *Omoo,* where, in fact, he was "improving" on his bare narrative with the fanciful products of his imagination. The Melville who steps forth in those pages is one very much like the author himself, only more resolute and compelling, and the same is true of such other characters as the Long Ghost; *Omoo* is the book in which Melville learned to draw the stark, slightly larger-than-life portraits that make later characters as different as Captain Ahab and Billy Budd visible to the mind's eye. As before, though, the ex-mutineer and deserter shrewdly appropriated whatever he needed to accomplish his ends, this time raiding William Ellis's *Polynesian Researches* and other works in order to create the backdrop against which his characters moved. *Omoo* was published in England by John Murray in April 1847 and in America by the Harpers a few weeks later. *Omoo* lacked the tension of the cannibal story that dominates *Typee,* but Melville had matured stylistically and also was able to capitalize on the earlier book's popularity; thus, both for intrinsic reasons and because of its status as an eagerly awaited sequel, *Omoo* became the most widely read of Melville's books during his lifetime.

Typee and *Omoo* sold well enough for Melville to think of himself, not as a rich man, but certainly one sufficiently well-off to contemplate marriage. On August 4, 1847, two days after his twenty-eighth birthday, he married Elizabeth Shaw in Boston; it is a mark of his celebrity at the time that the *New York Tribune* announced the event as the marriage of MR. HERMAN TYPEE OMOO MELVILLE.[5] Elizabeth was the daughter of Chief Justice Lemuel Shaw of the Massachusetts Supreme Court, and Carolyn L. Karcher points out that Melville the deserter and mutineer had evidently decided to exchange his adventurous ways for status, financial security, and a family life that was more stable than the one that Allan Melvill's widow and waifs had endured.[6] As it turns out, Melville's fictions are full of orphans, loners, and picaros rather than happily married patriarchs; on one level, at least, he knew that his own fortunes were destined to be more like his father's.

The couple enjoyed a two-week honeymoon in New Hampshire and Canada; upon their return, however, the exigencies of family life required the new husband to adopt something like bankers' hours in order to write *Mardi.* Clearly intended to build upon and extend the success of the two earlier books on Polynesia, what strikes many present-day readers as *Mardi*'s greatest strengths turned out to be, in the minds of much of Melville's contemporary readership, its greatest flaws. If *Typee* was more or less a barebones narrative and *Omoo* a narrative further embellished with more vivid portraits of individual characters, *Mardi* represents the next logical step: a narrative featuring characters with complex, active minds — too complex and too active, in the opinions of some — and distinctive personalities. In addition, Melville let his own mind run more freely, engaging in the speculations and digressions that would become a hallmark of his mature style, rhetorical fillips and disquisitions of the type that continue either to charm or enrage readers of such classics as *Moby-Dick.*

Of course, virtually every present-day reader will have read *Moby-Dick* first and then come to *Mardi* in order to deepen his or her knowledge of Melville, which gives this readership the advantage of treating the earlier book as a "rehearsal" for the later classic. But Melville's contemporaries had no such advantage and can hardly be blamed for the bewilderment that attended their thwarted expectations. Today we can say that *Mardi* was a necessary stage in the composition of *Moby-Dick,* but readers accustomed to cannibal tales must have wondered if the career of their favorite author was taking a disastrous direction or even sputtering to a halt.

Even Melville's previous publisher was discouraging. A less-preoccupied author might have intimated something sinister from the refusal of John Murray to publish a "romance." John R. Brodhead, a member of the American legation in London and a childhood friend of Melville's older brother Gansevoort, acted as the author's agent and reported bluntly: "It is a *fiction* & Mr. Murray says it don't suit him."[7] The English edition was published, in three volumes, by Richard Bentley in March 1849 and the American, under the usual arrangement, by Harpers in April.

The more fanciful *Mardi* did not please aficionados of the earlier and more factual volumes; the *Boston Post* called it "not only tedious but unreadable," and in England the *Athenaeum* reported that of a hundred readers, ninety would stop reading by the end of the first volume and nine of the remaining ten before finishing volume two.

Generally, other reviewers concurred; almost without exception, the notices were, if not damning, no better than tepid in their praise or their willingness, as in the case of *Bentley's Miscellany* (the production of Melville's own publisher), to describe *Mardi* as a book "which the reader will probably like very much or detest altogether." The author solaced himself with condemnation of the critics as dunces and told members of his circle that time would vindicate him and his book.[8]

No doubt he was sincere in his self-confidence. Of late, Melville had begun to write and speak of other authors in terms that show he was beginning to think of himself as at least a potential equal of theirs. While he quibbled with much of Emerson, for example, he described him to his friend Evert A. Duyckinck in terms that were very much his own, saying he was one of the "whole corps of thought-divers, that have been diving & coming up again with bloodshot eyes since the world began." "I love all men who *dive*," he wrote. "Any fish can swim near the surface, but it takes a great whale to go down stairs five miles or more." He included Shakespeare in this mighty corps as well, calling him "the divine William" and "full of sermons-on-the-mount, and gentle, aye, almost as Jesus."[9] The cetological metaphor says it all, associating Emerson and Shakespeare with greatness on a gargantuan scale yet including them in the watery ken of Melville's own world.

Certainly he needed alliances of this kind, even if he alone perceived them. Reviewers had not been kind, and since his family was growing — Malcolm Melville was born on February 16, 1849, or about the time *Mardi* was published — Melville needed to think as well of his prospects as possible in a suddenly and surprisingly harsh world. If he had deceived himself about *Mardi*'s appeal to the public, at least he had no illusions about what to do next, that is, write exactly the kind of book that his readers had come to expect of him. Accordingly, he fell back on the reliable materials of his own life, this time going back even beyond his Polynesian adventures to his first shipboard experience. *Redburn: His First Voyage* would be, as he wrote Richard Bentley, "a plain, straightforward, amusing narrative of personal experience... no metaphysics, no conic-sections, nothing but cakes & ale."[10]

Based on Melville's experiences on the voyage to Liverpool, *Redburn* was published by Harpers in the US and Bentley in England; it was quickly followed by *White-Jacket,* which dealt with his days aboard the *United States* on his way home from the Pacific. Written in four months, the two books reestablished much of Melville's credibility with his publishers and his readers, though he himself viewed them with a jaundiced eye. He had hoped that *Mardi* would establish him on a level of diver-writers comparable to Emerson and Shakespeare, and now he was being made to please an unsophisticated audience who wanted only a "little nursery tale," as he called *Redburn* in a letter to Richard H. Dana, Jr.[11]

On October 11, 1849, Melville sailed to England (and from there to the Continent) to arrange in person for the British edition of *White-Jacket,* which would appear under the usual arrangement from Bentley prior to American publication by Harpers. His journals and letters from this trip give a picture of a new, more confident

Melville. This sharper portrait is partly due to the fact that the historical record is more complete for this stage of his life, but the clearer image is also due to Melville's increased sense of who he was. The Melville of *Typee* and *Omoo* is essentially context-less, a confused if exhilarated wanderer. But the Melville of the more recent books sees possibilities that the younger one did not. There is more control in Melville's life now and more opportunities for philosophical system building of the type alluded to in *Mardi* and *White-Jacket.* Whereas the younger Melville sought unsuccessfully his individual place in a larger world, this Melville is ready to make worlds of his own.

His personal writings at this time show Melville in his maturity, both as husband and paterfamilias and also as an author trying to split the difference between his own desires and the public's needs. He writes longingly of his "faerie queene" Elizabeth; his homesick recollection of his son Malcolm's query, "Where dat old man?" suggests how he must have really been — as bearded and aloof as an Old Testament prophet, yet responsible and loving in his own way. The faerie queene herself, now burdened with a princeling, was apparently a good deal dismayed at her king's extended absence.[12]

Though more assured, Melville was never entirely at home within himself. Regarding his journal entries during the voyage to England, Geoffrey O'Brien notes that Melville "seems as much a stranger to himself as to the people he meets through his letters of introduction." This personal quality accounts for an idiosyncratic style that O'Brien sees in the journals: "Melville daybooks offer nothing like the full-blown interior arias of Emerson or Thoreau. Melville, it might appear, was not quite so comfortably 'in touch' with himself. His thoughts do not run in well-oiled transitions and cadenzas; they start up without warning; at times they break his sentences apart." He did not write as did the other classic authors of his day, for "against the Transcendentalists' sustained flights of meditation and metaphysical argument, we have Melville's outbursts: jagged, flung from nowhere, belonging nowhere."[13] Though Melville aspired to be a fox, to use Isaiah Berlin's terms (discussed in the introduction to this book), temperamentally he seemed fated to be a hedgehog.

He thought pragmatically of turning out another "nursery tale," this one based on the *Life and Remarkable Adventures of Israel R. Potter,* an account of a Revolutionary soldier who was captured by the British and taken to England, where he spent most of his adult life as an outcast and political suspect. It is easy to imagine the appeal of such a story to one of Melville's divided temperament, and eventually he did write the Potter story. For the moment, though, the sea voyage seemed to have awakened memories of shipboard life, and he was stirred to embark on a much grander enterprise, the writing of *Moby-Dick*.[14] One factor in the composition of his masterpiece was Melville's meeting Hawthorne. The earlier encounter with the captain who may or may not have been whaler-writer Owen Chase was without doubt an epic moment in Melville's self-creation. But Hawthorne was a fleshly embodiment of the kind of genius represented by the distant and all-but-divine Shakespeare; it is not too much to say that Melville looked at Hawthorne and thought, however consciously, What he is, I can be.

The immediate token of his response is his essay "Hawthorne and His Mosses," an encomium to the more accomplished author but also a championing of American genius.[15] Melville likens his new hero to an old one, saying that Hawthorne and Shakespeare share a sense of mirth but an even greater sense of tragedy, that the American novelist's work too is characterized by subtleties evident in Shakespeare: "deep far-away things," "flashing-forths of... Truth" that go unnoticed by those who think of the playwright "as a mere man of Richard the Third humps and Macbeth daggers." And should the reader think the comparison too grandiose, Melville issues a trumpet blast of democracy, cautioning that too much Shakespeare worship is no attitude "for an American, a man who is bound to carry republican progressiveness into Literature, as well as into Life" and contending that "Shakespeares are this day being born on the banks of the Ohio."

In the present age of canon breaking, in which the works of writers who once seemed provincial are now being read with the same reverence once accorded only the so-called masters, it is astonishing to note Melville's prescience as he says, "Let America first praise mediocrity even, in her own children, before she praises... the best excellence in the children of any other land." (Among other things, Melville saw the need for a more professional corps of reviewers, for "there are hardly five critics in America; and several of them are asleep"![16]) In Melville's eyes, of course, there was nothing mediocre about Hawthorne.

The rapport between the two writers was instant and cordial, and the accounts of their meetings ring with jollity. Their kindred spirits

soared in tandem, for the talk was as effervescent as the drink —
champagne is mentioned virtually every time. Sophia Hawthorne,
the novelist's wife, gives a sense of Melville's vivacity during the authors' rendezvous: "Nothing pleases me better than to sit & hear
this growing man dash his tumultuous waves of thought up against
Mr. Hawthorne's great, genial, comprehending silences...such a
love & reverence & admiration for Mr Hawthorne as it is really
beautiful to witness." The telling phrase "growing man" suggests
how obvious it was, even to a casual listener, that Melville was
rapidly making up for lost time in his simultaneous disputation with
and veneration of one whom he regarded as his "innermost Father
Confessor."[17] Too, upon his return, he found that *Redburn* had sold
nicely and *White-Jacket* promised to do as well or better, though he
had to borrow money from his father-in-law to make the down pay-
ment on "Arrowhead," the farm near Pittsfield, Massachusetts, that
became the new Melville home in September 1850.

Melville's confidence in his abilities swelled, as did his certainty
that the materials of his own life could be made into fiction that
the public would buy. From August 1850 to August 1851, then, he
kept mainly to his writing desk, supplementing his own knowledge
of the arcana of whale lore with the usual accounts by other seamen
and impelled all the while by the Shakespearean-Hawthornesque
drive to write a big book, a tragedy in the epic mold; the editors
of the standard edition of *Moby-Dick* have noted that, in writing
his masterpiece, Melville was waging "the most intense aesthetic
struggle yet waged in the English language on this continent."[18]
He had reached the peak of his powers, which is to say that he
wrote better than he knew, producing at last the perfect blend of
autobiographical materials, borrowings from others, and pure fiction in a volume that not only marked the apex of his own career
but became, along with *Adventures of Huckleberry Finn,* one of
two works that are invariably mentioned whenever the idea of "the
Great American Novel" is broached. *Moby-Dick* appeared in 1851
under the usual arrangement with Richard Bentley in England and
Harpers in the US.

In Irons

Melville followed his best book and the one that would make him
famous with a book that all but destroyed his reputation. Cer-

tain that *Moby-Dick* would be displeasing to his feminine readers and possibly the English as well, he decided to serve them up "a rural bowl of milk," as he described *Pierre* in a letter to Sophia Hawthorne.[19] How is it that the genius behind one of the greatest American classics was insufficient to inform its possessor that he was no longer capable, even if he ever had been, of pouring mere rural bowls of milk for his public?

Far from being a bucolic love story, *Pierre* is a bizarre hybrid, something vaguely reminiscent of the romances Charles Brockden Brown had written half a century before, long before Hawthorne had perfected the American form of that genre in *The Scarlet Letter*, yet freighted, especially in the final chapters, with personal grousings. Reviewers were not pleased — even Melville's friend Evert Duyckinck, writing in the *Literary World*, condemned *Pierre's* inconsistencies and overreachings, observing that "the combined power of New England transcendentalism and Spanish Jesuitical casuistry could not have more completely befogged nature and truth, than this confounded Pierre has done."[20]

Fortunately, there was an escape available to the beleaguered would-be romancer, and this was the opportunity of magazine publication, which was both plentiful and even daring in the nineteenth century. Works by Poe and Hawthorne and, later, Twain, James, and Crane, works that today seem unusual and experimental in some way, appeared regularly in a variety of literary journals whose numbers were widely distributed, cherished by their owners, read and reread with care. Although he had published occasionally in magazines, Melville had never really taken advantage of the occasion as these other authors had or would. But this seemed to be the time, and he capitalized on his chance with both industry and inventiveness.

Perhaps the birth of a son (Stanwix, October 22, 1851) and a daughter (Elizabeth, May 22, 1853) helped to quicken his pace. At any rate, within the next two years he wrote and published two of his three best short fictions: "Bartleby the Scrivener," one of the most enigmatic tales of any literature, and "Benito Cereno," a story as adventurous and action-packed as "Bartleby" is (on its surface, at least) staid and tranquil. These two, along with the posthumously published "Billy Budd," are Melville's most widely read works. And deservedly so, for they represent not only his mastery of craft but also the considerable range of his abilities as a writer.

Following the almost universal condemnation of *Pierre,* Melville worked on two projects that were intended to be books: the shadowy "Agatha story," based on an account a lawyer had given him of a woman deserted by her seafaring husband, and another of his autobiographically based tales, this one on tortoise hunting; the material for this book is almost certainly the same as that used in the series of sketches called "The Encantadas," which appears as one of *The Piazza Tales.*[21] Melville even received an advance from Harpers for this latter book, but it, like the "Agatha story," was apparently never completed. However, his difficulties with these two book-length projects and his success as a writer for journals suggested a new approach to publication, and for the first (and last) time, Melville serialized a full-length book in a magazine before publishing it in book form.[22] *Israel Potter; or, Fifty Years of Exile* appeared in *Putnam's Monthly Magazine* before it appeared as a book in 1855, published by Putnam in this country and Routledge in England. On March 2 of that year, a fourth child, Frances, joined the author's hungry brood.

Melville's next novel, *The Confidence-Man,* is not quite as startling in form as *Pierre,* though it rivals the earlier work in its seemingly willful bafflement of the reader. Its greater readability may be a matter of the more flexible plot device, a river journey during which the protagonist appears and reappears in various guises, testing the other characters' grasp of basic Melvillean themes: appearance and reality, good and evil, self-knowledge and self-deception. And there are flashes of humor along the way, although often of a decidedly private kind.

In the end, though, many readers felt that they too had become *The Confidence-Man*'s victims. The themes are launched into the air like so many Indian clubs, with the expectation that the novelist/juggler will catch them all at the end, but Melville could not have been less accommodating. Nothing is resolved at the novel's conclusion, and what has seemed to be an ironic tone turns out to be a sour one. *The Confidence-Man* is an ambitious book — to many readers, an overly ambitious one. As in *Pierre,* the author goes down one discursive alley after another, mapping uncharted territory, at least in his own mind.

From the standpoint of a book-buying readership, *Pierre* and *The Confidence-Man* are failures. Yet both works contain rewards for the serious reader, as chapter 4 will argue. Besides, to Melville, failure was one of the hallmarks of the true thought-diver. In "Hawthorne and His Mosses," he notes that "it is better to fail in originality, than to succeed in imitation. He who has never failed somewhere, that man cannot be great. Failure is the true test of greatness."[23] Certainly anyone who has read *Pierre* and *The Confidence-Man* will not deny their originality.

Measured against his undeniable successes, ambitious yet not entirely successful books like *Pierre* and *The Confidence-Man* make clear what Melville did best. His finest work is based on a firm external structure, either his own experience (*Typee, Omoo*) or another's experience as recounted in a nonfiction narrative ("Benito Cereno"). And he was at his transcendent best when he combined these two types of structure, as he did in *Moby-Dick*. He was less effective as a romancer, though. In his preface to *The House of the Seven Gables,* Hawthorne notes that "when a writer calls his work a Romance, it need hardly be observed that he wishes to claim a certain latitude ... to bring out or mellow the lights and deepen and enrich the shadows of the picture." But he goes on to warn that the same author "will be wise, no doubt, to make a very moderate use of the privileges here stated, and especially, to mingle the Marvelous rather as a slight, delicate, and evanescent flavor than as any portion of the actual substance of the dish offered to the public."[24]

In books like *Pierre* and *The Confidence-Man,* Melville serves up liberal portions of the marvelous, which is, however, never "slight, delicate, and evanescent" but always substantial and robust; the ideas that Hawthorne used as spice to his narrative tend, in Melville's less-successful writing, to take the narrative's place. Paradoxically, the limits of experience not only served to free Melville from the prison of his self-regarding discursiveness but also to inspire his headiest flights of imagination. He used his own materials so well that when he succeeded, no one succeeded better, and if Hawthorne never wrote romances as unmarketable as *Pierre* and *The Confidence-Man,* he never even came close to writing a novel as triumphant as *Moby-Dick.*

Melville's confidence in himself, never very strong anyway, was shaken by the poor critical reception of most of his books and the mediocre sales of nearly all of them — and this the fate of one who had decided to style himself "a man of letters." So it was that Melville embarked on an extended "sabbatical" on October 11, 1856. The trip to Europe and the Holy Land was justified partly by business matters (he was to arrange for an English edition of *The Confidence-Man*), but its main purpose was to allow Melville some distance from the personal and professional problems that deviled him. No doubt his wife had her husband's best interests in mind, but it is also clear that she had no desire to be trapped in a house with four small children and a bearish spouse as well; a sketch entitled "I and My Chimney" and written the year before describes a husband-wife conflict in terms too personal to be entirely invented. So it was that she arranged for a loan from her father so that Melville could make the trip and possibly find the solace that seemed to escape him on his native soil.

He encountered his old friend Hawthorne in Liverpool; the more successful novelist had gone there some months earlier to serve as consul. An excerpt from Hawthorne's journal reveals something of Melville's state of mind at the time:

We took a pretty long walk together, and sat down in a hollow among the sand hills (sheltering ourselves from the high, cool wind) and smoked a cigar. Melville, as he always does, began to reason of Providence and futurity, and of everything that lies beyond human ken, and informed me that he had "pretty much made up his mind to be annihilated"; but still he does not seem to rest in that anticipation; and, I think, will never rest until he gets hold of a definite belief. It is strange how he persists — and has persisted ever since I knew him, and probably long before — in wandering to-and-fro over these deserts, as dismal and monotonous as the sand hills amid which we were sitting. He can neither believe, nor be comfortable in his unbelief; and he is too honest and courageous not to try to do one or the other.[25]

Here Hawthorne takes a pen portrait of Melville that captures him at the height of his intellectual and artistic maturity. Putting aside for the moment the varying degrees of craftsmanship he brought to his individual works, it can be said that all of them bear the hallmarks of their maker's mind as enumerated in this passage: his intellectual courage, his persistent love of inquiry, and above all, his engagement with everything in nature and beyond it, including "everything that lies beyond human ken."

As this is one of the best-known descriptions of Melville's passionate skepticism regarding faith and other religious matters, it would be appropriate here to note that, regarding organized religion, Melville's own daughter is quoted as having said, "I never knew him to go to church but twice that I can remember — All Souls' Unitarian."[26] And as Frances Melville was married in that church, we may presume that at least one of these two occasions was social and familial rather than religious.

Melville's travels took him not only to England but also Greece, the Holy Land (where he gathered material for the long poem *Clarel* that he would eventually write), and Italy. In good spirits, he returned to New York on May 20, 1857, and, as he had done before with magazine writing, Melville took up another profession corollary to authorship that had proved profitable to many of his contemporaries: lyceum lecturing. He hoped to benefit from the national desire to see live authors give animated readings of their works before organizations devoted to the advancement of ideas, and so worked up talks drawing from his recent experiences ("Statues in Rome") as well as the ones he was renowned for ("The South Seas").

A few decades hence, Twain would make a considerable amount of money giving just such talks, but Melville lacked the Twain touch: though he toured the North and the Midwest three times in 1857–60 and netted several hundred dollars each time, Melville clearly had little interest in his new career. Although most of his notices were favorable, some reviewers commented on his low-key delivery and shy refusal to look up from his manuscript; one critic noted "his inexcusable blundering, sing-song, monotonous delivery. It was the most complete case of infanticide we have ever heard of; he literally strangled his own child."[27] Merton M. Sealts, Jr., notes that Melville's lectures are a link between his professional writings of the 1840s and early 1850s and his later private writings in that they represent the author's "skepticism about man's 'progress,' disgust with contemporary institutions, and preoccupation with ancient and primitive societies."[28] But for the moment Melville realized that the lecture hall was not a congenial environment, and so the writer returned to writing.

This time, it was to be poetry. By 1860, he had written enough single poems to comprise a volume. Then, as now, the publication of a first volume of poems is likely to go unheralded, and Melville entertained no illusions about fame and gain as he had with such earlier efforts as *Pierre* and *The Confidence-Man*. He made it clear to family and friends that his hopes were modest and his chances for success so small as to be unworthy of consideration.

He left the poetry collection with his brother Allan, who, as before, looked into the practical matter of publication on Herman's behalf. And, as seems to have become the custom on finishing a manuscript, the novelist-turned-poet turned traveler once more, this time on the clipper ship *Meteor,* bound for Cape Horn.

The *Meteor* docked in San Francisco, and Melville returned to New York by steamer, passing through the Isthmus of Panama. As he had all but predicted, the poetry project had not been favorably received by any publisher. He continued not only to write his own poetry but to read that of others systematically (his markings in the volumes he bought are still in evidence) and to seek, unsuccessfully, a foreign consulship. Melville's personal disquietude was not lessened by the outbreak of the Civil War, although eventually the various battles and their aftermaths provided subjects for his poems. In 1864 he secured a pass to visit the front in Virginia, where he accompanied a scouting party on horseback — as with his shipboard adventures, he undertook the challenge both for its own sake and also for the hope of finding something to write about. The old formula worked again, and in 1866, *Battle-Pieces and Aspects of the War* was published by Harper and Brothers.

Battle-Pieces found the sort of fate Melville had imagined for its earlier, unpublished predecessor; reviews were kind but not enthusiastic, and less than half of the first (and only) edition of 1,260 copies were sold. In need of income, Melville sought government work and was no doubt aided more by his acquaintance with influential people than by the fact that he had just published a volume of patriotic verse. He had already abandoned the unprofitable "Arrowhead," exchanging it in 1863 for the New York City home of his brother Allan, and at age forty-seven, Herman Melville was appointed deputy inspector of customs for the New York harbor, taking the oath of office as 1866 came to a close.

Now celebrated even by those who have never read him, in his own lifetime Melville all but disappeared from public view for nearly two decades. He continued to write, certainly, but without hope of being widely read or even published as other authors were. One wonders what this long period was like for him, and it is easy to imagine Melville as a brooding, self-hating failure. To put it another way, it is almost impossible to imagine him as turning cheerfully to government service and bringing to his duties as customs inspector the same qualities of professionalism that he once brought to his art. It would be a mistake, though, to think of Melville as the stereotypical *poète manqué,* gnashing his teeth as he stares in frustration at the unsullied page. John Updike praises him for "abstaining from a forced productivity"; by doing so, "Melville preserved his communion with greatness."[29]

Besides, Melville the government employee was evidently honest and constant in his labors. A description of Melville at work, though written by his brother-in-law John Hoadley, is so detailed as to suggest a certain amount of objectivity:

Proud, shy, sensitively honorable, — he had much to overcome and has much to endure; but he strives earnestly to so perform his duties as to make the slightest censure, reprimand, or even reminder, — impossible from any superior — Surrounded by low venality, he puts it all quietly aside, — quietly declining offers of money for special services, quietly returning money which has been thrust into his pocket behind his back, avoiding offence alike to the corrupting merchants and their clerks and runners, who think that all men can be bought, and to the corrupt swarms who shamelessly sink their pride; — quietly, steadfastly doing his duty, and happy in retaining his own self-respect — .[30]

Indeed, this work description illuminates qualities that are absent from more literary accounts by such contemporaries as Hawthorne: Melville's integrity, his steadfastness, and his quiet pride.

Melville still "had much to overcome," however. The next year was marked by a personal tragedy of the most wounding kind. His son Malcolm, who had otherwise seemed normal and happy, was found dead in bed with a bullet hole in his temple. The act looked so much like a suicide that a coroner's jury could hardly rule otherwise, but the family was convinced that the act was accidental, as it may well have been: as a member of a volunteer military company, Malcolm had a pistol that he handled carelessly and kept beneath his pillow.

Malcolm's was not the only death during this period; numerous friends and relatives died, including Melville's cousin Henry Gansevoort in 1871 and both his brother Allan and his mother in 1872. In late life Melville was naturally skeptical and dour in outlook, and these deaths impelled him to grapple again with the relation of happiness and belief, this time in a two-volume poem entitled *Clarel.* Clarel is a young American theological student who travels to Palestine (as Melville did in 1857), falls in love, but spends most of his time in extended philosophical conversation with other similar-minded pilgrims. At the conclusion of the poem, Clarel arrives at neither happiness nor belief but at the realization that his means of inquiry — his skepticism — can be an end in itself, that a certain detached uncertainty is the hallmark of a healthy mind. Reviewers seemed more puzzled by this long poem than appreciative of it, and more than one offered the view that it should have been written in prose.

Final Voyage

In the final years of his life, Melville was unknown to the public at large. However, four of his novels remained in print (*Omoo, Redburn, White-Jacket,* and *Moby-Dick*), and he was occasionally mentioned in print as an unappreciated genius. Ironically, various legacies from deceased relatives now made it possible for him to write full-time — just as he seems to have perfected the detachment that left him oblivious to the spurious calls of fame and fortune. At least he was able to resign his customs post in 1885 and prepare his final writings for publication. One of these was *John Marr and Other Sailors* (published privately in an edition of twenty-five copies in 1888), a collection of poems, several of which are preceded by prose headnotes, including the title piece. John Marr is a sailor who retires to a life on the prairie, where the ocean is but a matter of hearsay to the farmers; as isolated as Melville himself was, Marr finds that "the growing sense of his environment threw him more and more upon retrospective musings" in which his departed shipmates become "spiritual companions ... lit by that aureola circling over any object of the affections in the past for reunion with which an imaginative heart passionately yearns."[31] The last book Melville would see into print was *Timoleon*, a collection of poems. It appeared in 1891; like *John Marr, Timoleon* too was issued in a private edition of twenty-five copies.

Though his publishing career was over and though the strains of his personal life continued (his other son, Stanwix, died after a long illness in 1886), during this period Melville completed the work for which he is probably best known after *Moby-Dick*, although it would not be published until several decades after his death. As with other prose works, Melville's long-gestating memory was put into action by someone else's published memoir. He had brooded over the *Somers* affair and his cousin Guert Gansevoort's role in the technically legal yet morally repugnant hanging of the alleged mutineers, including the popular young sailor Elisha Small, who had died shouting, "God bless the flag!" But the appearance of an article called "The Mutiny on the Somers" in the June 1888 issue of the *American Magazine* resolved him to render the incident in fiction.

Evidently he intended to follow his old method of working up the essential plot of the story (though he moved the action from an American to a British ship and eliminated some of the characters) and then giving philosophical and historical weight to it by adding factual material and homiletic disquisitions. But just as he made a more ambitious book of *Moby-Dick* in midcomposition, so too did Melville change the fundamental nature of "Billy Budd" while he was writing it. The stimulus was the appearance of another article, "The Murder of Philip Spencer" (one of the three hanged mutineers and the son of the then secretary of war) in the June 1889 number of *Cosmopolitan Magazine*. This second article painted the characters of the mutiny in even more garish colors, and while it is uncertain that Melville relied on it to any great degree, at least his own characters took on more dramatic stature, with Captain Vere becoming more bookish and philosophical than most naval officers and the villain, Claggart, more complex and sinister than before. A draft of "Billy Budd" was not completed until 1891. Having earlier been placed under the care of a physician who diagnosed him as suffering from an "enlargement of the heart," Melville died on September 28 of that same year.

As a young man, Melville once made a self-mocking yet prescient entry in his journal. On November 4, 1849, the author of *Typee, Omoo,* and *Mardi* described himself in his journal as "H. M. Author of 'Peedee' 'Hullabaloo' & 'Pog-Dog.' "[32] Sounding much like the epitaph on a headstone, this short note proclaimed, with canny accuracy, the sorry state to which Melville's reputation would decline at the time of his death. In effect, Melville guessed that his readership would remember him for the wrong works, and that even these would be misapprehended.

And so it was: when the *New York Times* lamented his passing in an editorial, the author was presented to an oblivious public as "Henry" Melville.[33] Other death notices praised *Typee* and neglected *Moby-Dick;* for a time, at least, Melville had gone down to posterity, as he told Hawthorne he would many years before, as the "man who lived among the cannibals."[34]

"Billy Budd" was not published until 1924. A few years earlier, a number of articles were published commemorating the centenary of his birth; these plus the appearance of a new work, and especially one so attuned to the Modernist temper of the times, impelled a Melville revival that shows no sign of abating. From the 1920s forward, Melville's work has been interpreted every possible way, and "Billy Budd" — which can be taken as a tale of openhearted acceptance, stoicism, or bitter cynicism, depending on the reader — only illustrates once again the richness of Melville's art. More than any other author of his century, and, indeed, of any time, Melville is the consummate literary chameleon, changing shape on the page as surely as the Confidence Man took on different guises during his baffling night journey. Let us learn from his transformations.

2

The Early Novels

As distinctive a writer as he is, Melville shares some concerns with the other authors of his day. His (and their) books are shot through with individuals fighting for control over the ownership of their own minds and bodies: seekers of freedom, in essence. Yet these would-be autonomous individuals usually discover that autonomy has its limits, even its drawbacks. One of the great dangers of nineteenth-century life lay in the commodification of the individual, the turning of a human being into a thing: for example, a factory worker who figures as an insignificant and easily replaced cog in a giant manufactory, or even (in America) a slave. So the writings of this period often show persons clinging to their personhood, sometimes at great cost, even the cost of a life.

This zeal for individual freedom explains the vast number of escape novels in the nineteenth century. As industry developed in the northern United States and agriculture in the South, images of commodification (being turned metaphorically into something like a tool in a factory, say, or turned literally into a slave) begin to recur in the fiction. To avoid becoming the property of someone else, whether a manufacturer or a plantation owner, one often has little choice except to exchange "civilized" life for the wilds; hence the importance of the picaro or vagabond to the fiction of this period.

Thus the hero of Poe's *The Narrative of Arthur Gordon Pym of Nantucket* escapes his neoclassical heritage and makes a headlong romantic flight to the South Pole, just as the protagonist of *The Adventures of Huckleberry Finn* leaves the suffocating town he was born in for the freedom of the river (not the river towns, which are as bad as his own, but the river itself). In more domestic fiction, the pattern of flight is often replaced by the complementary one of suffocation: Henry James's novels are full of prisoners and jailers, such as the wealthy Isabel Archer and the sinister Gilbert Osmond who snares her in *The Portrait of a Lady,* and even a "popular" novel like Harriet Beecher Stowe's *A Pink and White Tyranny* shows how husbands and wives vie for control over one another.

The characters in each of these novels want freedom, yet they want to escape the loneliness that accompanies complete independence. Each, therefore, seeks a companion: Pym finds Dirk Peters, Huck finds Jim, the spouses in the other two novels find each other, however unsatisfactory the liaison. Egalitarian companionship has its perils, especially the spousal variety (the greater the intimacy, the greater the risk), but it is the only worthwhile middle position between the oppressive condition of being owned by someone else and the lonely condition of self-ownership.

Work after work from this period examines this paradox, and many of them dramatize extremes. For example, Walt Whitman's *Leaves of Grass* is among the most joyful texts of the century, urging the twin pleasures of roving and friendship. And one of the saddest stories is that of poor Hyacinth Robinson, protagonist of James's *The Princess Casamassima,* who sees no way out of his static life and kills himself when he is betrayed by his former companion Paul Muniment.

As we have seen, the search to be free and yet intimate with others was more than a literary idea to Melville, since his days as a sailor were considerably brightened by his discovery of fellows like himself, the learned menials who hauled lines and kept watch yet talked of books in their off hours. His memories of these men ascribe to them a preciousness that cannot be overstated in a universe in which each of us is an orphan doomed to oppression or loneliness or both. As Ishmael will tell us in the next chapter of this study, to Ahab sailors are "tools" to be used in his destructive quest; the individual sailor's only hope of escaping this fatal objectification is friendship and solidarity among others of his kind.

Even friendship has its limits, however, and the aging Melville seems to have taken philosophy as his best and, finally, his only companion. As we see him now, though, he is still young, and his view of human relations is considerably more sanguine. The individual, the larger world that wants to own him, the friend who provides intimacy without ownership — these are Melville's concern, beginning with his first book.

Typee

Based more on fact than on fantasy, *Typee* is nonetheless most conveniently called a novel, made up, as it were, like the bulk of Melville's productions, from his own experiences, his borrowings from other authors in the same field, and his skill as a creator. While *Typee* is more fact-based than *Mardi*, say, its author nonetheless took considerable liberties, expanding his four weeks on the island to four months. Melville's first novel was inspired by the events that took place between July 9, 1842, when he and a companion deserted the *Acushnet* (called the *Dolly* in the book) and August 9, when he was rescued by the *Lucy Ann* (which became the *Julia*).

Finding life aboard the *Dolly* intolerable, the narrator resolves to run away once the ship is safely docked in the harbor of Nukuheva in the Marquesas.[1] Aware that a deserter will invariably appear to be in the wrong, however, he takes pains to justify his cause: "When I entered on board the Dolly, I signed as a matter of course the ship's articles, thereby voluntarily engaging and legally binding myself to serve in a certain capacity for the period of the voyage; and special considerations apart, I was of course bound to fulfill the agreement. But in all contracts, if one party fail to perform his share of the compact, is not the other virtually absolved from his liability?"[2] Overlooking the fact that law and custom were not only entirely on the side of the ship and against the individual sailor but also extremely severe in their punishment of even the slightest infraction (as Melville himself well knew), the narrator answers his rhetorical question with a resounding affirmative. Melville would be concerned throughout his career with the conflict between the letter of the law, which is against him in this case, and its spirit; indeed, his last work, "Billy Budd," is also his most thorough examination of this conflict. For the moment, though, the spirit of the law is clear, for life on the *Dolly* had been terrible indeed: "The usage on board of her was tyrannical; the sick had been inhumanly neglected; the provisions had been doled out in scanty allowance; and her cruizes [*sic*] were unreasonably protracted" (21). There is no choice, then, but desertion.

However, the narrator's choice is complicated and his narrative given tension by the presence on the island of the Typees, who are "irreclaimable cannibals" — the very word "signifies a lover of human flesh" (24). Our narrator is quick to note that the stereotype of the "savage" is a false one, for there are both good and wicked islanders as surely as there are good and wicked whites. And the possibility of ending up as the main course in some native feast notwithstanding, he fairly wriggles with pleasure when he first steps foot on the island; rushing into a shady grove, he exclaims, "What a delightful sensation did I experience!... How shall I describe the scenery that met my eye, as I looked out from this verdant recess! The narrow valley... seemed from where I stood like an immense arbor disclosing its vista to the eye, whilst as I advanced it insensibly widened into the loveliest vale eye ever beheld" (28). Surely such an Eden is worth the risk of being devoured by aborigines, certainly a risk of which there is, as of yet, no evidence.

All that is lacking to our flight-minded narrator is a kindred spirit, a companion to share the fruits of Paradise and mitigate its loneliness. Such a one is Toby, an introspective and increasingly melancholy tar whom the narrator correctly guesses to be, like himself, a would-be deserter. A certain air of mystery sets him apart from the common run of sailors, for Toby is "one of that class of rovers you sometimes meet at sea, who never reveal their origin, never allude to home, and go rambling over the world as if pursued by some mysterious fate they cannot possibly elude" (32). Indeed, "Toby" is a pseudonym, "for his real name he would never tell us" (31). This vaguely sinister assertion is of little import to a narrator who is variously known as Tomtoo, Typee, Paul, and Taji in the Polynesian trilogy and who is joined in his pseudonymity by other notable characters in American literature: Chillingsworth of Hawthorne's *Scarlet Letter,* the Huckleberry Finn who changes his name so often during his river voyage that he himself becomes confused, the "Daisy Miller" of Henry James who is actually Annie P. Miller, and the protagonist of *Moby-Dick,* who adopts the name of an Old Testament outcast and introduces himself by saying, not "My name is...," but "Call me Ishmael." (Other Melvillean protagonists will take on new names, including those of *Redburn, White-Jacket, Israel Potter,* and *The Confidence-Man.*) What more like-minded companion to accompany one on the search for a new life?[3]

And a true friend will prove necessary on the quest our narrator undertakes. Trying to put distance between themselves and the ship, the two deserters scale a mountain with the expectation of descending into a manageable landscape, one the eye can encompass and the feet traverse. Instead, they find themselves in a kind of cloud forest, with no pathway ready to hand and, worse, none of the fruit they had expected in abundance. This is, on the surface, an occurrence so common in ordinary life as to seem unworthy of comment. But it presages much of the rest of *Typee* and of Melville in general as well as many books by other authors of this period. For what the two men encounter is neither what they expect (a wild yet negotiable landscape) nor its opposite (a desert, for example, or a village) but an almost-impossible-to-characterize state of formlessness that suggests no one form of action over another. In this sense *Typee* recalls novels as different as *The Narrative of Arthur Gordon Pym of Nantucket* and *The Scarlet Letter,* novels in which the characters often seem stuck in a dreamworld in which the most tangible reality is their own helplessness.

In their miserable aimlessness the two wanderers finally discover a footpath but realize, as did Robinson Crusoe in another novel, that the human presence suggested by this sign may, in fact, be a hostile one. Night descends, and rain begins to pour down on the two hapless adventurers, whose attempts at hut building have proved as inept as their other skills: "The rain descended in such torrents that our poor shelter proved a mere mockery. . . . I have had many a ducking in the course of my life, and in general cared little about it; but the accumulated horrors of that night, the death-like coldness of the place, the appalling darkness and the dismal sense of our forlorn condition, almost unmanned me." And "as for poor Toby, I could scarcely get a word out of him. It would have been some consolation to have heard his voice, but he lay shivering the live-long night like a man afflicted with the palsy, with his knees drawn up to his head" (46). So much for the benefits of companionship.

However, just as Dante had to descend into the Inferno before rising to Paradise, so it is with the two wanderers, who, the next day, find themselves in a landscape so beautiful as to suggest "enchanted gardens" (49). But whose gardens are they? The narrator fears that they are looking into the valley of the ferocious Typees, while Toby insists that so beautiful a place could only be the environs of the benign Happars, the Typees' peace-loving counterparts. At length they come upon a native couple, a slender, naked boy and girl whom they follow to a village. Their attempts to communicate with the villagers prove to be futile, yet the two friends find themselves slipping rather easily into the rhythms of village life. Before long, they befriend any number of these gentle, graceful, artistically inclined people — who turn out to be, of course, the much-maligned Typees. The narrator's favorite among these is the beauteous Fayaway, whose charms are enumerated at length. In one episode, Fayaway removes her single garment of tapa cloth and uses it as a sail; the narrator reflects that "we American sailors pride ourselves upon our straight clean spars, but a prettier little mast than Fayaway made was never shipped a-board of any craft" (134). This is an inoffensive phrase by present-day standards, but it was sufficiently risqué in Melville's day to trouble both his publishers and reviewers.

The two sojourners vacillate between fear and contentment; at one point they wonder if they will be eaten during a great feast, but as it turns out they are merely fed. A far greater danger is posed by the narrator's increasing lameness from a leg injury that does not respond to the Typees' herbal remedies. Toby sets out to obtain effective medicine from the surgeons of the French fleet anchored in the bay of Nukuheva, but before long he returns with a grievous head wound; he has been attacked by the Happars, who are guilty of the blood lust wrongly attributed to the Typees. Within a few days, Toby recovers enough to investigate reports of a boat sighting; at this point he disappears from the narrative, never to return. The narrator cannot decide whether Toby has gone for the medicine or simply left him in the lurch, and since the natives are silent on the subject, he wonders if his erstwhile shipmate has met with foul play. As when he found himself on the mountaintop the first day, the narrator is in a moral and epistemological fog symptomatic of his overwhelming feeling of helplessness. This profound anxiety must be seen as part of the narrator's lack of identity; in *A Connecticut Yankee in King Arthur's Court,* Hank Morgan is able to act decisively in a much more daunting situation precisely because he knows who he is and what he can do, but not our uncertain narrator. Unable to do anything, then, he does nothing.

Except narrate — crippled and dispirited, the narrator becomes a passive eye at this point, and the bulk of the remaining chapters are given over to the island's natural history as well as Typee manners and mores. The story proper is abandoned; instead, there are descriptions of feast-day dances and rituals, Typee theology, burial customs, tattooing, and makeup. This is not to say that Melville has abandoned his authorial duty, for one traditional purpose of

the novel has always been to inform, usually with the effect of let-
ting the reader know that he or she is rather better off than the
characters described. Certainly this is a requirement of travel literature of the early nineteenth century, and it is a requirement that
is amply met in *Typee:* readers come away with both a full knowledge of island life and the certainty, thanks to the narrator's subtle
if unmistakable condescension, that their own lives are superior.

For the most part, the narrator is treated with courtesy and defer-
ence, yet he is given to understand that he is a prisoner, even though
there is no apparent reason for his captivity: "Had I been in a situation to instruct them in any of the rudiments of the mechanic
arts, or had I manifested a disposition to render myself in any way
useful among them, their conduct might have been attributed to
some adequate motive, but as it was the matter seemed to me inexplicable." His confusion is made the greater by his solitude, and
in his despair he turns on his old shipmate: "No language can describe the wretchedness which I felt; and in the bitterness of my soul
I imprecated a thousand curses on the perfidious Toby, who had
thus abandoned me to destruction" (120). And their general benign
treatment of him notwithstanding, the narrator has reason to wonder if some of his earlier fears of the Typees are not well-grounded:
in one of the later chapters he comes across some islanders hastily
putting away three shrunken heads (one a white man's) and also
discovers the remnants of a cannibal feast. A less-troubling threat
yet one he resists vociferously comes when the Typees indicate they
wish to tattoo him. To be tattooed would mean submitting to the
authority of the "state," such as it is, and just as the narrator does
not want to give his body to be eaten, so too does he oppose anyone
else's domination of his soul.

In the final chapter, the narrator makes a mad dash onto a whaleboat that has been sent on a rescue mission; the islanders try to
restrain him, but he makes good his escape, and in short order he
finds himself aboard the *Julia,* whose captain is short of crew and
therefore desirous of recruiting every available hand, regardless of
the circumstances. Delighted as he is to be free again, the narrator
concludes his story on a note of loss; the final paragraph reads, in
its entirety, "The mystery which hung over the fate of my friend and
companion Toby has never been cleared up. I still remain ignorant
whether he succeeded in leaving the valley, or perished at the hands
of the islanders" (253). An appendix reports on Toby's fate: himself

recruited to an undermanned ship, he is forced to sail while the narrator is still in the hands of the Typees, and the two men, each of whom believes the other to be dead, will not be reunited for years. What began as an adventure ends as a meditation on humankind's solitary condition.

Book after book of Melville's will begin and end just this way. In time, his grasp of the individual's essential loneliness will become part of a larger metaphysic. For the moment, though, his thoughts are emotional and autobiographical rather than philosophical. In later books, loneliness will become a condition the Melvillean persona acknowledges and even cultivates. For the moment, though, it is a decidedly disagreeable state that has only one cure: another adventure.

Omoo

The first-person narrator who introduces himself at the beginning of *Omoo* is clearly the same one who figures in the pages of *Typee*. Indeed, the second novel begins with a brief summary of the conclusion of the first, as though reminding the reader of the pleasures of that earlier text and thereby promising even greater pleasures to come.

But how changed this narrator is! He appears as a kind of half-breed, no longer an American sailor but a peculiar sui generis jungle creature whose "appearance was calculated to excite curiosity [among the crew of the whaler that has rescued him]. A robe of the native cloth was thrown over my shoulders, my hair and beard were uncut, and I betrayed other evidences of my recent adventure."[4] So the book opens, at least, with a narrator more sure of himself than the one the reader leaves behind in *Typee* — more self-created, as it were, one who appears to act as least as much as he is acted upon.

This is not an atypical Melville opening; often his main characters begin as dauntless adventurers and end as helpless waifs. For the moment, though, and indeed, throughout most of the text, the *Omoo* narrator is drawn with bolder strokes than his predecessor. *Omoo,* or "rover," is a fitting sobriquet for the peripatetic hero-narrator, a much more active protagonist than the captive one of *Typee*.

His story, too, has more literary qualities than the often merely episodic *Typee.* As before, Melville manipulated time as he saw fit, for example, expanding the narrator's two-week stay on the island of Imeeo to two months. But whereas *Typee* often read as a journal might, *Omoo* benefits from fully developed characters and highly crafted dialogue. The dramatis personae include a somewhat effete Captain Guy, an alcoholic though able mate named Jermin, a learned doctor with egalitarian principles who will become the narrator's closest friend, and an extraordinarily ugly ship's carpenter called "Chips" and, ironically, "Beauty." The following dialogue is from a scene in which the captain discovers an irascible Jermin in the act of struggling with Chips, who has neglected his watch:

"Why, why," he began, speaking pettishly, and very fast, "what's all this about? — Mr. Jermin, Mr. Jermin — carpenter, carpenter; what are you doing down there? Come on deck; come on deck."

Whereupon Doctor Long Ghost cries out in a squeak, "Miss Guy, is that you? Now, my dear, go right home, or you'll get hurt."

"Pooh, pooh! you, sir, whoever you are, I was not speaking to you; none of your nonsense. Mr. Jermin, I was talking to *you*; have the kindness to come on deck, sir; I want to see you."

"And how, in the devil's name, am I to get there?" cried the mate, furiously. "Jump down here, Captain Guy, and show yourself a man. Let me up, you Chips! Unhand me, say! Oh! I'll pay you for this, some day! Come on, Captain Guy!"

At this appeal, the poor man was seized with a perfect spasm of fidgets. "Pooh, pooh, carpenter; have done with your nonsense! Let him up, sir; let him up! Do you hear? Let Mr. Jermin come on deck!"

"Go along with you, Paper Jack," replied Beauty; "this quarrel's between the mate and me; so go aft, where you belong!" (18)

The silly names, false voices, mixture of high and low styles, and general irreverence recall the interplay among any of Shakespeare's "rude mechanicals." That the officers are made to sound like members of a lower class may be a sign of Melville's greater sympathy for that group, although clearly he is more attracted to the doctor than to any other individual, and that because of the doctor's most unegalitarian erudition and learning.

The narrator's enhanced awareness of class distinctions is another characteristic that sets *Omoo* apart from *Typee.* The situation of the latter book, after all, is rather static, for the most part. Here, however, the narrator not only finds himself within the rigid class structure of the ship but also has the opportunity to witness encounters of all sorts between larger groups: ships' crews, island authorities, missionary society, native tribes, and so on. From all these interactions, one moral may be drawn: whenever distinctions can be made between one group and another, people will act badly. A typical incident closes chapter 6, when the otherwise mild Captain Guy fires a pistol into a crowd of natives, wounding one and prompting the narrator to remark that "wanton acts of cruelty like this are not unusual on the part of sea captains landing at islands comparatively unknown.... The islanders coming down to the shore have several times been fired at by trading schooners passing through their narrow channels; and this too as a mere amusement on the part of the ruffians," for "it is almost incredible, the light in which many sailors regard these naked heathens. They hardly consider them human. But it is a curious fact, that the more ignorant and degraded men are, the more contemptuously they look upon those whom they deem their inferiors" (25).

Withal, the South Pacific seems largely inhabited by a rough race of men. On meeting a "renegado," a once-poor and orphaned Englishman named Lem Hardy who has gone native and become an important military leader in one of the tribal wars, the narrator observes that "it is just this sort of men — so many of whom are found among sailors — uncared for by a single soul, without ties, reckless, and impatient of the restraints of civilization, who are occasionally found quite at home upon the savage islands of the Pacific. And, glancing at their hard lot in their own country, what marvel at their choice?" (28). The narrator seems both horrified at Hardy's life among the islanders and reconciled to it; a onetime deserter who appears in native garb at the beginning of this book, perhaps he sees in the tattooed and wolfish "renegado" a version of himself.

The narrator's affinity for the solitary and the fatherless suggest that he is returning to a realization of that sense of isolation that marks so much of *Typee*. Thus chapter 12 begins with his observation that the mirthfulness of some of the sailors often contrasted shockingly with the grave illness of others and concludes, "Thus, at least, did it seem to me, though not to others" (44). In this same mood, he witnesses the sea burial of one of his former shipmates just two pages later and observes, "Behold here the fate of a sailor! They gave him the last toss, and no one asks whose child he was" (46). In part because of humankind's innate solitary nature and in part because of the inevitable friction between distinct classes, communities do not seem to hold together very well in Melville's novels, and before long there is a mutiny aboard the *Julia*.

The circumstances are these: the captain himself being too sick to command, Mr. Jermin the mate takes charge for the sail from the Marquesas to Tahiti, which latter appears as "a fairy world, all fresh and blooming from the hand of the Creator" (66). The plan is to put the captain ashore for a period of recuperation while the others resume the search for whales as quickly as possible. But the would-be Adams aboard the *Julia* will not be denied their Eden, so they refuse to work at all.

The men make an appeal for justice to the English consul, a disagreeable fellow who sides with Jermin, and instead the sailors find themselves incarcerated in a rude "Calabooza Beretanee" (from Spanish *calabozo,* or "dungeon," and the pidgin word for "Britain"). Captain Guy regains his health, recruits a new crew to replace the imprisoned one, and the *Julia* sails away.

As it turns out, life in the "Hotel de Calabooza" is a good deal merrier than one might suppose: the men seem to be able to come and go with relative freedom, and liquor, if not especially choice, nonetheless seems to be in good supply. As when he was captured on Nukuheva, the narrator reverts to observation and reporting, as, for example, when he decries the deleterious effects of the so-called civilizing process imposed upon the Tahitians by the European authorities and the "mickonarees" (missionaries). William Braswell notes that Melville "showed when he wrote *Typee* and *Omoo* that what he had seen had convinced him that some people would have been better off if they had never heard of Jesus Christ. He had learned a great deal about the incompetence and even insincerity of many who professed to guide others to Christian salvation."[5]

The year after Melville arrived on Tahiti, it became a French protectorate and later a colony, but at this time there were both British and French (or "Wee-Wees," as the Tahitians called them) on the island. Here, as in *Typee,* the narrator details the Europeans' prohibition of the harmless and colorful pastimes of the natives and the replacement of these pleasant activities with the listlessness and sensuality that are inevitable by-products of boredom. The islanders were discouraged from the practice of handicrafts because such items as clothing and eating utensils were replaced by similar articles of European manufacture. And more seriously, the narrator points out how imported disease has decimated the indigenous population. His criticism of the Europeans notwithstanding, though, our adaptable protagonist cheerfully (if briefly) converts to Catholicism and attends Mass regularly in order to enjoy the good food and drink served by the Wee-Wees. Ever uncertain of profession or legal status or even his own name, the thirsty narrator abandons his dry morals as easily as he jumps ship.

Facing up once more to his chronic dissatisfaction with communal life, the narrator decides to strike out on his own, but, as in *Typee*, with a companion: "For my own part, I began to long for a change; and as there seemed to be no getting away in a ship, I resolved to hit upon some other expedient. But first, I cast about for a comrade; and of course the long doctor was chosen" (199). The English consul is eager to get rid of his merry charges, who seem to be enjoying life in the "Hotel de Calabooza" more than he had intended; so it is that, in the manner of the pseudonymous characters who appear in all nineteenth-century American fiction and seem especially populous in Melville's South Pacific, Doctor Long Ghost and the narrator are reborn as Peter and Paul and contract to work as field laborers on the nearby island of Imeeo.

Whereas work aboard ship was an all-or-nothing proposition, in which spasms of frenetic activity alternated with long periods of inaction ideal for our dreamy and meditative narrator, field labor proves to be hot, arduous, and constant. Worse, the planters soon begin to pamper Doctor Long Ghost, whom they see as "a man of science," whereas the narrator strikes them as "a mere ditcher" (231). This rank class discrimination goes against the grain of democratic companionship, but as the doctor is an egalitarian at heart, he is easily persuaded to conclude this unfair episode by setting out with the narrator for the nearby island of Tamai — with, as it turns out, the good-natured planters' cheerful acquiescence.

But the class discriminations of the nineteenth century are not so easily eluded and Paradise not so easily found, even in the South Pacific. No sooner are the two adventurers agreed on settling down among the accommodating Tamai islanders than they are compelled to flee before the advancing mickonarees, who threaten to seize them under an act designed to suppress vagrancy, for "as friendless wanderers over the island, we ran the risk of being apprehended as runaways, and, as such, sent back to Tahiti. The truth is, that the rewards constantly offered for the apprehension of deserters from ships, induce some of the natives to eye all strangers suspiciously" (249). Armed with a kind of passport from one of the planters, who testifies to their good characters, they continue their tour, making friends among the natives, dining well everywhere, and gazing on beautiful island women with young men's sense of connoisseurship.

Our footloose democrats seem to find democracy everywhere on the road and nowhere among the established communities that beckon yet ultimately reject them; they are indeed a pair of "omoos." An impromptu audience with the reclusive Queen Pomaree of the village of Partoowye not only results in the banning of strangers from the palace but also seems to remind the wanderers that they are white men and sailors, not the islanders they admire and often wish to dwell among. Accordingly, the narrator arranges to ship out on the *Leviathan* (the *Charles and Henry*, in Melville's actual experience), whose captain does not trust the doctor, correctly believing him to be from Sydney, a city notorious for its rowdies ("If there be a mutiny on board a ship in the South Seas, ten to one a Sydney man is the ringleader" [313]). So the two part company. As Doctor Long Ghost steps into the canoe that will take him back to Imeeo, the narrator says, "I shook the doctor long and heartily, by the hand. I have never seen or heard of him since" (316). As at the end of *Typee*, the narrator who joined with a kindred soul to flee the injustice of maritime authority finds himself where he started. That is to say, he finds himself among humanity again, yet utterly alone.

Mardi

Mardi is the last novel of the so-called Polynesian trilogy; paradoxically, it is the most ambitious, yet, at least in the eyes of Melville's contemporary reading public, the least successful of his works to date, the book that is clearly a rehearsal for *Moby-Dick*, yet one so outsized and ambitious that it left much of Melville's readership sputtering in its wake. In length, *Mardi* is bigger than both its predecessors combined: *Typee* runs to 271 pages in the standard edition of Melville's works, and *Omoo* to 316, while *Mardi* is 654 pages in length. More substantive differences are set out in an uncharacteristically brief preface:

Not long ago, having published two narratives of voyages in the Pacific, which, in many quarters, were received with incredulity, the thought occurred to me, of indeed writing a romance of Polynesian adventure, and publishing it as such; to see whether, the fiction might not, possibly, be received for a verity; in some degree the reverse of my previous experience. This thought was the germ of others, which have resulted in Mardi.[6]

In making a "romance" of his experiences in the South Seas, Melville availed himself of the authorial latitude invoked by Hawthorne in his preface to *The House of the Seven Gables;* that is to say, he indulged his whim to graft a personal philosophical stamp onto what would otherwise be barebones photographic observations of life among the islanders. If he failed to heed Hawthorne's advice to indulge this whim minimally, at least he used his new status as a romancer to practice techniques that would become Melville trademarks in *Moby-Dick* and the great short works of his late career.

For instance, there is a new narrative voice in *Mardi,* one more rhapsodic than reportorial. Related to this heightened tone is a greater erudition — by freeing himself from the confines of observed reality, Melville was not only able to sound a new note on the page but also to draw on the considerable accumulation of esoterica he had acquired during years of avid reading and conversation with like-minded shipmates. Frequently, the poetry and the learning come together in passages like this, a meditation on death:

And to yield the ghost proudly, and march out of your fortress with all the honors of war, is not a thing of sinew and bone. Though in prison, Geoffry Hudson, the dwarf, died more bravely than Goliath, the giant; and the last end of a butterfly shames us all. Some women have lived nobler lives, and died nobler deaths, than men. Threatened with the stake, mitred Cranmer recanted; but through her fortitude, the lorn widow of Edessa stayed on the tide of Valens' persecutions. 'Tis no great valor to perish sword in hand, and bravado on lip; cased all in panoply complete. For even the alligator dies in his mail, and the swordfish never surrenders. (30–31)

This confident new voice, at once lyrical and learned, will be tried out several times, especially in the earlier part of *Mardi,* yet will fall silent after a while and not receive its full expression until it comes to dominate the pages of *Moby-Dick.*

Other aspects of *Mardi* are more familiar, such as the adoption of a pseudonym; whereas the narrator was intermittently called

Tommo in *Typee* and Typee (and then Paul) in *Omoo,* here he is
named Taji by islanders who mistake him for an absent deity come
home. Another aspect in common with the earlier books is the selection of a soul mate, in this case an older sailor from the Isle of
Skye named Jarl, with whom he'll jump ship (and who will later
disappear, as did Toby and Doctor Long Ghost). The captain of the
Arcturion (the *Leviathan* in *Omoo*) proposes to visit the polar regions; therefore the two sailors, who find the Mardi archipelago
more to their liking, slip away on the little "Chamois." Following
a series of adventures, notably the finding of the brigantine *Parki,*
which seems abandoned yet is found to have on it the island couple
Samoa (who later bravely amputates his own injured arm) and An-
natoo, the narrator and Jarl have an encounter that develops into
the novel's central plot device. They meet with a boat manned by
priestly figures and bearing a veiled maiden who will be sacrificed
to an island deity. The narrator resolves to save the maiden; in the
ensuing fray, he impetuously kills the priest, who has menaced him
with a dagger, and is smitten hard by remorse, though he perseveres
in his mission.

The maiden he rescues is named Yillah, a creature of great beauty
who has been raised in a dreamy vale that recalls such Romantic environs as the pleasure dome in Coleridge's "Kubla Khan." A lovely
innocent, she falls rather quickly for her doughty rescuer, who, once
they make land, is mistaken by the Mardi islanders for Taji, "a sort
of half-and-half deity, now and then an Avatar among them, and
ranking among their inferior ex-officio demi-gods" (164). To find
both love and a place of honor among the amiable islanders — what
twin triumphs, following the sporadic loneliness and confusion over
identity of the first two-and-a-half books of the Polynesian trilogy!
The self-exiled narrator variously known as Tommo and Typee now
has the companionship, acceptance, and sense of identity for which
he has been searching all along.

This might have been a perfect place for the trilogy to conclude,
with the narrator satisfied at the end of his long quest and the overall dramatic structure now complete. As it is, the narrative reaches
the point described above in chapter 53, whereas the book as a
whole is comprised of 195 chapters. The remaining three-quarters
of the novel is taken up with the search for Yillah, who disappears
inexplicably. In the company of four allegorical figures — the judi-
cious King Media, a storyteller named Mohi or Braid-Beard, the

philosopher Babbalanja, and Yoomi the minstrel — the narrator searches for Yillah from island to island.

There is little tension to the search for Yillah, however, no sightings or near misses or close calls. Instead, the narrative becomes a travelogue in which every stop is described in detail and the local legends recounted; when these are not forthcoming, the narrator's windy companions fill the empty space with their own stories, philosophical disquisitions, and songs. Every isle has its own monarch and court; these, too, are presented down to the last fold in their clothing. Thus the reader is treated to an extended social commentary in the course of a narrative that is ostensibly about the search for a lost lover. As Michael Paul Rogin observes, in *Mardi* "Melville introduced two new subjects, politics and women. They destroyed *Mardi,* but one would form the basis for *Moby-Dick,* the other for *Pierre*" (62). For the patient reader, then, *Mardi* is understood as an absolutely essential way station in Melville's career, though its unique joys are reserved for the specialist.

Part of the problem for the general reader is that Melville tends to employ a curious tone in the middle and late chapters, one that equates island society with the Western variety in a manner comic yet too affected to be either genuinely tender or truly satiric:

> And now to describe the general reception that followed. In came the Roes, the Fes, the Lol-Lols, the Hummee-Hums, the Bidi-Bidies, and the Dedidums; the Peenees, the Yamoyamees, the Karkies, the Fanfums, the Diddledees, and the Fiddlefies; in a word, all the aristocracy of Pimminee; people with exceedingly short names; and some all name, and nothing else. It was an imposing array of sounds; a circulation of ciphers; a marshaling of tappas; a getting together of grimaces and furbelows; a masquerade of vapidities. (409)

The narrator seems to feel an affection for this collection of fuddy-duddies, as one might for an eccentric relative or peculiar-looking pet, yet clearly he loves nothing so much as the sound of his own voice as he describes them. The confident narrator of the earlier lyrical-yet-learned passages has been replaced by the coxcomb of the first "Fragments from a Writing Desk" (see chapter 1 of this study). For better or worse, the heading of chapter 152 — "They Sail round an Island without Landing; and Talk round a Subject without Getting at It" — is applicable to the book as a whole. The islands they visit have satirical equivalences in real life: Vivenza is clearly the United States, as Dominora is Great Britain. Typically, Taji, like his picaresque predecessors in the two earlier Polynesian novels, is dissatisfied with the practices of the inhabitants of Serenia, the isle of Christian love, even though Babbalanja believes them to be the embodiments of earthly wisdom.

This is not to say that the bulk of *Mardi* is pure wind. If the search for Yillah provides little tension, there are nonetheless moments of terror and beauty. From time to time the searchers are menaced by the vengeful sons of the priest slain earlier; during the search for Yillah, the sons kill Jarl, who has remained behind on one of the island kingdoms, having become a much less significant figure than either of his counterparts, Toby in *Typee* and the doctor in *Omoo*.

And additional mystery is provided by the strange heralds of Queen Hautia, who appear from time to time bearing flowers and other gifts. Hautia herself appears briefly in midnarrative as a sort of alter ego to Yillah. Similarly veiled and even more enigmatic, she is a more aggressive, sexual creature than the innocent Yillah; reminiscent of Keats's Lamia and Belle Dame Sans Merci as well as the Geraldine of Coleridge's "Christabel" (and, before her, the false Duessa of Spenser's *Faerie Queene),* this seductive, vampiristic woman suggests that Melville had been reading the English Romantics and that, like them, he saw good and evil intertwined:

In some mysterious way seemed Hautia and Yillah connected. But Yillah was all beauty, and innocence; my crown of felicity; my heaven below; — and Hautia, my heart abhorred. Yillah I sought; Hautia sought me. One, openly beckoned me here; the other dimly allured me there. Yet now I was wildly dreaming to find them together. (643)

Near the end of *Mardi,* Melville abandons his travel notes and satires and philosophical digressions to become the adroit storyteller once again. Hautia herself appears and makes her final bid for the narrator: "Come! let us sin, and be merry. Ho! wine, wine, wine! and lapfuls of flowers!...Damsels! dance; reel, swim, around me: — I, the vortex that draws all in. Taji! Taji! — as a berry, that name is juicy in my mouth!" (650). But when he touches her hand, a dead bird falls from the sky.

In the novel's final chapter, the narrator breaks away from Hautia and pursues the fleetingly glimpsed Yillah out to the open sea, while his companions first beg him to take a more prudent course and then abandon him altogether and swim to shore. Bound for the horizon, the narrator barely has time to note that the sons of the dead priest are dashing after him. The last sentence reads, "And thus, pursuers and pursued flew on, over an endless sea" (654). Whereas *Typee* and *Omoo* ended with the narrator alone and friendless in a static situation, here he is last seen in a much more active dynamic, chasing love while death chases him into a world without boundaries. The satirical parts of *Mardi* suggest that institutions and ideas are all lacking in one way or another, but throughout, and most emphatically at the end, one concept is preeminent: the individual quest for fulfillment through action.

An overlong, loosely organized, yet occasionally thrilling tale, *Mardi* is a fitting centerpiece to the first third of Melville's career. It recalls such encyclopedic narratives as Spenser's *Faerie Queene,* Dante's *Divine Comedy,* Burton's *Anatomy of Melancholy,* Sir Thomas Browne's *Religio Medici,* and Rabelais's *Gargantua and Pantagruel* (which includes a voyage taken by the giant Pantagruel and his loquacious companions to various islands). Yet *Mardi* was not what the readers of *Typee* and *Omoo* had expected. Whereas the former was governed by a strict unity of place and the latter by a strong central character, *Mardi* was pulled in three directions at once: toward straightforward adventure narration; toward stylized literary romance in the manner of La Motte-Fouqué's *Undine,* which bears many resemblances to the Yillah story; and toward the allegory sustained by Taji's four companions. The novel calls at all these ports yet finds safe harbor in none of them.

Charles Roberts Anderson, author of *Melville in the South Seas,* the authoritative guide to the early novels, notes that, while *Omoo* is the most strictly autobiographical of all of Melville's books in the literal sense, *Mardi* was "the first of his books to be written entirely in New York City under the full influence of his new [literary and intellectual] associations" and was therefore "at least in part a reflection of the new world of ideas in which the young author was now moving."[7] Thus *Mardi,* too, is autobiographical, certainly insofar as ideas are part of one's life. Of course, most contemporary readers of the first two Polynesian tales did not share Melville's interest in esoterica.

In a sense, though, Melville taught himself how to write when he wrote *Mardi,* learned what worked well for him and what did not, and mastered strategies without which *Moby-Dick* would not be the work of genius that it is. But even geniuses need to be practical. Stung by *Mardi*'s poor reception, Melville quickly wrote two more books that were, like the popular *Typee* and *Omoo,* based more on his experiences than his imaginings.

Redburn

Written after the Polynesian trilogy, *Redburn* is based on events that occurred before the experiences of the earlier books. And though Melville noted in his journal that *Redburn* was "a thing, which I, the author, know to be trash, & wrote it to buy some tobacco with," it is nonetheless the kind of book that many authors write following a certain period of accomplishment, namely, a look at beginnings — at the roots whence accomplishment sprang, as it were.

Such a book is often anomaly-ridden. Since it deals with beginnings, it necessarily describes a callow protagonist; but since the book is composed in midcareer, its author often endows that youthful protagonist with qualities better suited to the more mature characters whose stories have already been related (in Melville's case, the more experienced heroes of *Typee, Omoo,* and *Mardi,* all of whom were created before Redburn yet are older than he is). Thus Redburn's philosophical disquisition on the sailor's mystical position within God's grand scheme (chapter 29) would be more suited to the mature protagonist of *Mardi,* for example, than to a teenager who has not been fully seasoned by the maritime life.

Putting aside these occasional incongruities, however, *Redburn* is of a piece with the rest of Melville's work. Notwithstanding the scope of Melville's inquiry, the breadth of his experience, and the variety in the forms of his expression (romance, poem, essay, etc.), Melville treats a handful of ideas with notable consistency throughout his career, and thus it is possible to see inside Redburn the mature Melvillean protagonist in his chrysalis. That fatherless, friendless character who learns to accept his fate philosophically appears here frightened and all but overwhelmed by his orphan status. Significantly, Redburn is spurred to travel by memories of his dead father's accounts of foreign exotica. And he is further impelled by the presence in his town of a bug-eyed man who supposedly wandered starving through the Arabian desert until he spied a date tree hanging with ripe fruit and at which he stared so gluttonously that he deformed himself.

And so Redburn goes to sea, where he hopes to discover the marvelous and also make a place for himself in the social scheme:

> I frequently fell into long reveries about distant voyages and travels, and thought how fine it would be, to be able to talk about remote and barbarous countries; with what reverence and wonder people would regard me, if I had just returned from the coast of Africa or New Zealand; how dark and romantic my sunburnt cheeks would look; how I would bring home with me foreign clothes of a rich fabric and princely make, and wear them up and down the streets, and how grocers' boys would turn back their heads to look at me, as I went by.[8]

At both ventures, the discovery of the exotic and the search for acceptance by others, Redburn is singularly unsuccessful. The *Highlander*'s destination is Liverpool, a foul, pestilential city most dramatically characterized by the incident in chapter 37, where Redburn discovers a mother and her children dying in a cellar; all of his efforts to secure help from the police and from passersby are rebuffed, and the little family is left to die (see the discussion of the factual basis for this episode in chapter 1 of the present study). Liverpool turns out to be a good deal less than "the coast of Africa or New Zealand," and Redburn quickly acquires a sense of the true nature of the sailor's life.

As far as his own place in the world is concerned, Redburn learns an equally harsh lesson. The captain of the merchant ship, so friendly and even paternal during Redburn's initial interview, turns out to be an aloof, ill-tempered tyrant at sea, where Redburn finds himself at the very bottom of the maritime hierarchy. But if he is too shabby for the captain, he is too wellborn for the men, and the sailors abuse this self-styled son of a gentleman for taking the bread out of the mouths of honest fellows like themselves.

As always — or at least whenever possible — the Melville protagonist finds his solace in philosophy, and by midbook he has found at least some sense of identity and of a venerable ancestry in the very fact of being American: "Our blood is as the flood of the Amazon, made up of a thousand noble currents all pouring into one. We are not a nation, so much as a world. ... We are the heirs of all time, and with all nations we divide our inheritance. On this Western Hemisphere all tribes and people are forming into one federated whole; and there is a future which shall see the estranged children of Adam restored as to the old hearth-stone in Eden" (169). The brotherhood of humankind is not altogether palpable; for the moment, however, it will suffice in the absence of more immediate companionship.

Too, all freshmen eventually become sophomores, and on the return voyage, a tanned and callused Redburn is able to look with both pity and self-congratulation on the travails of one Harry Bolton, a dandified Briton who joins the ship's crew in Liverpool and becomes the rank novice that Redburn had been earlier. Harry meets in Redburn in Liverpool and travels with him to London, where the two are involved in a never-fully-explained adventure that results in Harry's abrupt resolve to flee to America, possibly to escape some sort of trouble resulting from gambling losses. Harry joins the crew of the *Highlander* and innocently makes himself even more objectionable to the crew than Redburn was, for instance, turning out for his first morning watch "in a brocaded dressing gown, embroidered slippers, and tasseled smoking-cap" (253). Redburn and Harry are thrown together by their past history and the crew's distaste for them both, but as the perplexing escapade in London might have suggested to Redburn, Harry is too guarded to become a true soul mate. Besides, as in *Typee* and *Omoo,* all companionship seems temporary, and when the voyage is over, Redburn says, in words that recall his farewells to Toby and Doctor Long Ghost in the earlier novels, "I never saw Harry again" (311).

It is interesting to note that Melville's oddest and least-successful book to date, *Mardi,* is the only one that ends differently from the other three. In producing Redburn, Melville decided to write a "safe" book that would satisfy the demands of his rebellious readership, even down to the ending. So whereas *Mardi* ends with the protagonist in hopeful pursuit of a woman, *Redburn,* like the first two books, ends with him regretting the loss of a male companion. This is not to say that Melville's readers preferred one type of ending to the other. More likely, the difference can be explained this way: that whereas *Mardi* represented in every way a challenging new artistic direction for Melville, *Typee, Omoo,* and *Redburn* represented a more familiar mode of writing, a mode in which many techniques had been used to the point of overuse, including a certain kind of ending. Certainly it was a mode of which Melville himself was weary, even if his readers were not.

However, although *Redburn* does not rank with Melville's best work, it is far from being the potboiler its author claimed it was. Its

chief interest to students of Melville lies in its presentation of themes
and images that recur elsewhere in his writing and reach a peak
in his masterpiece, *Moby-Dick*. Chief among these is the matter of
identity. When the callow Redburn pretends to be well-off in order
to impress the captain of the *Highlander,* he is chagrined when his
pretense results in a meager salary, leading him to conclude that
"poor people make a very poor business of it when they try to seem
rich" (17). Later, the matter of his identity is taken out of his hands
entirely when he becomes a "boy" (the sailors aboard ship were
divided into able seamen, ordinary seamen, and boys) and is given
contemptuous names by the officers and crew; at various times he is
called Pillgarlic, Buttons, Jimmy Dux, and Boots.

Like Ishmael, then, whose true name the reader never knows,
Redburn takes on a pseudonym (several, actually) when he goes
to sea; he gives up his old name just as he gives up his old life.
Portentously, this youthful protagonist "Beholds a Herd of Ocean-
Elephants," as the subtitle of chapter 20 reports, though he finds
them a disappointing sight (95). Still, and while it is inadvisable to
believe that every event in Redburn's life is based on a correspond-
ing one in Melville's, it is significant to catch the author who wrote
the greatest whale story of all time in the act of reminiscing over
what may have been his own first sight of the creature that would
make him famous beyond the wildest desires of his youth.

White-Jacket

An extraordinary book for several reasons, *White-Jacket* can be
understood as two works in one. First, it is an eloquent examination of both the ideal of democracy as well as its corrupt shipboard
form, with special attention given to the practice of flogging, a punishment Melville viewed not only with a reformer's skepticism but
also a genuine visceral horror. In Melville's own day, *White-Jacket*
received nearly universal critical approval in large part because of
Melville's attack on naval abuses, his humanitarian tone, and his
championing of democracy. "It was a book in tune with the times,"
note the editors of the standard edition of the novel.[9] And Charles
Roberts Anderson observes that with *White-Jacket* Melville "got
on the bandwagon of reform; he had an eye for the public taste,
in his earlier years, as keen as that of Defoe and Cotton Mather"
(431). While the novel did not lead to the abolition of flogging in

the US Navy, as some readers have opined, it was certainly part of the growing tide of agitation against this barbaric practice.

But, in addition to being a passionate political tract, *White-Jacket* is also a novelist's novel, shaped by a refined literary self-consciousness that gives depth and coherence to what might otherwise be a merely chronological sequence of terrifying and (Melville being Melville, no matter how solemn his agenda) comic moments. After describing the ranks and functions of his shipmates, the protagonist of *White-Jacket* concludes,

> Most of us man-of-war's-men harmoniously dove-tail into each other, and by our very points of opposition, unite in a clever whole, like the parts of a Chinese puzzle. But, as in a Chinese puzzle, many pieces are hard to place, so there are some unfortunate fellows who can never slip into their proper angles, and thus the whole puzzle becomes a puzzle indeed, which is the precise condition of the greatest puzzle in the world — this man-of-war world itself. (164)

The most significant puzzle piece is the white jacket the hero wears throughout; its lengthy treatment makes clear not only the jacket's importance to this novel but also Melville's maturing sense of the value of a symbol. The jacket appears on the book's first page: finding himself without a "*grego,* or sailor's surtout" or even a pea jacket, the narrator exercises the powers of invention that are indispensable to every sailor and fashions "an outlandish garment of my own devising," a frock or shirt doubled at the bosom and slit lengthwise to produce "a coat! — a strange-looking coat, to be sure; of a Quakerish amplitude about the skirts; with an infirm, tumble-down collar; and a clumsy fullness about the wristbands; and white, yea, white as a shroud." And his "shroud it afterward came very near proving, as he who reads further will find" (3): the evening after the ship's cooper dies, the white-jacketed narrator is mistaken for a ghost and nearly plunges to his death when his affrighted shipmates hastily furl the rigging in which he has been spied (chapter 19). In chapter 47 he tries to get rid of the jacket, but a superstitious sense of fate leads the narrator to believe that if the jacket survives, tattered as it has become, then so will he.

Finally he manages to rid himself of this garment that both offends and redeems; in the novel's second-to-last chapter, the narrator falls into the sea and begins to sink, yet he succeeds in cutting the jacket "as if I were ripping open myself" (394). It is, as Michael

Paul Rogin points out, as though he "gives birth, as by a cesarean, to himself" (97–98). And, indeed, it is roughly from this moment in Melville's life that White-Jacket the man, having freed himself from the white jacket that signified his life as a sailor, reclaimed his actual name and became an artist — "roughly" because the fall from the mast is one of a number of invented episodes that stud an otherwise-factual narrative.

In addition to this simple equation of jacket with narrator, however, there is a more complex association among a variety of elements that seem disparate yet share a fundamental sameness: jacket, book (*White-Jacket* itself but other books as well), narrator, ship, world. Melville announces a new sophistication in his method of inquiry on the novel's first page, where he notes that the slitting of his shirt/jacket was like the cutting of a page in a new novel, which is, of course, what his nineteenth-century readers would have just done. Thus to open the book is to open the jacket is to open the man and so on. Here the Melvillean narrator begins by speaking of such small things as jackets and books and then moves on to larger considerations of the man-of-war and, ultimately, the world itself; the narrator stands at the center of focus, with the small and great things to either side.

At different points throughout the novel, Melville seems to be saying that all of these things are varied yet coherent, complicated yet, in the end, readable. Just as the parts of a person or a book or a ship or the world itself somehow make a whole despite their difference, so too does a jacket acquire a single distinct personality even though it is cobbled together out of various unrelated bits. Much of the distinct character of Melville's writing derives from his agile movement among items as common as a book or a tattered jacket and as grand as a man-of-war or even the wide world itself; since all things suggest a variety as well as a simplicity that is fundamental, then nothing is too great or too small, nothing is unworthy of his or his readers' consideration.

This idea — that all things have their own complex, multipartite character yet, for that very reason, share a fundamental sameness of structure — is key to an understanding of Melville. But this idea is also preliminary to an even more important one, namely, that all things are ultimately readable, even if "many pieces [of the puzzle] are hard to place." Among the things that cry out for a reading are the White Whale, eventually, as well as Herman Melville himself. But in *White-Jacket* Melville is mainly perfecting his method of inquiry rather than applying it, and one senses his pleasure as he moves nimbly from such superficially unrelated yet ultimately similar objects as jacket, man, book, ship, and world.

At his best, Melville treats more than one of these entities simultaneously and in a manner that is both jokey and philosophical, as when he describes the ship's library-in-a-barrel whose contents are unceremoniously dumped on deck by an irritable "librarian" whenever one of the sailors wants to make a selection (chapter 41). After poking gentle fun at this primitive method of distributing fine literature and mentioning some of his own favorite volumes, the narrator concludes the chapter in a manner that recalls his Chinese-puzzle musings earlier: "My book experiences on board of the frigate proved ... that though public libraries have an imposing air, and doubtless contain invaluable volumes, yet, somehow, the books that prove most agreeable, grateful, and companionable, are those we pick up by chance here and there; those which seem put into our hands by Providence; those which pretend to little, but abound in much" (169). One can almost visualize the books making their way haphazardly into the narrator's hands and confirming in yet another way that, though "many pieces are hard to place," sometimes the puzzle does in fact come together.

A similar episode is found in chapter 45, which recounts a funny, woeful tale of shipboard "publishing": a bard of the gun-deck named Lemsford, who had the habit of hiding his work in the mouths of one of the cannons, watches with horror as his poems are blasted into oblivion when the ship, which has docked in Rio de Janeiro, returns a shore salute. Lemsford has been described at length earlier in a chapter aptly entitled "The Pursuit of Poetry under Difficulties" (chapter 11), and the narrator describes his latest difficulty in typical jokey-philosophical manner, citing the brotherly Jack Chase, who says, "That's the way to publish ... fire it right into 'em." This advice leads to a discussion that begins with a lament for the inevitable heartbreak associated with publishing (something about which Melville knew a great deal) and ends with Lemsford and his friends accepting this calamity with rueful cheer. Once again the puzzle pieces have moved together to form a whole, at least in the minds of the characters.

Earlier it was said that *White-Jacket* could be read as either a treatise on democracy or an exercise in literary self-awareness, but on a more profound level it is both. Throughout his career, Melville was consumed with the inseparable issues of personal freedom and the individual's place within larger groups. What better context in which to examine these issues, then, than that of a crowded man-of-war? Much of the book is given over to shipboard practices, both benign (the issuing of the daily ration of grog) and horrific (brutal, often fatal floggings for seemingly minor infractions). The narrator's horror of flogging is so pronounced that when he himself is falsely accused of neglecting his post and ordered flogged, he prepares to embrace the captain and leap overboard with him in a desperate murder-suicide: "Locking souls with him, I meant to drag Captain Claret from this earthly tribunal of his to that of Jehovah, and let Him decide between us" (280). Fortunately, the incident comes to a peaceful conclusion when some of his superiors testify that this narrator is not the sort of sailor who would desert his station. As Charles Roberts Anderson points out, this incident, like that of the "cesarean" rebirth described above, was almost certainly invented; the white jacket itself may well have been an invention, too, since Melville could have drawn a pea jacket and had it charged against his pay or procured a similar garment at any of the ship's ports of call (411–12, 413–15, 417–18). But the episode dramatizes Melville's visceral horror of shipboard discipline in a way that no mere polemic could, and it also relieves what would have been a rather flat narrative otherwise.

For, while the sailor's life has its moments of joy and its times of terror, most often that life is merely tedious. Given the highly structured nature of life aboard a naval vessel, the tedium often assumes bizarre patterns, as when one entire watch has to nap on deck but pressed together to conserve space, "heel and point, face to back, dove-tailed into each other at every ham and knee." Even the shifting common to sleepers is regimented: "Three or four times during the four hours I would be startled from a wet doze by the hoarse cry of a fellow who did the duty of a corporal at the after-end of my file, 'Sleepers ahoy! stand by to slew round!' and, with a double shuffle, we all rolled in concert, and found ourselves facing the taffrail instead of the bowsprit" (83). Here the reader is reminded that the puzzle we call the world often assembles itself in noisome and unpleasant ways. One comes away from *White-Jacket* with a sense of the sailor as chess piece, moved here and there at the whim of his uncaring superiors.

But on another level, to Melville we are all sailors and we are always sailing — the last chapter reminds us that, "as a man-of-war that sails through the sea, so this earth that sails through the air. We mortals are all on board a fast-sailing, never-sinking world-frigate, of which God was the shipwright. . . . And though far out of sight of land, for ages and ages we continue to sail with sealed orders, and our last destination remains a secret to ourselves and our officers; yet our final haven was predestinated ere we slipped from the stocks at Creation" (398). And as we sail, to use the metaphor cited at the beginning of this section, the most alive among the crew are those aware of themselves simultaneously as individual puzzle pieces and as parts of the whole puzzle.

Though *White-Jacket,* like the other autobiographically based works, remains fairly faithful to the actual events of Melville's life, it does not end the way they do. *Typee, Omoo,* and *Redburn* conclude on an I-never-saw-him-again note, referring to the narrator's loss of a faithful companion. In *White-Jacket,* too, the narrator loses a friend, but his departure is announced in chapter 4: recollecting Jack Chase, the narrator says, "Wherever you may now be rolling over the blue billows, dear Jack! take my best love with you; and God bless you wherever you go!" (14). But the story proper ends more in the manner of *Mardi,* with the image of a boat or ship sailing for an unknown destination.

White-Jacket and *Mardi* are related in another way as well. Both prefigure *Moby-Dick;* while *Mardi* is often mentioned as an obvious precursor to Melville's masterpiece, the evidence cited is usually of a stylistic and rhetorical nature. But if the Melville of *Mardi* is beginning to sound like the Melville of *Moby-Dick,* the Melville of *White-Jacket* is beginning to think like that later author. *Mardi* has more of the style that the mature Melville will use, *White-Jacket* the vision.

Moby-Dick

Immensity

"Call me Ishmael": is there any better-known first sentence? Dickens's "It was the best of times, it was the worst of times" (*A Tale of Two Cities*) and Tolstoy's "Happy families are all alike; every unhappy family is unhappy in its own way" (*Anna Karenina*) are more frequently quoted by politicians and other speechmakers, though it is doubtful that their audiences are familiar with the novels that these sentences begin. Not that *Moby-Dick* is any more widely read than these two. But of the great unread books, *Moby-Dick* is probably the most celebrated. Its larger-than-life characters, themes, and symbols are ready fare for filmmakers, cartoonists, and ad designers. As a result, Melville's masterpiece, like the great works of Freud and Marx, is thoroughly familiar to the literate many who have nonetheless never read a word of it. But just as everyone "knows" about the Oedipal complex or the basic tenets of communism without having read *The Interpretation of Dreams* or *Capital,* so too are they thoroughly familiar with Melville's great tale of . . . what?

Though Ishmael steps up boldly in the novel's first sentence and, in the paragraph that follows, establishes himself as a multidimensional character, he rather quickly retreats in the succeeding chapters and spends the rest of the book as a more-passive-than-most protagonist, one shaped by events rather than a shaper of them. So *Moby-Dick* is not "about" Ishmael. Nor is it "about" Ahab, though certainly Ahab's maniacal obsession is the novel's source of power, the engine, as it were, that drives the narrative forward. *Moby-Dick* is not even "about" Moby Dick or whales, for that matter. Its subject is this: immensity.

The dozen or so pages that precede the famous first sentence of *Moby-Dick* suggest the book's unique nature. Instead of starting the way most novels start, *Moby-Dick* begins with a brief "Etymology (Supplied by a Late Consumptive Usher to a Grammar School)" and an extensive list of "Extracts (Supplied by a Sub-Sub-Librarian." These two devices, whimsical yet portentous in nature, might have various effects on the reader; indisputably, though, they distance the reader from any traditional idea of story. The pseudoacademic aspect of the "Etymology" (of the word *whale*) and the "Extracts" (of references to whales in world literature from the Bible forward) remind the reader that *Moby-Dick* is, first, last, and always, a book: not a slice of life, not a realistic portrait, not any of the things that a traditional novel, heavy on plot and character, pretends to be. In fact, throughout *Moby-Dick*, it often seems that, whenever the reader is on the verge of "identifying" with Ishmael and sinking almost mindlessly into the events of the story, Melville wakes that reader up with a little nudge, a reference of some kind to the book's bookish nature and to the fact that his world is not made up of ships and sailors but of black marks on white pages.

These two prefatory devices, and especially the "Extracts," also suggest that something big is to come. And the big thing to come, of course, is bigness. The "Extracts" spell this out very clearly, often clinically: while there are the expected references to the whale swallowing Jonah, for example, Melville also quotes *Stowe's Annals* to the effect that "this whale's liver was two cart-loads."[1] He cites as well "John Hunter's account of the dissection of a whale" (noting that it was "a small sized one") to the effect that "ten or fifteen gallons of blood are thrown out of the heart at a stroke, with immense velocity" (xxiii). Melville also enlists the considerable authority of "Scoresby" (William Scoresby, Jr., was the author of *An Account of the Arctic Regions*) as testimony to the whale's immensity; according to Scoresby, one whale drew 10,440 yards, or "nearly six English miles," of rope from the boats involved in its capture, and whales in general crack their tails like whips and so loudly that "the sound can be heard three or four miles away" (xxv). And not one but two texts, *Sibbald's Fife and Kinross* and the familiar *Twice-told Tales* of Hawthorne, are cited because of their references to whale jaws being used as garden gates (xxi, xxiv).

These references to the enormous size of whales are more than mere window dressing, for they are echoed amply in the text proper. And as with everything else in Melville, the characterizations alternate between the ridiculous and the sublime. Chapter 81, for example, treats a flatulent old bull who causes "the waters behind him to upbubble" and prompts Stubb, the second mate, to call for paregoric, saying, "Lord, think of having half an acre of stomach-ache!" (352). The very next chapter, however, entitled "The Honor and Glory of Whaling," exalts the whale by listing the larger-than-life figures who have pursued him in myth and legend: "Perseus, St. George, Hercules, Jonah, and Vishnoo! there's a member-roll for you!" (363).

There is method in all this enumeration, of course. If the whale is a creature so big as to require a barrel of paregoric to quiet its dyspepsia or a foe as godly as Hercules to bring it to heel, then what is the reader being told about the nature of so marvelous a beast? Melville answers this fundamental question, but his answer comes in pieces and is scattered throughout the text in a way that suggests fundamental questions are not answered easily. For instance, it is clear that Melville is getting at something significant in chapter 104 when the narrator's voice evokes

that wondrous period, ere time itself can be said to have begun; for time began with man.... Then the whole world was the whale's; and, king of creation, he left his wake along the present lines of the Andes and the Himmalehs. Who can show a pedigree like Leviathan? Ahab's harpoon had shed older blood than the Pharoahs'. Methuselah seems a schoolboy. I look round to shake hands with Shem. I am horror-struck at this antemosaic, unsourced existence of the unspeakable terrors of the whale, which, having been before all time, must needs exist after all humane ages are over. (457)

We see Melville quavering before the *mysterium tremendum et fascinans* here, the naked face of the "unsourced" and the "un-speakable," terms used traditionally in every scripture to describe God Himself. When, in the "Extracts," Melville quotes the *New England Primer* as saying, "Whales in the sea / God's voice obey," he is suggesting in another way that creatures so immense must have a connection to God that lesser creatures do not. Compiled and published in Boston during the last years of the seventeenth century, the *New England Primer* is estimated to have sold more than five million copies; it helped form the mind of the Hawthorne-Melville generation with its simple, Old Testament–based moral texts, the "Now I lay me down to sleep" prayer, and, to at least one Albany, New York reader, the meaning, grasped only in adult life, of the whale's existence.

As Hawthorne concluded after his walk with Melville on the English shore, "He can neither believe, nor be comfortable in his unbelief; and he is too honest and courageous not to try to do one or the other."[2] Melville was never sure of the existence of God. But if God did exist, the only way to Him was through the greatest of His creatures. As James Barbour points out, "The whale, like life itself, resists man's intellectual efforts and remains a mystery: it is too huge, too vital, too transcendentally other for man's reductive intelligence to 'capture' it. The whale is the symbol of that which is beyond man's intellectual and imaginative reach, beyond art and language." That is to say, the whale is like God Himself: as Barbour notes, in writing *Moby-Dick* Melville may have been thinking of God's statement to Moses in Exodus 33:20, 23: "Thou canst not see my face: for there shall no man see me, and live.... And I will take away mine hands, and thou shalt see my back parts: but my face shall not be seen."[3] At any rate, the whale is the bridge between our petty lives and *something*, though what that something is, is not easily named — if it can be named at all.

An immense treatment of immensity: quite a task for a novelist. But is *Moby-Dick* a novel? Certainly the student who thinks it will be a novel like *Great Expectations* or *Anna Karenina* is heading for heartbreak. It is important to know what genre a work is before beginning it; the reader who has been told by a prankish friend that *Macbeth* is a comedy will perhaps chuckle at the doings of the "weird sisters" but suffer increasing bafflement and frustration when other comedic elements fail to materialize and events begin to take a marked turn toward the tragic. *Moby-Dick* has been described variously as an epic, a novel, a tragedy, a satire, and so on. But it might be best described as an encyclopedic narrative, a form that includes all these others and much else besides.

In fact, there is little that an encyclopedic narrative does not include. Edward Mendelson writes that this genre "gathers from the full range of a culture's knowledge," including, "in ways that other large books do not, detailed accounts of a science and a nonverbal art, as well as a theoretical exposition of statecraft" and "an encyclopedia of rhetoric, ranging from compendia of proverb lore to the most euphuistic of high styles." And of course the encyclopedic narrative always includes "giants or gigantism," as in Mendelson's examples: the *Divine Comedy, Gargantua and Pan-*

tagruel, Don Quixote, Faust, Ulysses, Gravity's Rainbow, and, of course, *Moby-Dick.*[4]

Since an encyclopedic narrative is about everything, it is also about itself, and *Moby-Dick* contains plenty of references to books. For example, in chapter 32, aptly named "Cetology," where Melville attempts to define the whale, he begins by calling it "a *spouting fish with a horizontal tail*" but divides his subject into "three primary BOOKS (subdivisible into CHAPTERS)," namely, the folio, octavo, and duodecimo whale (137). In bookmaking, large pieces of paper are used; folded once, they make two good-sized pages for a folio volume. Folded twice and then cut, the large piece of paper yields eight smaller pages for a book of octavo size. To make a duodecimo volume, one folds the paper in half from left to right and then in thirds from top to bottom, thus making twelve pages (and therefore a book) of the smallest size. So, too, with whales: the folio whale includes the sperm whale, the right whale, and other true leviathans, while the octavo and duodecimo categories include the lesser whales.

Melville goes on at some length with his taxonomy but admits at the end of the chapter that his system of classification is imperfect, for while "small erections may be finished by their first architects . . . grand ones, true ones, ever leave the copestone to posterity. God keep me from ever completing anything." And if the reader is beginning to think that Melville is talking not merely about his cetological taxonomy but also about the entire enterprise of *Moby-Dick* itself, the author confirms as much in the next sentence when he says, "This whole book is but a draught — nay, but the draught of a draught." And he concludes the chapter with every writer's self-encouraging howl of despair: "Oh, Time, Strength, Cash, and Patience!" (145).

Moby-Dick contains a number of observations of this kind, little epithets or self-hypnotic mantras of the kind that other authors leave in their notebooks or include in letters to friends. "Out of the trunk, the branches grow," writes Melville at the beginning of chapter 63; "out of them, the twigs. So, in productive subjects, grow the chapters" (289). So a book evolves, he might have said — as the whale does, or the world itself, that is, not systematically, but organically, for "there are some enterprises in which a careful disorderliness is the true method" (361).

There is one more point that should be considered regarding Melville's intent in writing *Moby-Dick,* and that is his metaphorical association of whales with superior human beings. In letters to Evert Duyckinck (discussed in chapter 1 of this study), Melville associates Emerson and Shakespeare with a "corps of thought-divers," saying "any fish can swim near the surface, but it takes a great whale to go down stairs five miles or more."[5] Great thinkers are to the ordinary run of humankind what great whales are to other fish; in that sense, Melville not only wanted to write about whales but to be one in the metaphorical sense of accomplishing something enormous.

We have seen in *White-Jacket* that Melville is fond of universes and that he takes a certain pleasure out of studying and even constructing them. But in his other books Melville is concerned with such lesser universes as man, ship, and world, whereas in *Moby-Dick* he is contemplating the universe itself and constructing a parallel to it. Melville the Unbelieving Believer may have felt faintly blasphemous in ascribing to himself not merely a mortal capacity for bookmaking but a divine one for world making, something he seems aware of at the conclusion of the "Cetology" chapter, where he states deliberately that "I now leave my cetological system standing thus unfinished, even as the great Cathedral of Cologne was left, with the crane still standing upon the top of the uncompleted tower" (145). This is an important passage and one that will be discussed again near the end of this chapter, but for the moment suffice it to say that Melville is hedging his bet here by alluding to an ambitious system of inquiry that approaches God's own knowledge yet deliberately stops just short. The history of literature is rife with tales of heaven-stormers who were punished for their ambition; Adam, Prometheus, and Faust are the best-known examples from other cultures, and Melville's friend Hawthorne wrote more than one story about a scientist who tried to appropriate God's knowledge and came to a bad end as a result ("Rappaccini's Daughter" is an example). There is method, then, in Melville's deliberate imperfection.

Elsewhere, he comments cheerfully on his own untidiness; more than two hundred pages into *Moby-Dick,* he begins chapter 45 by saying, "So far as what there may be of a narrative in this book..." and then announces yet another digression (203). He deflates genuine pomposity with mock pomposity, as in chapter 104, where he brings together his fascination with immensity and with bookmaking in a reference to his use of Dr. Johnson's dictionary, "because that famous lexicographer's uncommon personal bulk more fitted him to compile a lexicon to be used by a whale author like me" (456). Like bold Ahab (as we shall see), Melville can lay claim to a limitless effrontery and seek the knowledge that only God has. But like wily Ishmael, he can also say, "I am simply writing a book — a big book, to be sure, but a book nonetheless."

Two Men and a Whale

"Call me Ishmael," says the narrator. But why "call me"? Poe's 1838 novel *The Narrative of Arthur Gordon Pym of Nantucket* begins, "My name is Arthur Gordon Pym. My father was a respectable trader in sea stores at Nantucket where I was born. My maternal grandfather was an attorney," and so on.[6] Whereas Pym establishes his bona fides in a straightforward manner, Ishmael gives the reader, not his name, but what he is "called," and then continues: "Some years ago — never mind how long precisely — I thought I would sail about a little and see the watery part of the world" (3). Where Pym draws us toward himself and his forebears, Ishmael, after telling us that he has a tendency to become surly after too long a period on land, quickly points us toward "the watery part of the world," the men and ships on its surface and the whales beneath. What is it that this Ishmael does not want us to know?

"Ismail" is a holy name in Arab countries. The half-breed son of Abraham and the Egyptian slave Hagar, he was conceived when Abraham and his wife Sarah feared that there would be no heir to carry on the line but banished when Sarah bore Isaac. To Jews and Christians, then, Ishmael was a bastard and an outcast. To Arabs, however, he was the father of twelve sons who themselves led twelve tribes from which all present-day Arabs are descended. Moreover, Ishmael and the Ishmaelites, as distinct from Isaac and the Israelites, were archers and fighters, warlike and unsubdued. (In chapter 16 of Genesis, an angel tells the pregnant Hagar that her son "will be a wild man; his hand will be against every man, and every man's hand against him.")

Edwin Haviland Miller makes the point that "Abraham sent Ishmael off to the wilderness as the boy entered puberty, presumably when he was twelve or thirteen" just as Allan Melvill "abandoned his son when he was but twelve years old."[7] As important as Melville's identification with a boy prematurely pitchforked into the world of men, however, is the fact that he chose as protagonist one who is not merely an outsider but one whose hand is forever raised against anyone not of his tribe. To Jews and Christians, Ishmael simply disappears as their own rich history unfolds; to Arabs, "Ismail" is the founder of another sort of history altogether, one defined at least in part by conflict with what the other two groups would call "orthodoxy."

While it is remarkable the Melvillean narrator has chosen the name of, in Western eyes, a bastard and an outcast, it is equally noteworthy that this narrator has named himself and in the novel's first words. As Miller observes, earlier narrators wait to be called Tommo by islanders (*Typee*) or Buttons by sailors (*White-Jacket*), but Ishmael "performs the baptismal rite himself" (193). Other readers have decried an element of self-deprecation in this taking of a bastard's name, but why not see Ishmael as the Arabs do, as the father of the Bedouins, wild as an ass, forever at war with the dominant creeds?[8]

The wild, warlike Ishmael rather quickly pacifies himself, however; after his first-paragraph talk of knocking people's hats off, within three pages he is speaking of the simple joys of a sailor's life. He uses a curious yet apt metaphor in his self-presentation, noting in the first paragraph of *Moby-Dick* that "with a philosophical flourish Cato throws himself upon his sword; I quietly take to the ship" (3). Perhaps Ishmael is killing that part of himself that threatens physical violence, even though he retains his feistiness of spirit throughout.

His initial outburst would suggest that Ishmael is absolutely unemployable, yet within paragraphs he is musing philosophically on the necessity of taking orders. Why? It is interesting to note that Ishmael identifies himself, in chapter 10, as a Presbyterian, possibly suggesting, considering that he lived in the period that followed the great Scottish migration to America, that he practiced a form of Presbyterianism influenced by the Church of Scotland with its strong Calvinist bias and its emphasis on the virtues of industry, frugality, and sobriety. His wild talk notwithstanding, Ishmael, like his maker, is a seasoned sailor who knows that hard work rather than impulsive action is the stuff of ordinary life. As children of Adam and Eve, all dwellers in this vale of tears must needs earn their bread by the sweat of their brows, and while it is harmless and even natural to speak of knocking people's hats off, eventually it is best to face up to life's vagaries with an accepting attitude.

Thus, even though he is terrified of Queequeg at first, Ishmael quickly adjusts to his future shipmate, a tattooed peddler of shrunken heads and tomahawk-wielding worshiper of pagan idols. Indeed, Ishmael feels an almost-instant affection for Queequeg; the two share a bed previously identified by the landlord of the Spouter-Inn as the one in which he and his wife shared on their wedding night, and when Ishmael awakes the next morning to find "Queequeg's arm thrown over me in the most loving and affectionate manner," he confides to the reader that "you had almost thought I had been his wife" (25). Some readers have made much of the homosexual overtones of this passage, but Carolyn L. Karcher observes that "Whatever sexual predilections it may indicate in Melville, he knew he could get away with dramatizing a happy interracial marriage by disguising it as a male comradeship which his public would dare not interpret as homosexual."[9] The larger point of Ishmael's and Queequeg's mutual regard is thematic in nature, then, rather than sexual.

For this radical joining together of two very different character types is part of a larger theme of universal acceptance that will be discussed in some detail below. Suffice it to say here that Ishmael's generous instincts are right on the money, for Queequeg will turn out to be one of the more capable mariners on board the *Pequod* and will save more than one life during the voyage. And his initial, startling appearance notwithstanding, Queequeg's strengths are those of, not some outlandish demigod, but a moderate and self-disciplined professional. It would be hard to imagine a better Presbyterian than the pagan Queequeg.

But Ishmael has more than the business of whaling on his mind. There is another and more existential reason to go to sea, for the life of a sailor seems necessary to escape the zombie lives of the greater part of shore dwellers, "thousands upon thousands of mortal men" who are "posted like silent sentinels all around the town . . . fixed in ocean reveries" (4). Humankind is drawn to water because "meditation and water are wedded for ever" and the greatest body of water, the sea, is "the image of the ungraspable phantom of life" (4, 5). Thus the general run of humanity is drawn to the ocean the way Melville is drawn to the whale, as a bridge to greater knowledge. And for those without the social advantage that leads to a captaincy or the wherewithal to buy a ticket, the sailor's life is the only way to confront the mysteries represented by a marvelous image that echoes the comments on the transcendent nature of whales in the "Extracts" that begin *Moby-Dick*. By signing on for a whaling voyage, says Ishmael in the last sentence of chapter 1, "the great flood-gates of the wonder-world swung open, and in the wild conceits that swayed me to my purpose, two and two there floated into my inmost soul, endless processions of the whale, and, midmost of them all, one grand hooded phantom, like a snow hill in the air" (7).

But in chapter 133, it is not Ishmael but Ahab who, sensing the proximity of a whale, is hauled into the air by the crew and cries, "There she blows! — there she blows! A hump like a snowhill! It is Moby Dick!" (547). The difference in the two passages, of course, is that the snow hill is an object of contemplation to the peaceable Ishmael but an abomination to the hostile Ahab. That is, each regards the "snow-hill" that is Moby Dick in a very different fashion: to Ishmael the white whale is a source of limitless wonder, but to Ahab it is a concentrated and one-dimensional malignancy.

Elsewhere Melville contrasts Ishmael and Ahab by means of another distinctive image that is used much in the manner of the snow-hill one. In chapter 4, Ishmael, who would have already been identified as an orphan by any Bible-smart reader (as more readers of Melville's day than our own would have been) tells of his punishment at the hands of a stepmother "who was all the time whipping me, or sending me to bed supperless." In this instance the miscreant boy is sent to bed at two o'clock in the afternoon, where he falls into a dream that "a supernatural hand seemed placed in mine," the hand of a "nameless, unimaginable, silent form or phantom" (25–26). Following an unjust punishment, then, Ishmael is contacted by a supernatural being. Similarly, in chapter 132, a long-suffering Ahab is soothed by the clement weather of a beautiful day: "That glad, happy air, that winsome sky, did at last stroke and caress him; the step-mother world, so long cruel — forbidding — now threw affectionate arms around his stubborn neck, and did seem to joyously sob over him, as if over one, that however willful and erring, she could yet find it in her heart to save and to bless" (543). Thus both Ishmael and Ahab are stepchildren, are unfairly punished, and are described as being approached by supernatural beings (phantom, "step-mother world") in the course of their suffering.

The difference is in their reactions to their analogous experiences.

Ishmael does not know what to make of his ordeal: "for days and weeks and months afterwards I lost myself in confounding attempts to explain the mystery. Nay, to this very hour, I often puzzle myself with it" (26). But whereas Ishmael is able to put aside his sense of injustice and instead ponder the mystery of the phantom hand, Ahab swiftly rejects the embrace of the stepmother world and sinks again into his profound rage and self-pity. "What is it," he asks, "what nameless, inscrutable, unearthly thing is it; what cozening, hidden lord and master, and cruel, remorseless emperor commands me; that against all natural lovings and longings, I so keep pushing, and crowding, and jamming myself on all the time; recklessly making me ready to do what in my own proper, natural heart, I durst not so much as dare?" (545). Whereas Ishmael is drawn out of his self-absorption to contemplate his supernatural visitor, Ahab turns his back on his miraculous encounter and retreats into a thicket of familiar fears and resentments. Considered together, the snow-hill and stepmother passages remind the reader that, while Ishmael and Ahab are both searchers — and, indeed, searchers after the same object — their motivations are altogether opposed.

Let us consider the object of their pursuit for a moment. Moby Dick is a sort of absent presence in the book, the target toward which the other characters lumber. He is always on the next page, in the next chapter; like the Holy Grail, the white whale is one of those great offstage shapers of action that determines what happens because of its importance to the other characters rather than because of anything it does itself. Indeed, when the whale finally appears at the novel's end, it is something of a disappointment, since it is simply a whale: a prodigious whale, to be sure, a whale more picturesque than any other, yet something much less than the embodiment of all meaning in the universe (if Ishmael is to be believed) or all evil (according to Ahab).

One object, two pursuers. As the chief action figure in the novel, Ahab supplies the story; as resident philosopher, Ishmael provides the commentary and little else. Given Ishmael's feisty self-presentation in the first paragraphs of *Moby-Dick,* it is rather startling to see how rapidly and completely he not only pacifies himself but then disappears entirely once the *Pequod* is at sea. Instead of the truculent landlubber turned sailor, we are given a voice: Ishmael's voice, we think, yet a voice so separate from a body that it is difficult not to think of it as anything other than the voice of Herman Melville, especially considering how similar it is in sound to the Melville of his journals, letters, and autobiographical writings.

When Ishmael does reinsert himself into the narrative, the effect is surprising: in chapter 41, for example, which begins "I, Ishmael, was one of that crew" and again in chapter 54, "The *Town-Ho's* Story (As Told at the Golden Inn)," where our narrator depicts himself as something of a dandy in the company of some young Spanish cavaliers (179, 243). Yet the dilemma of the two voices is solved once we remember that Ishmael's story is told in retrospect and that there are, in fact, two Ishmaels in the story: the callow one who sets out on an adventure and the mature one who tells the callow Ishmael's story. The reader sees these two characters diverge in such scenes as the one that concludes chapter 7, where Ishmael regards the memorial tablets for dead whalemen. The Ishmael who survived the sinking of the *Pequod* discourses profoundly and feelingly on death; the Ishmael who has not sailed yet is merely present physically.

Insofar as *Moby-Dick* is a story, then, it is Ahab's story after the *Pequod* sets sail and before Moby Dick is sighted: Ahab supplies the narrative and Ishmael the encyclopedic elements, with Moby Dick as the stimulus to both. Given his larger-than-life status and his easily caricatured appearance — the missing leg, the dour, pale, scarred face, the somber attire, the sulks, the rages — Ahab calls attention to himself in a way that the disembodied Ishmael cannot. We know what Ahab looks like, as well as Queequeg and Tashtego and Stubb and any number of the other characters, but who can describe Ishmael? The invisibility of Ishmael underscores both his physical passivity and his mental activity. To put it another way, he is not really "in" the book so much as he is writing the book much more self-consciously than is usual for a first-person narrator. Huckleberry Finn, for example, gives the impression of telling his story rather than writing it and gives as much attention to his own actions as anything else, whereas Ishmael refers constantly to the act of writing and, once the *Pequod* is under way, all but disappears from the narrative.

Yet the greater visibility of Ahab should not detract from the mystery of him. When Ishmael signs on as a crew member and asks to see the captain, Peleg, one of the owners of the *Pequod,* tells him that Ahab "keeps close inside the house; a sort of sick, and yet he don't look so.... He's a queer man.... Ahab's been in colleges, as well as 'mong the cannibals; been used to deeper wonders than the waves; fixed his fiery lance in mightier, stranger foes than whales.... *He's Ahab,* boy; and Ahab of old, thou knowest, was a crowned king!" (79).

Ishmael knows his Bible, however, and tells Peleg that if Ahab was a king, he was "a very vile one. When that wicked king was slain, the dogs, did they not lick his blood?" A king of Israel, Ahab is vilified in the First Book of Kings for having done more evil in the sight of the Lord than any king who preceded him. His chief crime was to marry the Phoenician princess Jezebel, who encouraged the worship of Baal and persecuted such prophets of the true faith as Elijah; when he was slain in battle, the dogs licked the blood that ran from his chariot.

Just as the reader might ask what kind of mother would name her child Ishmael, so might one wonder who would give her infant the name of one of the great villains of the Judeo-Christian tradition. Peleg tells Ishmael that Ahab's name was "a foolish, ignorant whim of his crazy, widowed mother, who died when he was only a twelve-month old." But there may be more to it than that: Peleg also notes that the "old squaw Tistig, at Gay-head, said that the name would somehow prove prophetic." The sanguine Peleg sees no dark meaning in Ahab's name, noting only that the captain was "a little out of his mind for a spell" following his first encounter with Moby Dick and, since then, "a kind of moody — desperate moody, and savage sometimes." But "that will all pass off," promises Peleg, especially since Ahab "has a wife — not three voyages wedded — a sweet, resigned girl," and "by that sweet girl that old man has a child: hold ye then there can be any utter, hopeless harm in Ahab?" (79).

Peleg is right in suggesting that connectedness can save one from the madness that comes of isolation. But that is a general principle, and Ahab is a particular case. He will recall his wife and child fondly at one point late in the novel, but for the most part he is one more orphan-bachelor in Melville's world of orphans and bachelors. Too, he lives in a world of men, not a domestic world, and even there he is isolated by his rank.

More than that, though, Ahab is cut off from *everything:* Ishmael too is an orphan-bachelor, yet his connections with both the natural world and the world of ideas are substantial. Ahab's only concern is Ahab; even his detestation of the white whale comes across more as an extreme form of self-indulgence than anything else. In describing the paucity of dealings even between Ahab and other members of the upper echelon of maritime society, that is, the mates and harpooners, Ishmael says that, "socially, [Ahab] was inaccessible. Though nominally included in the census of Christendom, he was still an alien to it. He lived in the world, as the last of the Grisly Bears lived in settled in Missouri." And he compares Ahab to a legendary woodsman who is both trapped yet sustained by his self-isolation: "And as when Spring and Summer had departed, that wild Logan of the woods, burying himself in the hollow of a tree, lived out the winter there, sucking his own paws; so, in his inclement, howling old age, Ahab's soul, shut up in the caved trunk of his body, there fed upon the sullen paws of its gloom!" (153).

In saying that Ahab is alien to Christendom, Melville is using that term in its general and geopolitical sense, that is, denoting the civilized world or that part of the planet in which Christianity prevails. But *Christendom* is a loaded word, and if Melville did not mean to imply that Ahab was not merely an outsider but also a pagan, he might have phrased his characterization of Ahab differently. The reader knows from the Polynesian trilogy and other Melville writings that the author mistrusted organized religion and its representatives, such as the missionaries he assails in *Typee* and *Omoo*. But there is a powerful link in Melville's mind between God Himself and democracy, and to imply that Ahab is, by being alien to Christianity, also alien to God, is to suggest that Ahab has removed himself from a belief system far more vital and significant to humankind than any church.

For each of us bears "that democratic dignity which...radiates without end from God," who is "the center and circumference of all democracy!" Chapter 26 concludes with a stirring paean to democracy that is also a characteristically quirky association of figures that only Melville would attempt; it is worth quoting in full. Commenting on the *Pequod*'s crew, he asks for the reader's indulgence in exalting the anonymous, the unsung, even the criminal:

If, then, to meanest mariners, and renegades and castaways, I shall hereafter ascribe high qualities, though dark; weave around them tragic graces; if even the most mournful, perchance the most abased, among them all, shall at times lift himself to the exalted mounts; if I shall touch that workman's arm with some ethereal light; if I shall spread a rainbow over his disastrous set of sun; then against all mortal critics bear me out in it, thou just Spirit of Equality, which hast spread one royal mantle of humanity over all my kind! Bear me out in it, thou great democratic God! who didst not refuse to the swart convict, Bunyan, the pale, poetic pearl; Thou who didst clothe with doubly hammered leaves of finest gold, the stumped and paupered arm of old Cervantes; Thou who didst pick up Andrew Jackson from the pebbles; who didst hurl him upon a war-horse; who didst thunder him higher than a throne! Thou who, in all Thy mighty, earthly marchings, ever cullest Thy selectest champions from the kingly commons; bear me out in it, O God! (117)

It is unlikely that any author other than Melville would exercise his breadth of learning and originality of observation in linking Bunyan, Cervantes, and Andrew Jackson. That he did so is testament not only to his craft but to his feelings about human dignity — that the admirable person is no semi-divine descendant of the gods nor even some pious merchant of the Republic, but the renegade and castaway, the meanest mariner. These are the ones more likely to accomplish the task at hand, whether it be to write an epic, lead an army in battle, or catch a whale. Melville once wrote to Hawthorne that he considered a "thief in jail . . . as honorable a personage as Gen. George Washington."[10] Ishmael's evident affection for characters as different as Queequeg and Stubb reflects Melville's belief that this type of person is more reliable than some highborn and properly-schooled aristocrat.

A spirit of fellow feeling among all creatures permeates *Moby-Dick,* a spirit alternately (and sometimes simultaneously) described in terms of both religion and democracy, and it is this spirit from which Ahab has excluded himself. When Starbuck chides Ahab for wishing "vengeance on a dumb brute . . . that simply smote thee from blindest instinct," saying that "to be enraged with a dumb thing, Captain Ahab, seems blasphemous," Ahab replies, "Talk not to me of blasphemy, man; I'd strike the sun if it insulted me" (164). In Starbuck's mind, to strike down at the whale is to strike up toward heaven. And Ahab agrees, even seeming to relish the sacrilege.

The height of Ahab's egotism is that he equates Moby Dick with himself: "Ahab had cherished a wild vindictiveness against the whale, all the more fell for that in his frantic morbidness he at last came to identify with him, not only all his bodily woes, but all his intellectual and spiritual exasperations." The whale engendered everything that is hateful in Ahab because it is hateful itself; only by destroying the loathsome creature can Ahab free himself of the whale-born demons that possess him, for "all that most maddens and torments; all that stirs up the lees of things; all truth with malice in it; all that cracks the sinews and cakes the brain; all the subtle demonisms of life and thought; all evil, to crazy Ahab, were visibly personified, *and made practically assailable* [emphasis mine], in Moby Dick" (184). By killing the whale, then, Ahab can kill the ugliest parts of his own character. To Ronald T. Takaki, Ahab represents the worst of the American expansionistic character, the imperialist who conquers and kills others and, without realizing it, destroys himself as well.[11] This seems to be something that Ahab has not fully considered — or, more typical of one who knows what blasphemy is yet commits it anyway, has considered and set aside.

It is a cliché of college teaching to ponder the meaning of the White Whale, but in chapter 43, "The Whiteness of the Whale," Melville is very explicit, if characteristically subtle, on that very subject. Suffice it to say that, having considered the hundreds of ideas, positive and negative, that Moby Dick represents, Ishmael concludes simply, "And of all these things the White Whale was the symbol" (195). That is, the whale is everything and nothing, a concept that is graspable by the agile mind. But not a monomaniacal mind — Ahab narrows and reduces Moby Dick to a concentrated evil and thus similarly narrows and reduces himself.

Ultimately, any betrayal of the democratic-religious spirit of *Moby-Dick* is a betrayal of oneself. Just as the beautiful islands of Polynesia are surrounded by vast waters populated by monsters, just as "this appalling ocean surrounds the verdant land, so in the soul of man there lies one insular Tahiti, full of peace and joy, but encompassed by all the horrors of the half known life. God keep thee!" says the voice of Ishmael. "Push not off from that isle, thou canst never return!" But Ahab has pushed off from the Edenic isle of inner joy and tranquility to participate in the "universal cannibalism of the sea," where "sharks" and other "remorseless tribes . . . prey upon each other, carrying on eternal war since the world began" (274). Ahab is not entirely alone in his self-hating blasphemy since he is assisted by the sinister Fedallah and his four equally suspect associates. But Melville takes pains to describe these apparitions as uncivilized, devilish, tigerlike, and so on — more like members of one of the "remorseless tribes" of the sea, that is, than conventional human beings.

Is there any hope at all for Ahab in this book, any chance that he will abandon his view of a universe occupied only by himself and the whale — at bottom a single creature, in Ahab's view, not two — and participate instead in the universal democratic-religious fellowship? At moments, yes. At times there are hints that the captain has tried to heal and domesticate a ferocity that antedates by a good many years his maiming encounter with Moby Dick. The reader is given to understand that Ahab has always been quite a handful; in chapter 19, aptly titled "The Prophet," a shabby stranger named Elijah tells Queequeg and Ishmael that while Peleg may have told these new crew members that Ahab was an able whale hunter, he said nothing "about that thing that happened to him off Cape Horn, long ago, when he lay like dead for three days and nights; nothing about that deadly skrimmage with the Spaniard afore the altar in Santa," and "nothing about the silver calabash he spat into" (92). These events are among the never-to-be-told chapters of world literature and as such rank with Dr. Watson's account of Sherlock Holmes's encounter with the Giant Rat of Sumatra, a story "for which the world is not yet prepared."[12] In the Old Testament, Elijah was a foe of Ahab the king, and it may be that the mutterings of this Elijah are born of some hate-driven dementia, although his characterizations of Captain Ahab are consistent with the tortured figure who acts out his agony on the deck of the *Pequod*.

But Ahab is human, after all, neither the god he wants to be nor the devil he appears to be, and he tries to cure himself via what Bruno Bettelheim calls "that which alone can take the sting out of the narrow limits of our time on this earth: forming a truly satisfying bond to another."[13] In explaining away the horrific connotations of Ahab's name, Peleg assures that, though Ahab may be "stricken" and "blasted," the fact that he has wife and child is proof that "Ahab has his humanities!" (79). But it may be that he has his humanities only onshore — the literal shore (which is, after all, where Peleg has observed him) but also that "insular Tahiti" of peace and joy in the soul. When Ahab shoves off into the encompassing horrors, he reverts to his stricken, blasted self and forgets the lessons that wife and child have taught him.

Ahab remembers his family late in *Moby-Dick* and perhaps too late. The moment itself is shocking, not because it is horrifying in any way but for precisely the opposite reason, for this horrific old man, this sulphurous raging tyrant shocks the reader with his sentimentality and, moreover, his genuine affection. It occurs in chapter 132, just paragraphs before Moby Dick is sighted and the book begins its final, fatal sequence. Buoyed up by the light and breezes of a beautiful day (the one on which "the step-mother world" throws its arms around his neck), Ahab begins to reminisce with Starbuck and recalls "that young girl-wife I wedded past fifty, and sailed for Cape Horn the next day, leaving but one dent in my marriage pillow." Warming to his own oratory, Ahab bids the mate, "Close! stand close to me, Starbuck; let me look into a human eye; it is better than to gaze into sea or sky; better than to gaze upon God. By the green land; by the bright hearth-stone! this is the magic glass, man; I see my wife and child in thine eye."

Starbuck, ever the voice of sense and moderation on the *Pequod,* responds to Ahab in his own terms: "Oh, my Captain! my Captain! noble soul! grand old heart, *after all!* [my emphasis] why should anyone give chase to that hated fish! Away with me! let us fly these deadly waters! let us home! Wife and child, too, are Starbuck's.... Away! let us away! — this instant let me alter the course! How cheerily, how hilariously, O my Captain, would we bowl on our way to see old Nantucket again!" (544). Still in the grip of his uncharacteristic affection, Ahab pictures his little boy waking from a nap and the mother promising the child that his father will return one day to dance with him.

Starbuck's belief that he has tapped a deeply buried well of humanity in Ahab is dashed, however. The chapter in which the foregoing conversation between Starbuck and Ahab takes place on a gorgeous day in which all the elements of nature seem to be working in concert is aptly titled "The Symphony," yet it ends on a discordant if familiar note, for within moments of Ahab's fond paternal reminiscence he shakes like a "blighted fruit tree" and casts "his last, cindered apple to the soil." The sweet memory of wife and son is thrown away as Ahab asks himself, "What nameless, inscrutable, unearthly thing is it; what cozening, hidden lord and master, and cruel, remorseless emperor commands me; *that against all natural lovings and longings,* I so keep pushing, and crowding, and jamming myself on all the time." This passage appears earlier as part of a general attempt to describe Ahab's character, but in this instance emphasis is placed on words that reveal how Ahab is doubly damned. It would be one thing if Ahab were utterly oblivious to the lure of domesticity — if he were an unthinking monster, that is — but here he consciously ponders and then rejects his humane qualities. In the face of this implacability, Starbuck steals away, having "blanched to a corpse's hue with despair" (545). And Ahab's tragic isolation seems all the more damnable in light of his having revealed that he knows how wrongheaded it is.

But, in fact, Ahab has been systematically isolating himself in other ways as well. Early in the book (chapter 30) he performs a simple act yet a startling one to any person versed in the ways of mariners: he tosses his pipe overboard. Tobacco is a rare consolation to men at sea, whose other appetites are doomed to unfulfillment. Lacking female companionship, alcohol, and fresh food, at least a fellow can enjoy a "chaw" or smoke. Elsewhere in *Moby-Dick,* smoking is seen as a token of fellowship (as when Ishmael and Queequeg share a pipe) or a hale and hearty attitude (the cheerful Stubb is a great smoker). But Ahab finds no more pleasure in smoking, just as he finds less and less pleasure in everything that is external to him.

This early casting away of the pipe has sinister implications that are borne out later in the book as Ahab casts off shipboard implements of considerably more importance. In fact, every instrument that will guide the *Pequod* on its search for Moby Dick (and safely to port again) is either deliberately destroyed, damaged, or lost: the quadrant in chapter 118, the compass in chapter 124, and the log used to measure the ship's speed in chapter 125.

Ironically, after Ahab dashes the quadrant to the deck and tramples it, saying, in effect, that this device looks questioningly to heaven but receives only inadequate answers, he cries, "No longer will I guide my earthly way by thee; the ship's compass, and the level dead-reckoning, by log and line; *these* shall conduct me, and show me my place on the sea" (501). Yet within a few pages the ship's compass is rendered useless in a thunderstorm, and then the log line snaps. "I crush the quadrant, the thunder turns the needles, and now the mad sea parts the log-line. But Ahab can mend all" (521). In fact, Ahab succeeds in fashioning a new compass by magnetizing a sail-maker's needle, yet his attitude toward his accomplishment suggests a destructive hubris that no technology can surmount. "Look ye, for yourselves," he shouts, "if Ahab be not lord of the level loadstone!" And the voice of Ishmael reflects that "in his fiery eyes of scorn and triumph, you then saw Ahab in all his fatal pride" (519). It is suggested throughout *Moby-Dick* that, as captains go, Ahab is among the best in terms of technique, know-how, and the ability to improvise. Weighed against all that, though, is his foolish, prideful belief that he is "lord" over the unforgiving, uncaring physical world.

In the chapter called "The Try-Works," a weary Ishmael describes how he dozes off at the tiller, having been hypnotized by the fires that render the whale blubber into oil. He awakes in time and avoids an accident but concludes, "Look not too long into the face of the fire, O man!" But Ahab has done precisely that — has looked too long into the fire of his rage and been hypnotized by it. Ahab bears out the wisdom of Solomon, who said that "the man that wandereth out of the way of understanding shall remain [i.e., even while living] in the congregation of the dead." This has Ahab done, though Ishmael does not mention him here, enjoining the reader only to "give not thyself up, then, to fire, lest it invert thee, deaden thee; as for the time it did me," for "there is a wisdom that is woe; but there is a woe that is madness" (424–25). The wise are always woeful, in Melville's scheme of things, yet the overly woeful are mad from having stared too long into the fire of that woe.

In putting aside the instruments that would keep him in "the way of understanding," Ahab is merely dramatizing the larger gulf between himself and the men who should be a means to his end yet become as superfluous to him as do the pipe, the quadrant, and so on. "To accomplish his object Ahab must use tools," says Ishmael, "and of all tools used in the shadow of the moon, men are most apt to get out of order" (212). First Mate Starbuck is the one character most consistently at odds with Ahab or, rather, with Ahab's vengeful mission; thinking at one point that Starbuck means to rebel, Ahab brandishes a musket, only to have the mate tell him, "I ask thee not to beware of Starbuck... but let Ahab beware of Ahab; beware of thyself, old man" (474). Sadly for Starbuck and the others, Ahab is not only aware of his self-destructiveness but uncaring of it. Only by killing the hated whale can he kill the pain in himself that the whale has caused; to die trying would be less gratifying yet just as conclusive. How should Ahab care for the lives of those "tools" called men when he has no care for his own?

An Anacharsis Clootz Deputation

Some attention must be given to these "tools" that Ahab uses so badly, and the democracy-loving spirit of Melville will forgive us if we take the mates and crew of the *Pequod* in order of the hierarchy that, after all, made sense to them, for while it is true that "there are some enterprises in which a careful disorderliness is the true method," whaling is not one of these (361). Indeed, it is not the failure of democracy per se that sinks the *Pequod* but the extension of tyranny to an illogical extreme; Ahab loses ship, crew, and self not because he is at the head of a hierarchy but because he cuts himself off from the natural order of things. For as we have seen, the right relation between the parts and the whole of any scheme is everything to Melville.

Just below the captain in this particular scheme are the three mates: Starbuck, Stubb, and Flint. Though secondary characters, each is crucial to a full understanding of Ahab, whom each in some way opposes, mocks, or parodies.

The first mate, Starbuck, is a Quaker some thirty years of age. He is described as "a staid, steadfast man...uncommonly conscientious for a seaman, and endued with a deep natural reverence"; Starbuck's byword is "I will have no man in my boat...who is not afraid of a whale," which means, we are told, merely that "an utterly fearless man is a far more dangerous comrade than a coward" (116). While Ishmael takes the long view and stands for broad philosophical observation, Starbuck is the epitome of good common sense, so much so that he is given to presentiments that would seem like rank superstition in a less-intelligent person; this is why the most telling revelations about Ahab occur in the captain's conversations with the first mate who is so opposite to him in character. It is Starbuck's grave, sensible dignity that prompts the paean (discussed earlier) to such noble commoners as Bunyan, Cervantes, and Andrew Jackson. This paean concludes two chapters appropriately entitled "Knights and Squires"; each knight or mate has a harpooner, and Starbuck's "squire" is Queequeg.

Stubb, the second mate, is as capable a mariner as Starbuck but in his cheerful fearlessness often sounds like the original inspiration for Popeye the Sailor Man, right down to the short, black pipe that is as much a part of his face as his nose. "Good-humored, easy, and careless," Stubb presides over his whaleboat "as if the most deadly encounter were but a dinner, and his crew all invited guests" (118). If Starbuck stands for good sense, Stubb represents good attitude. In contrast to Ahab, the tobacco-loving Stubb enjoys what little pleasures he can find on the sea and is indifferent to the troubles over which he has no control anyway. His harpooner is Tashtego, a Native American warrior-hunter who pursues whales now instead of the beasts of the forest.

Stubb is, though a minor character, one of the most bizarre and interesting of Melville's creations. In an original and comprehensive study of the age of Melville, David S. Reynolds identifies Stubb as an embodiment of "radical democrat" thought. According to Reynolds, the radical democrats, that is, such reform journalists and popular authors as George Lippard, were "so ardently devoted to the egalitarian ideals of the American democracy that their writings are filled with hyperbolic reverence for the Founding Fathers and, at the same time, with vitriolic bitterness against perceived inequities in nineteenth-century American society, which they regarded as a nightmarish realm of upper-class charlatans and political oppressors described in highly sensational images."[14] Clearly this is a group with whom Melville would have strong affinities, and his admiration of radical-democrat humor is evident in his creation of Stubb. Reynolds gives special significance to Stubb's frequent use of the word *queer,* a favorite word of this group because "it summoned up the skewed reality that these dark humorists perceived," as does the "bizarre, nightmarish ... kaleidoscopic imagery" that is characteristic of the radical democrats and was borrowed by Melville for his own subversive purposes.

A notable example of this hyperbolic and surreal imagery is Stubb's "queer dream" of being kicked by Ahab, who has turned into a pyramid, and then kicking the captain back, only to be stopped by a humpbacked old merman. When Stubb goes to kick the merman, that worthy exposes a backside full of marlinspikes. Momentarily stymied, Stubb is told by the merman to view Ahab's kicking of him as an honor comparable to a Knight of the Garter being tapped with a sword by the queen; Ahab's leg is ivory, after all, not mere flesh and bone. This cynical suggestion that one should accept gladly the abuse of one's superiors is redolent with radical-democrat humor, according to Reynolds: "In his portrayal of Stubb, Melville captures with marvelous concision the leering sarcasm and nightmarish imagery of popular humorists, particularly radical democrats," for "the comically churlish, grinning mate . . . represents the centrifugal forces of popular dark humor, the forces that fly quickly into the cynical and the chaotic as a result of a disillusion with perceived reality" (544, 546).

The third mate, Flask, is almost a parody of Ahab, for he is "a short, stout, ruddy young fellow, very pugnacious concerning whales, who somehow seemed to think that the great Leviathans had personally and hereditarily affronted him; and therefore it was a sort of point of honor with him, to destroy them whenever encountered." The difference between Flask and Ahab is that Flask's is an "ignorant, unconscious fearlessness," an aggression directed against all whales rather than one (119). While Flask seems as alien as Ahab to the democratic-religious covenant of living creatures, at least his unthinking animus is the kind that should prove profitable to Peleg and the other ship's owners, whereas Ahab's articulate obsession with Moby Dick would have meant financial disaster even if the *Pequod* had not sunk. Flask's harpooner is Daggoo, a gigantic African who towers over the little "knight."

Queequeg, Tashtego, and Daggoo are not the only harpooners aboard the *Pequod,* however. Much of the early tension in *Moby-Dick* is supplied by various hints that there are stowaways aboard the *Pequod;* figures are seen in the fog, sounds are heard as of rats below deck. These mysterious figures turn out to be the sinister Asiatic Fedallah and his four countrymen, "five dusky phantoms that seemed fresh formed out of air" as they appear suddenly around Ahab (216). Together they form one of the grander effects of *Moby-Dick,* a Gothic horror-novel convention that serve to flesh out Ahab's diabolism, throw into relief the genteel qualities of such orthodox mariners as Starbuck, and add excitement to a book heavily freighted with philosophy.

Fedallah is described as "tall and swart, with one white tooth evilly protruding from [his] steel-like lips. A rumpled Chinese jacket of black cotton funereally invested him, with wide black trousers of the same dark stuff. But strangely crowning this ebonness was a glistening white plaited turban, the living hair braided and coiled round and round upon his head." Here Melville cannot resist the creation of a fantasy figure who gives the lie to the democratic-religious sentiments that suffuse almost every other page of *Moby-Dick.* And this dark-skinned figure with his unfortunate orthodonture and his snaky locks is joined by companions "of that vivid, tiger-yellow

complexion peculiar to some of the aboriginal natives of the Manil-
las," a race "by some honest white mariners supposed to be the
paid spies and secret confidential agents on the water of the devil,
their lord" (217). In light of Melville's comments elsewhere on the
brotherhood of all humankind, it seems less likely that these lines
represent an unqualified animus for a particular racial group as
a surrender to a melodramatic impulse that has, unfortunately, a
racial bias at its base.

Importantly, Fedallah is, though tacitly described as Asiatic, a
character who seems to derive from the cabala and from Jewish
folklore more than from any country that might be recognized by
Melville's readers.

He was such a creature as civilized, domestic people in the temperate zone
only see in their dreams, and that but dimly; but the like of whom now
and then glide among the unchanging Asiatic communities, especially the
Oriental isles to the east of the continent — those insulated, immemorial
unalterable countries, which even in these modern days preserve much of
the ghostly aboriginalness of earth's primal generations, when the memory
of the first man was a distinct recollection, and all men his descendants,
unknowing whence he came, eyed each other as real phantoms, and asked
of the sun and the moon why they were created and to what end; when
though, according to Genesis, the angels indeed consorted with the daugh-
ters of men, the devils also, add the uncanonical Rabbins, indulged in
mundane amours. (231)

More than anything, Fedallah functions as a familiar between Ahab
and a traditional, historically based world of evil. For if there is a
God who has anointed figures as various as Bunyan, Cervantes, and
Andrew Jackson over a period of time (see the concluding paragraph of chapter 26 of *Moby-Dick* and my analysis of it, above),
then His counterpart must exist to perform parallel if antithetical
functions. It is important that Melville keep Ahab believable, after
all, and the presence of Fedallah aboard the *Pequod* allows Ahab to
give full vent to his demonism and still to appear verisimilitudinous.
If Ahab is, in the end, a man, Fedallah is the devil's man. Together
the two make a formidable, destructive, and self-destructive pair.

Collectively, Melville refers to the crew of the *Pequod* as "an
Anacharsis Clootz deputation from all the isles of the sea, and all
the ends of the earth" (121). Anacharsis Clootz or Cloots was a fa-
natical and eccentric French revolutionary who, in 1790, brought a

delegation of foreigners to the National Assembly as ambassadors of the human race; later he was executed during the Reign of Terror. In chapter 40 of *Moby-Dick,* a chapter made up of dialogue, snatches of song, and stage directions, this Anacharsis Clootz deputation appears to sing, quarrel, kid each other, and celebrate the world's diversity; among them are Tashtego, Daggoo, and sailors from Nantucket, Holland, France, Iceland, Malta, Sicily, Long Island, the Azores, China, India, the Isle of Man, Tahiti, Portugal, Denmark, England, Spain, and Ireland. Melville takes pains here to include men from all races and all lands, men naturally divided by innate prejudice yet capable of pulling together in a common cause; Daggoo and the Spanish sailor exchange racial insults and nearly come to blows, but when a squall develops up, all work together to save the ship and themselves. Unhappily, the sailors' cause is Ahab's, but as yet the fullness of his obsession is still hidden.

In addition to the crew members detailed above, certain ones among the crew of the *Pequod* stand out both because of their distinctive characters and also because of what they contribute to an understanding of Melville's worldview. These include the ship's carpenter and blacksmith and mad Pip, who is yet another of Melville's waifs and orphans. The description of the carpenter recalls the passages in *White-Jacket* that describe the "world-puzzle" (see chapter 2 of this study), for he is, not merely a jack-of-all-trades, but an all-in-one representative of every occupation, a one-man Anacharsis Clootz deputation of, not races, but jobs. Because a ship's carpenter is necessarily not only "experienced in numerous trades and callings collateral to his own" but also "singularly efficient in those thousand nameless mechanical emergencies continually recurring in a large ship, upon a three or four years' voyage, in uncivilized and far-distant seas" (including the making of a new ivory leg for Ahab when he accidentally shatters the old one), Melville likens the carpenter to what would today be called a Swiss army knife: "those unreasoning but still highly useful, *multum in parvo* [many in small], Sheffield contrivances, assuming the exterior — though a little swelled — of a common pocket knife; but containing, not only blades of various sizes, but also screwdrivers, cork-screws, tweezers, awls, pens, rulers, nail-filers, countersinkers" (466, 468). While the carpenter is clearly a unity, then, he is understood most of the time as a collection of parts, so that, "if his superiors wanted to use the carpenter for a screwdriver, all they had to do was open that part of him, and the screw was fast; or if for tweezers, take him up by the legs, and there they were" (168).

Significantly, Ahab does not appreciate the carpenter's versatility. Having made the coffin that Queequeg has ordered and then being ordered to convert it into a lifebuoy to replace one that was lost, the carpenter is interrogated by Ahab and asked, "Art thou not an arrant, all-grasping, intermeddling, monopolizing, heathenish old scamp, to be one day making legs, and the next day coffins to clap them in, and yet again life-buoys out of those same coffins? Thou art as unprincipled as the gods, and as much a jack-of-all-trades" (527). There is no practical reason for the captain to dislike this industrious, competent tradesman, so the animosity must stem from a perceived difference in temperaments; the carpenter is as broad in his goals as Ahab is narrow in his. Too, the carpenter, associated already with "gods" by Ahab, is likened to the Titans a page later, and is challenged when he uses the word *faith,* even though he says "it's only a sort of exclamation-like — that's all, sir" (528). To the mates and the crew, the carpenter figures as an admirable specimen of humankind. But to Ahab he is entirely too godlike in his self-sufficiency, and there is room for but one god aboard the *Pequod.* The carpenter is also a model of action rather than thought, so that when Ahab asks him what he "means" by his versatility, he replies, "But I do not mean anything, sir. I do as I do" (527). This response too is grating to the thought-tormented and envious Ahab.

The zombie gloom of Perth the blacksmith contrasts starkly with the unthinking efficiency of the carpenter. A once-happy landsman, Perth has fallen far: "He had been an artisan of famed excellence, and with plenty to do; owned a house and garden; embraced a youthful, daughter-like, loving wife, and three blithe, ruddy children; every Sunday went to a cheerful-looking church, planted in a grove." But Perth's Eden is invaded by a serpent, "a desparate burglar" who takes everything — "It was the Bottle Conjuror! Upon the opening of that fatal cork, forth flew the fiend, and shrivelled up his home." A drunkard, Perth hammered less and less; "the bellows fell; the forge choked up with cinders; the house was sold; the mother dived down into the long church-yard grass; her children twice followed her thither; and the houseless, familyless old man staggered off a vagabond" (485–86). Having destroyed his life on land, Perth now experiences a living death on the seas. Perth is both a reminder of the fragility of happiness as well as, like other Melville characters, notably Bartleby, one of those who seems to exist mainly as a protest against life as it is lived by the Starbucks of this world.

Of all the minor characters, though, none represents the quintessential solitude of the human condition as well as Pip. Like Stubb and Fedallah, Pip is a character who would be secondary and all-but-dispensable in a less-ambitious book but is essential in an encyclopedic narrative like *Moby-Dick*. Pip has cost the crew a whale by leaping into the sea in a moment of panic and becoming entangled in the line; Stubb orders Tashtego to cut the line but warns Pip to " 'stick to the boat... or by the Lord, I won't pick you up if you jump.' " But Pip does jump, and Stubb is true to his word. "It was a beautiful, bounteous, blue day; the spangled sea calm and cool, and flatly stretching away, all round, to the horizon, like gold-beater's skin hammered out to the extremest.... In three minutes, a whole mile of shoreless ocean was between Pip and Stubb." For a short while, a strong swimmer is as physically safe in the open ocean as he is a few yards from shore, "but the awful loneliness is intolerable. The intense concentration of self in the middle of such a heartless immensity, my God! who can tell it?" Stubb had not really meant to abandon Pip but assumed that one of the other whaleboats would see his dilemma and pick him up. The other mates are in pursuit of whales of their own, as it turns out, and by the time that Pip is rescued by the *Pequod* itself, he has gone quite mad: "From that hour the little negro went about the deck an idiot.... The sea had jeeringly kept his finite body up, but drowned the infinite of his soul. Not drowned entirely, though. Rather carried down alive to wondrous depths, where strange shapes of the unwarped primal world glided to and fro before his passive eyes; and the miser-merman, Wisdom, revealed his hoarded heaps; and among the joyous, heartless, ever-juvenile eternities, Pip saw the multitudinous, God-omnipresent, coral insects, that out of the firmament of waters heaved the colossal orbs." Pip sees what Ishmael himself wanted to see, but he is not strong enough to withstand the impact of the vision: "He saw God's foot upon the treadle of the loom, and spoke it; and therefore his shipmates called him mad" (413–14).

Throughout the rest of the book, Pip will refer to himself in the third person and inquire as to his own whereabouts, having left the self he knew in the depths. Together with the lines on the "insular Tahiti" and the chapter entitled "The Symphony" (see analyses, above), these paragraphs on Pip define the state of maddening solitude that each of us is but a step from. All three of these passages describe someone adrift on a sea, one that may be beautiful but beneath which lie unspeakable terrors. Or terrors speakable only in some new, incomprehensible tongue. As Starbuck says, concerning Pip's prattling, "I have heard...that in violent fevers, men, all ignorance, have talked in ancient tongues; and that when the mystery is probed, it turns out always that in their wholly forgotten childhood those ancient tongues had been really spoken in their hearing by some lofty scholars. So, to my fond faith, poor Pip, in this strange sweetness of his lunacy, brings heavenly vouchers of all our heavenly homes" (479).

Yet if Pip is a warning to Ishmael, he is a warning to Melville, too, since the author of *Moby-Dick* himself speaks of storming heaven. The problem is one of language, not one of Pip's strong points to begin with. Having seen God, he lacks the words to describe Him and so remains submerged in his inarticulate knowledge of things divine, unable to communicate with his shipmates. For "man's insanity is heaven's sense; and wandering from all mortal reason, man comes at last to that celestial thought, which, to reason, is absurd and frantic; and weal or woe, feels then uncompromised, indifferent as his God" (414). But Pip was just a boy when he jumped the second time, whereas Melville was writing in the fullness of his literary powers, convinced that he belonged to that "corps of thought-divers" that included Emerson and Shakespeare.

The Reader

The assumption is that the reader too is a deep diver. Melville never made it easy on his readers, and *Moby-Dick* is one of the great challenges in all literature. Novices may be tempted to skim or skip entirely such "digressions" as the chapters on cetology, but this is a failed strategy, since so many passages that seem at first glance to be mere glosses on some Melvillean whim turn out to be indispensable to the book as a whole.

Besides, his reputation as a difficult author notwithstanding, Melville is surprisingly seductive, if not ultimately accommodating; he was too insistent on his own views to make significant concessions to readers' desires. But there are a number of passages in *Moby-*

Dick that simultaneously announce the difficulty of interpretation while teasingly inviting a closer look. While waiting in New Bedford for the packet-boat that will take him to Nantucket, whence the whaling ships depart, Ishmael checks in at the Spouter Inn, where he sees "a very large oil-painting so thoroughly besmoked, and every way defaced, that in the unequal cross-lights by which you viewed it, it was only by diligent study and a series of systematic visits to it . . . that you could any way arrive at an understanding of its purpose." This is a portentous way to begin a book that will itself demand diligent study and a series of systematic visits by the reader who wishes to take in its entirety.

The painting Ishmael studies is "a boggy, soggy, squitchy picture truly, enough to drive a nervous man distracted," and yet "there was a sort of indefinite, half-attained, unimaginable sublimity about it that fairly froze you to it, till you involuntarily took an oath with yourself to find out what that marvelous painting meant." This is indeed a wondrous art work, at once puzzling and confounding yet somehow riveting as well. Its subject could be any number of things, and Ishmael lists some possibilities: a midnight gale on the Black Sea, a blasted heath (out of *King Lear,* presumably), and so on. But he finally decides that the "picture represents a Cape-Horner in a great hurricane; the half-foundered ship weltering there with its three dismantled masts alone visible; and an exasperated whale, purposing to spring clean over the craft, is in the enormous act of impaling himself upon the three mast-heads" (12–13). Ultimately, then, the painting offers a scene of menace and destruction, even though that interpretation is (a) only arrived at after many viewings and (b) but one of many possibilities. Implicit in this scene, however, is the suggestion that each of us must dissect the materials of our own lives to discover what, if anything, they can tell us.

For the great truths may never be revealed, or, if so, only at the viewer's peril. Melville discusses the matter of artistic representation in several other passages in *Moby-Dick* that recall this one, though often there is a warning as well. Chapter 55, for example, concludes:

Any way you may look at it, you must needs conclude that the great Leviathan is that one creature in the world which must remain unpainted to the last. True, one portrait may hit the mark much nearer than another, but none can hit it with any very considerable degree of exactness. So there is no earthly way of finding out precisely what the whale really looks like. And the only mode in which you can derive even a tolerable idea of his living contour, is by going a whaling yourself; but by so doing, you run no small risk of being eternally stove and sunk by him. Wherefore, it seems to me you had best not be too fastidious in your curiosity touching this Leviathan. (264)

But caution is not the same as refusal, and Ishmael will make his attempt at depiction, no matter how impossible or exhausting it may be: "Give me a condor's quill! Give me Vesuvius' crater for an inkstand! Friends, hold my arms! For in the mere act of penning my thoughts, they weary me, and make me faint" (456). Thus the reader struggling with *Moby-Dick* or any other difficult text should assume no willful authorial obfuscation; if the reader's task of decoding is laborious, the author's task of representing is even more so.

The search for answers takes many forms in *Moby-Dick,* and virtually every mode of inquiry is mentioned at one point or another: painting, science, philosophy, religion, adventure, literature. Similarly, many types of inquirers are depicted, from the aggressive Ahab to the pensive Ishmael. As one might expect in a book of this encyclopedic breadth and intent, there is also a variety of "artists," from the various artisans aboard the *Pequod* to Father Mapple, who recasts the instructive parable of Jonah in contemporary terms; Jonah's suspicious shipmates not only have American names but also colloquial speech patterns: "In their gamesome but still serious way, one whispers to the other — 'Jack, he's robbed a widow'; or, 'Joe, do you mark him; he's a bigamist'; or, 'Harry lad, I guess he's the adulterer that broke jail in old Gomorrah, or belike, one of the missing murderers from Sodom' " (43). All of these questers help to create a context of questing in which the reader partakes; the task is never made easy for the reader, but there is plenty of company. When Ishmael reports that Queequeg is from Kokovoko, he adds that this island "is not down in any map; true places never are" (55). Melville's crew of questers, the reader included, are trying to reach those true, if unmapped, places.

Thus the call to create, to read, to interpret is constant in *Moby-Dick.* In chapter 36, Ahab nails a doubloon to the mainmast and promises it to the man who sights Moby Dick; chapter 99 amounts to an essay on interpretation in which the principal characters in the drama study and then describe the coin in ways more revelatory of their own characters than of anything objectively true about the doubloon itself. Ishmael, for example, takes pains to be clear, precise, and noncommittal about what he sees, whereas Ahab sees repeated references to himself in the coin. Starbuck is saddened by what he sees, Stubb jokey, and the practical Flask imagines how many cigars he'll be able to buy should he win the prize. At the end of this procession of characters comes mad but wise Pip, who interprets the interpreters themselves by means of a verb conjugation: "I look, you look, he looks; we look, ye look, they look" (434). Pip's grammar lesson suggests that many look in *Moby-Dick,* though few see.

Ultimately, the various representations of looking, seeing, reading, creating, interpreting, and so on in *Moby-Dick* lead one to ask if there is not a single method of inquiry endorsed above others by the book's author. At first it would seem that this question has a simple answer — since *Moby-Dick* is an encyclopedia of sorts, and since Melville endorses encyclopedia writing in both explicit and implicit ways, one might conclude that the way to the truth is through data gathering. There is something to this suggestion; clearly *Moby-Dick* is an attempt to amass a vast amount of evidence that will lead to a conclusion of some sort. Yet data gathering, though crucial, is but the first stage in Melville's method. In chapter 74, following a description of the smallness and delicacy of the sperm whale's eyes and ears, Ishmael asks rhetorically if larger sense organs would enable the whale to see or hear more. Since the answer is clearly a negative one, he asks, "Why then do you try to 'enlarge' your mind? Subtilize it" (331). To gather the world's data is to reconstitute the world's immensity between the covers of a single book. The question then becomes, What is the reader to make of all this?

Using the practical example of the whaling industry to show the reader how to reconstitute and study the world's immensity, Melville chooses images from that same industry to give lessons in subtlety as well. Chapter 89, "Fast-Fish and Loose-Fish," explores the area of maritime law that determines whalers' rights in cases where more than one claimant asserts ownership of a single whale; for example, the crew from one ship might harpoon a whale only to have the crew of a second vessel seize it. Melville makes a metaphor of the concept and extends it to the domination of greater nations over smaller ones and beyond: "What are all men's minds and opinions but Loose-Fish? What is the principle of religious belief in them but a Loose-Fish? What to the ostentatious smuggling thoughts of thinkers but Loose-Fish? What is the great globe itself but a Loose-Fish?" He concludes: "And what are you, reader, but a Loose-Fish and a Fast-Fish, too?" (398). Each of us — each thing — is owned and free at the same time, and if we can appreciate this fundamental condition of existence, then we have "subtilized" our minds.

Melville was giving lessons in subtlety well before *Moby-Dick,* of course. As one reads his masterpiece, one recalls perforce the Chinese puzzle section of *White-Jacket* and sees numerous analogies in this later work. There are numerous passages in *Moby-Dick* where Melville points out how parts form wholes and where he characteristically juxtaposes different examples of this phenomenon. In chapter 2, for example, Ishmael thinks how his body is like a house and both are like the universe itself in its finished if imperfect state: "Yes, these eyes are windows, and this body of mine is the house. What a pity they didn't stop up the chinks and crannies though, and thrust in a little lint here and there. But it's too late to make any improvements now. The universe is finished; the copestone is on, and the chips were carted off a million years ago" (10). Whereas passages of this sort seemed in *White-Jacket* to be attempts at developing a means of grasping the subtlety of our complex existence in this world, here they not only seem fully developed but also take their place as part of that democratic-religious spirit (discussed above) that suffuses *Moby-Dick.* Each thing is a puzzle, consisting of parts that eventually make a whole; and since all things share this fundamental structure, each thing is therefore unique unto itself and simultaneously akin to all other things.

The *Pequod* itself is a central example of the Chinese puzzle idea. In chapter 16, "The Ship," the *Pequod* is described as "a ship of the old school," one that takes its character from every part of the globe: "Her old hull's complexion was darkened like a French grenadier's, who has alike fought in Egypt and Siberia." Her masts were "cut somewhere on the coast of Japan, where her original ones were lost overboard in a gale"; now they "stood stiffly up like the spines of the three old kings of Cologne," and her decks are as worn as "the pilgrim-worshipped flag-stone in Canterbury Cathedral where Becket bled." Yet to this "ship of the old school" have been added "new and marvelous features"; old Peleg, one of the owners, "had built upon her original grotesqueness, and inlaid it all over, with a quaintness both of material and device," so that she is now "apparelled like any barbaric Ethiopian emperor" and is both "a thing of trophies" and a "cannibal of a craft" with whale teeth in the bulwarks instead of pins and a tiller "curiously carved from the long narrow lower jaw of her hereditary foe." Thus the *Pequod* strikes Ishmael, who is seeing it for the first time, as a "noble craft, but somehow a most melancholy!" (69–70). Ishmael's assessment shows the subtlety of his own mind as well as that of his creator's in a way that has not yet been demonstrated in any Melville book, for there is both nobility and melancholy in the *Pequod*'s construction. In themselves, or as puzzle pieces, its parts suggest the world's variety; taken as a whole, however, the *Pequod* is clearly a death ship, as the last moments of its history make clear.

In the confident fullness of his artistic prowess, either Melville is careful to avoid the trap that snared Adam, Prometheus, Faust, and other prideful seekers (including Ahab) or else he is simply unable to lay his hand on the knowledge that he seems otherwise so eager to claim. As Ishmael says, though, his inquiry will be go unfinished, at least by himself, for "small erections may be finished by their first architects; grand ones, true ones, ever leave the copestone to posterity" (145). There is a certain not-altogether-serious modesty to this statement, but, in a sense, Ishmael's formulation *is* complete. That is, an inquiry based on action rather than results will be complete as long as the action continues; an inquiry based on action but one that achieves results and then ceases is necessarily a failure. As we have seen, *Mardi* and *White-Jacket,* the two books that have figured most significantly in Melville's preparation for the writing of *Moby-Dick,* end with searches in progress, whereas the others all end in static isolation.

Surprisingly, so does *Moby-Dick.* The last word of the text proper is "orphan": Moby Dick having dragged down not only the crew of the ship but the *Pequod* herself, Ishmael alone is by another ship that, looking for its own missing crew members, "only found another orphan" (573). Why? Given what seems to be a vital interconnection between the three books, one might reasonably expect *Moby-Dick* to end dynamically as do *Mardi* and *White-Jacket* rather than in the static manner of *Typee, Omoo,* and *Redburn.* But Ishmael's fate is the right one, after all, if one considers that he has accomplished what his creator intended for him to do, that is, perfect a system of inquiry, one that succeeds, as we have seen, by remaining imperfect. In his life as well as in his writings, Melville underscores again and again the loneliness of the human condition. But whereas the loneliness of Tommo, Typee, and Redburn is an impoverished and miserable one, that of Ishmael is rich and satisfying. To the very last, he is chanting poetry: "Now small fowls flew screaming over the yet yawning gulf; a sullen white surf beat against its steep sides; then all collapsed, and the great shroud of the sea rolled on as it rolled five thousand years ago" (572). Against the self-pitying lamentations of Tommo and the others, Ishmael puts an attitude of understanding and acceptance, for he has both enlarged his mind and subtilized it. James Barbour describes Melville's pursuit of "the ungraspable beast" as "a foredefeated venture."[15] Yet Ishmael's physical defeat is not the end of his story. It is, instead, the penultimate stage: Ishmael's physical defeat merely occasions the spiritual triumph that comes with the relation of his personal history. We must bear in mind always that Ishmael's story is, after all, a first-person narrative told long after the occurrence of its "events."

But if Ishmael's labors are done, the reader's are not. In a sense, one will never be done with reading *Moby-Dick;* it is one of those books that continually call into question everything that is best and worst about our culture, and each generation will need to examine it again. Each new generation of readers, of course, is a Chinese puzzle in itself, composed as it is of individual pieces that have the potential to be a whole. And though each reader is alone, each is connected to others in ways suggested by various passages in *Moby-Dick.* One of these is chapter 47, "The Mat-Maker"; here, Ishmael and Queequeg are using a wooden sword to weave mats that will be used to cushion the whaleboats from the ship, and Ishmael reflects that the woof (or horizontal rope) represents his own free will as it threads around the warp (the vertical thread) of necessity and is struck by Queequeg's sword, which represents chance. Until they end, our lives are governed by all of these factors, some of which are in our control, some not. In this way, says Ishmael, we are both free and chained simultaneously.

At rare moments, though, Ishmael gets utterly, blissfully lost in the democratic-religious spirit of Melville's world. One such incident occurs in chapter 94, where he and his fellows are squeezing the lumps out of spermaceti, a lumpy, waxy substance extracted from blubber and from a cavity in the whale's head (where it helps maintain the head's buoyancy) and used as a lubricant and in ointments, cosmetics, candles, and soap. "It was our business to squeeze these lumps back into fluid," says Ishmael, and "a sweet and unctuous duty" it is:

Such a clearer! such a sweetener! such a softener! such a delicious mollifier....

As I sat there at my ease, cross-legged on the deck ... under a blue tranquil sky; the ship under indolent sail, and gliding so serenely along; as I bathed my hands among those soft, gentle globules of infiltrated tissues, woven almost within the hour; as they richly broke to my fingers, and discharged all their opulence, like fully ripe grapes their wine; as I snuffed up that uncontaminated aroma, — literally and truly, like the smell of spring violets; I declare to you, that for the time I lived as in a musky meadow; I forgot all about our horrible oath [to slay the white whale]; in that inexpressible sperm, I washed my hands and heart of it....

Squeeze! squeeze! squeeze! all the morning long; I squeezed that sperm till I myself almost melted into it; I squeezed that sperm until a strange sort of insanity came over me; and I found myself unwittingly squeezing my co-laborers' hands in it, mistaking their hands for the gentle globules. Such an abounding, affectionate, friendly, loving feeling did this avocation beget; that at last I was continually squeezing their hands, and looking up into their eyes sentimentally....

Would that I could keep squeezing that sperm for ever! ... In thoughts of the visions of the night, I saw long rows of angels in paradise, each with his hands in a jar of spermaceti. (416)

Occurring late in the book, this rhapsodic passage seems very much like the other side of a coin whose face is that passage in chapter 1 in which Ishmael says he does not mind if "some old hunks of a sea-captain" should "thump and punch him," for "everybody else is one way or another served in much the same way — either in a physical or a metaphysical point of view, that is; and so the universal thump is passed round" (6). In this world of universal thumps, the individual pieces of the Chinese puzzle seem destined not to come together satisfactorily. But in the world of affectionate squeezes, the puzzle pieces come together at last, if only briefly.

Carolyn Karcher points out that "despite the comic homoerotic spirit of this passage, it serves as serious a purpose as the comic account of the friendship with Queequeg that reaches its consummation in the landlord's conjugal bed" (75). The very exuberance of the passage compels all but the most literal minded of readers to surrender to the barrier-dissolving (albeit temporary) passion of the sailors, who are here likened to angels.

No single reader or generation of readers will ever be satisfied with a single interpretation of this immense book whose subject is immensity. In rare moments, Melville's readership will squeeze hands affectionately and come to some sort of consensus about *Moby-Dick;* more frequently, it will pass around those thumps that echo often in the halls of academe. But then that is what it means to be a thought-diver.

4

The Later Novels

Pierre

In his exultation over the completion of *Moby-Dick,* Melville wrote a letter to Hawthorne (probably on November 17, 1851) that suggests he had even bigger works in him. "Lord, when shall we be done growing? As long as we have anything more to do, we have done nothing. So, now, let us add Moby Dick to our blessing, and step from that. Leviathan is not the biggest fish; — I have heard of Krakens."[1] The kraken is a legendary sea monster said to inhabit the waters off Norway; did Melville really think his thought-diving would take him past the realms of whales to depths inhabited by creatures even more marvelous? It is true that in *Pierre* he meant to present his female readers with a "rural bowl of milk" to compensate for the masculine world of *Moby-Dick.*[2] But Harrison Hayford and the other editors of the standard edition of Melville's work speculate that, confident in his now fully-developed abilities, Melville may have intended to write a pleasing romance on the surface, yet to enrich and fortify his simple tale with a psychological profundity hitherto unapproached by himself or by any other author.[3] Yet his perception of the failure of *Moby-Dick* (an incorrect perception, yet a hurtful one at the time) altered the writing of *Pierre*. The result is, if not a kraken, exactly, at least one of the strangest and most provocative books of the American nineteenth century.

As Michael Paul Rogin notes, Alexis de Tocqueville believed that in this country "poets, not finding the elements of the ideal in what is real and true, abandon them entirely and create monsters," that "productions of democratic poets may often be surcharged with immense and incoherent imagery, with exaggerated descriptions and strange creations; and that the fantastic beings of their brain may sometimes make us regret the world of reality"; this is because "nothing conceivable is so petty, so insipid, so crowded with paltry interests — in one word, so antipoetic — as the life of a man in the United States."[4] Rogin himself observes that there is a powerful distinction between the European novel of this period and the American romance, that the "novel presents a society's waking activities, the romance its dream life"; further, whereas "characters develop in a novel from the texture and limits of lived experience," the characters of romances, who tend to be possessed and "driven by obsessional quests, reveal the melodramatic underside of consciousness" (15). Certainly Pierre and his intimates occupy a landscape that seems as much mental and emotional as physical.

However, it is not quite correct to suggest that *Pierre* began as a bucolic romance and then took a turn for the grotesque, as some readers suggest. The text's outlandishness is present from the very beginning and only intensifies as the narrative progresses. Within a few paragraphs the reader learns that Pierre Glendinning and his mother "were wont to call each other brother and sister" and that, further, there is an "inexpressible tenderness and attentiveness" in the "lover-like adoration of Pierre" for his mother.[5] The protagonist's unusual attitude toward his mother is partially explained by the "strange yearning of Pierre for a sister," which emotion is itself complicated by a confusion of the idea of sister with that of wife: "the solitary head of his family" and "the only surnamed male Glendinning extant," Pierre experiences an early crippling, "for surely a gentle sister is the second best gift to a man; and it is first in point of occurrence; for the wife comes after. He who is sisterless, is as a bachelor before his time. For much that goes to make up the deliciousness of a wife, already lies in the sister" (7). This, then, is Melville's pleasing romance for the ladies, a story that begins with a son/brother/lover making up to a mother/sister/wife. A narrative that begins with such explosive tensions is likely to be something more than a "rural bowl of milk."

But in addition to his complicated relationship with his mother, Pierre is also romantically attached to a more conventional type of sweetheart, a Lucy Tartan. But this linking, too, has its bizarre qualities; for example, when Pierre becomes rapturous over Lucy's beauty, he is given to bursting forth with "some screaming shout of joy," which causes Lucy to shrink from him in the realization that "the extremest top of love, is Fear and Wonder" (35). As it turns out, Pierre is troubled by more than his impassioned relations with his mother and Lucy. Pierre is haunted by the apparition of a woman's face, an apparition that takes tangible form when his half sister appears, a sibling hinted at in the incoherent words of Pierre's dying father. Pierre had been in the habit of contemplating his father's portrait and "unconsciously throwing himself open to all those ineffable hints and ambiguities, and undefined half-suggestions, which now and then people the soul's atmosphere." But when he receives a letter from Isabel, "Pierre saw all preceding ambiguities, all mysteries ripped open as if with a keen sword, and forth trooped thickening phantoms of an infinite gloom" (84–85). The effect of this revelation on Pierre is catastrophic: "On all sides, the physical world of solid objects now slidingly displaced itself from around him, and he floated into an ether of visions" (85). Heretofore he has only inferred the ambiguities created by his father's sin; hereafter he must shoulder a sort of Hawthornesque curse caused by that misdeed, a curse that blights his entire being.

The news about his sister strikes like a flash of lightning that reveals the shabbiness of the whole world: "Not only was the long-cherished image of his father now transfigured before him from a green foliaged tree into a blasted trunk, but every other image in his mind attested the universality of that electral light which had darted into his soul" (88). For a high-minded fellow like Pierre, the dilemma is all but insoluble. To acknowledge Isabel is to admit that his father was an adulterer as well as one who abandoned his own child; the admission would also break the heart of the proud Mrs. Glendinning. But to deny Isabel is to refuse a blameless young woman her rightful place socially and financially.

Pierre takes to the woods to ponder his dilemma and seats himself on a rock he calls the Memnon Stone after the king's son slain by Achilles in the Trojan War. There he thinks of another king's son, Hamlet, and of "that nobly-striving but ever-shipwrecked character in some royal youths" (136). Later he concludes that if "the pregnant tragedy of Hamlet convey any one particular moral at all fitted to the ordinary uses of man, it is this: — that all meditation is worthless, unless it prompt to action; that it is not for man to stand shillyshallying amid the conflicting invasions of surrounding impulses; that in the earliest instant of conviction, the roused man must strike, and, if possible, with the precision and the force of the lightning-bolt" (169). Pierre decides that his only recourse is to deny his own happiness and rescue Isabel by pretending to espouse her; while this sham marriage will inflict "his living mother with a wound that might be curable," better that "than cast world-wide and irremediable dishonour ... upon his departed father" (173). Earlier, Pierre has a premonition that he might "feel himself driven out an infant Ishmael into the desert, with no maternal Hagar to accompany and comfort him" (89). This prophecy is swiftly realized when the socially aware Mrs. Glendinning casts out Pierre for shaming Lucy and bringing a "thing" and "slut" into her once-proud family (193, 194).

Every other orphan and outcast in Melville has made a new family to replace the one he is excluded from; usually this new family is all male and nautical. In *Pierre,* the one Melville novel set entirely on land and concerned with heterosexual love, the protagonist's new family is closer to the traditional nuclear unit, though an expectable Melvillean quirkiness makes it seem like more a refraction than a reflection of the stereotypical combination of mother, father, and child. In his flight from the innocent rural world to the complications and turmoils of the city, Pierre is accompanied by his chaste "wife," Isabel, as well as Delly Ulver, a seduced-and-abandoned farm girl who becomes a sort of surrogate daughter as a result of Pierre's high-minded sense of obligation.

On the coach ride to the city, Pierre finds a tattered pamphlet by one Plotinus Plinlimmon, which purports to be a "scientific" critique of the Christian practice of returning good for evil, a doctrine which can only be enacted by divine beings, not mortal ones; unfortunately, the pamphlet's concluding paragraphs have been torn off, leaving Pierre reliant on his own ad hoc sense of morality. Pierre looks to his cousin Glen Stanly for welcome, but Glen, who loves Lucy, despises Pierre. In swift succession, Mrs. Glendinning dies, her entire estate goes to Glen instead of the disinherited Pierre, and Glen begins to woo Lucy, who, though jilted, has come to town to be near her former lover, to whom she promises to be as a "nun-like cousin" (311).

Troubled already, Pierre finds no comfort in his new domestic arrangement and instead descends into a nightmarish torpor haunted by a vision of Enceladus, the "doubly incestuous" Titan whose father, the product of an incestuous match, has married his own mother (347). The theme of incest, never very far from the surface of the novel, recurs when Pierre, Isabel, and Lucy visit a gallery where they view portraits of Beatrice Cenci, who was guilty of parricide as well as incest, and also an Italian who bears a close resemblance to the father of Pierre and Isabel. At this point "the ambiguities" have closed in on Pierre once more and are all but smothering him. The pamphleteer Plinlimmon makes a brief appearance in the novel but is clearly a charlatan rather than a genuine thought-diver; neither he nor any other thinker can save Pierre from his increasing confusion. Too, his unstable emotional life has been made even more tumultuous by Pierre's unsuccessful attempts to make his living as an author.

The crisis reaches its climax on the day that Pierre receives two hateful letters. The one is from the publishing firm of "Steel, Flint & Asbestos" which, in a clear reference to *Moby-Dick* (and, generally, all of Melville's books), avers that, "upon the pretext of writing a popular novel for us, you have been receiving cash advances from us, while passing through our press the sheets of a blasphemous rhapsody." The second letter is from Glen Stanley and Lucy's brother Fred who, convinced that Pierre has somehow hypnotized Lucy into following him, call him a "villainous and perjured liar" and vow their eternal enmity (356). His professional life come to smash and his personal life aswirl in hopeless confusion, Pierre stuffs this last letter into the barrels of the pistols he kills Glen with; Lucy collapses and dies when she visits Pierre in prison, and he and Isabel kill themselves by swallowing poison.

The personal letter seems to be the one that pushes Pierre over the brink into madness, but the one from the firm of Steel, Flint & Asbestos represents another strain of discord that has been nearly as troubling to Pierre as his unhappy family relations. Like Melville himself, Pierre resolves to write a book "which the world should hail with surprise and delight" (283). Another character asks playfully if Pierre is not writing a kind of *Inferno*, but while Pierre's work may have the scope and ambition of Dante's masterpiece, in the end it is denounced as blasphemy by the very firm that has agreed to publish it.

At the time that these chapters of *Pierre* were being written, there was every indication that *Moby-Dick* would likely be misunderstood and ill received by public and critics alike, and Melville clearly refers here to his dashed expectations for that book.[6] Yet he seems to be aware as well of the failure of his hopes for *Pierre*, the putative "rural bowl of milk" that in so many ways recalls Hawthorne's *Blithedale Romance* (both books appeared in 1852) yet which, in the end, is so different from that novel. Both books are characterized by highly episodic structures and a common town-versus-country theme as well as such plot elements as false prophets (Hollingsworth/Westervelt, Plinlimmon), chaste, artificial relationships (Hollingsworth and Zenobia/Priscilla), and failed Utopias (Blithedale, the colony of the Apostles where Pierre lives when he tries to make his living as a writer). But the highly idiosyncratic *Pierre* is not a more or less conventional novel of the *Blithedale Romance* type. And Melville's ambitions notwithstanding, his tortured authorship bore less and less resemblance to Hawthorne's comparatively calm professionalism as the years passed and the personal divide between the two writers grew wider.

Carolyn L. Karcher believes that Melville tried sincerely to write conventionally in *Pierre* but could not help producing "a novel about how a patriotic and sensitive young American, born to the social position the Melville family had inherited, comes to recognize the disparity between the democratic and religious ideals his peers and mentors profess and the poverty, exploitation, and injustice they sanction. Even more, *Pierre* is a novel about the entrapment of a young American who, unlike Ishmael, cannot transcend his discredited world view by finding a meaningful way of acting on his new perceptions and affirming his solidarity with downtrodden humanity."[7] And Ishmael had only his obsessed captain to deal with; Melville was dealing with the much greater horror of his professional setbacks.

One of Melville's best-known self-criticisms is contained in a letter to Hawthorne in which he writes, "What I feel most moved to write, that is banned, — it will not pay. Yet, altogether, write the *other* way I cannot. So the product is a final hash, and all my books are botches."[8] A book like *Pierre* shows exactly what Melville meant when he said that he "cannot" write conventional romances. Clearly he means, not "will not lower myself," but simply "am unable to." That is, he felt himself compelled (at least this once) to write a book that met his readers' expectations yet found that he had lacked the means to write conventionally.

Melville was clearly writing autobiographically in the chapters that deal explicitly with authorship, and one wonders if he was not doing so earlier when he reflected that Pierre tended to "lose himself in the most surprising and preternatural ponderings, which baffled all the introspective cunning of his mind. Himself was too much for himself. He felt that what he had always before considered the solid land of veritable reality, was now being audaciously encroached upon by bannered armies of hooded phantoms, disembarking in his soul, as from flotillas of spectre-boats" (49). The Melville who, following the failure of the fanciful *Mardi*, was able to draw on his "introspective cunning" and approximate the success of the bare-boned narratives *Typee* and *Omoo* with the similar *Redburn* and *White-Jacket*, was now finding himself irresistibly drawn to the "blasphemous rhapsody" of *Moby-Dick* and *Pierre*.

Thus *Pierre* is in one way the most autobiographical of Melville's writings, since it deals with his principal concern, the driving force of his very existence, namely, authorship. Yet Melville's true feelings about writing are placed in an invented setting. According to Michael Paul Rogin, "Four of the six books Melville published before *Pierre* are autobiographical. There is invention in each, but each is faithful in broad outline to the events from which it derives. *Pierre* wrote a finish to Melville's autobiographical fiction"; indeed, "*Pierre* is bourgeois family nightmare, not autobiography" (166). Yet it is Melville's most extended commentary on his professional aspiration and disappointment.

In dramatizing the inevitable disastrous end of the "blasphemous rhapsody" style of authorship, Melville has his protagonist stuff words down a gun barrel and blast them into the body of his enemy. A similar scene was the occasion of mirth in *White-Jacket*, when the bard Lemsford sees his verse shot from a cannon's mouth. But in *Pierre* the analogous action is grotesque rather than whimsical, fatal instead of funny. This is not to say that Melville lost his sense of humor as he pondered *Moby-Dick*'s poor reception and looked ahead toward the readily foreseeable failure of *Pierre*. But in *Pierre* and the two novels that followed it, the transcendent and optimistic humor that characterizes the earlier works is replaced by a humor that is grim and biting — perhaps, in *The Confidence-Man*, even murderous.

Israel Potter

Throughout his career, Melville alternated between narratives that were largely fact-based and others that were largely invented. Whereas *Typee* and *Omoo* followed his own adventures closely, *Mardi* was almost entirely fanciful; whereas *Redburn* and *White-*

Jacket remained more or less true to the events of his own life, *Moby-Dick* and *Pierre* were mainly exercises of the artist's imagination. *Israel Potter* marked a return to true adventures, but with this difference: the exploits were someone else's this time, not Melville's own. *Israel Potter; or, His Fifty Years of Exile* was based, at least in its early chapters, on an 1824 narrative, Henry Trumbull's *Life and Remarkable Adventures of Israel R. Potter,* the biography of a man who fought at the Battle of Bunker Hill yet failed to reap the rewards due a Revolutionary hero and ended his days as a peddler in London. Ostensibly the literal biography of an obscure figure and therefore a work that has not received the attention of Melville's other writings, *Israel Potter* is more than it seems at first glance and, indeed, deserves a more exalted status than it has customarily been given.

In order both to separate *Israel Potter* from the *Life and Remarkable Adventures* and to give it its proper place in the Melville canon, three points might be made initially. The first is that Melville adhered to his historical source mainly in the early chapters, inventing episodes after that and also interpolating historical material from other sources. Melville's Potter serves as a spy for Benjamin Franklin, has his boldest naval adventures while serving under John Paul Jones, and encounters Ethan Allen in captivity; the original Potter spoke to Franklin once and never encountered these other Revolutionary heroes.[9]

The other two points do not involve changes in the narrative; instead, they suggest the irresistible attraction of the Potter story for Melville and its resonance with events and ideas already central to Melville's very being. For one thing, the real-life Israel Potter shared a birthday with Melville; as Melville would have seen immediately upon opening the *Life,* the caption beneath the frontispiece reads, "Israel R. Potter / Born in Cranston (R.I.) August 1.st 1744."[10] Interestingly, in Melville's narrative the hero's home is not located in the Cranston, Rhode Island, of the original Israel Potter but in Melville's own Berkshire country near Pittsfield, Massachusetts, suggesting a further identification between the author and his protagonist.

The remaining point involves the protagonist's distinctive name. "Potter" is a common name denoting a common profession and connoting the ignominy associated with the phrase "potter's field," the burial place of paupers, the anonymous dead, and criminals.

Such an association would hardly be lost on the Melville who had enjoyed literary fame, had seen his hopes for greater glory dashed, and now wondered if he would even be able to support his family. However, this luckless Potter's given name would have conjured an entirely different set of ideas. "Israel" is the nation of the chosen, the saved, the children of Abraham's legitimate son, the pure-blooded Isaac; it bears a mocking resemblance to "Ishmael," the name of the half-breed bastard outcast who was excluded from God's Covenant. Melville had already told the story of an Ishmael whose struggles with orthodoxy had yielded decidedly mixed results, a character who dramatized his creator's spiritual adventures more than anything else. And now he would tell (or retell) the story of an Israel whose life, like Melville's own, was poised between ignominy and glory, a figure destined for the one, perhaps, yet ever hopeful of the other. If Melville was going to tell someone else's story, he might have done better to choose a more celebrated figure with greater appeal to the reading public. As it was, he was drawn to a twin of sorts, someone who shared a birthday with him and had a name that not only bore a superficial resemblance to that of the central character of his most ambitious book but also suggested Melville's own greatest hopes and fears.

Israel Potter's story begins on the familiar notes of orphanage and solitude; breaking with his father over the love of a neighbor's daughter, he is spurned by the girl and then cheated out of his wages by an unscrupulous employer. Thus the young Israel quickly finds himself as bereft of family, love, and money as Tommo or Typee or Ishmael and without so much as a Toby or Dr. Long Ghost or Queequeg to call friend. Like the professionless Melville, he turns sailor, shipping aboard several vessels, including a whaler. Following his return, Potter becomes a soldier and fights at the historic battle of Bunker Hill, a highly ambiguous British "victory" that turned into a triumph for the other side because of spirited American resistance and British failure to break the siege of Boston, where their own troops were starving.

With characteristic whimsy, Melville dedicated *Israel Potter* "To / His Highness / The / Bunker-Hill Monument," which he describes with no little irony as "the Great Biographer: the national commemorator of such of the anonymous privates of June 17, 1775, who may never have received other requital than the solid reward of your granite" (vii–viii). Melville's self-appointed mission is to

rescue from anonymity one of these unsung privates, a palpable
mortal who contrasts sharply with the quasi-religious, quasi-royal
abstraction of the battle as it has been immortalized both in the
history books and as the indifferent granite monument itself. And
Melville confers further significance on "Bunker-Hill" by hyphen-
ating it as he did the subjects of *White-Jacket, Moby-Dick,* and
The Confidence-Man. Though the novel's ostensible subject is the
adventures, largely overseas, of Israel Potter, the battle of Bunker
Hill looms large as background; this negative victory or positive
defeat that had been unthinkingly and antidemocratically memo-
rialized in the popular mind is invoked throughout and serves as
a stark contrast to the smaller, human-scale ambiguities of Israel
Potter's life.

The patriotic Potter volunteers for service aboard one of the vessels intended to intercept ships bringing provisions to the starving
British, and here his adventures begin with a vengeance: within a
few pages he is captured and taken aboard a British vessel, leads an
unsuccessful rebellion, is put in irons, escapes, is recaptured, escapes
again, is taken once more, and finally escapes for good, by this time
having made his way nearly to London. Within these opening pages,
Melville demonstrates not only his hero's tireless ingenuity but also
the overall pattern of his existence, the frenzied, ultimately fruitless
activity of one who clearly deserves better.

For a time, Potter makes his living as a gardener. His employees
include the kindly Sir John Millet, whom the grateful but resolutely
democratic Potter insists on calling "Mr." Millet. Eventually he gets
a berth as a laborer at Kew Gardens where, in a chapter appropriately entitled "Israel in the Lion's Den," he encounters none other
than George the Third himself. Here (and only the most credulous
of Melville's readers could have imagined he was still adhering to
the events of the actual Potter's life) the doughty hero reveals that
he is a runaway rebel, but the dotty monarch admires his honesty
and promises to say nothing.

George the Third is only the first of several larger-than-life figures
encountered by Potter, figures who make him (and by extension, all
ordinary mortals) seem genuinely if unfairly trivial in comparison.
The next such personage is Benjamin Franklin, to whom Potter is
sent by some pro-American Englishmen; before putting him on the
boat to France, the conspirators outfit Potter with a pair of hollow-
heeled shoes that contain papers important to their cause. Franklin

is full of apothegms and homilies, sayings that ring true yet that, in their pastoral simplicity, do little to help Potter deal with the unpredictable complexities of his life. Besides, there is something of the hypocrite in the sage; he pretends to save Potter from temptation by warning him against sugar, cologne, brandy, and the attentions of a pretty chambermaid, leaving the hero to reflect that "every time he comes in he robs me . . . with an air all the time, too, as if he were making me presents. If he thinks me such a very sensible young man, why not let me take care of myself? . . . Depend upon it, he's sly, sly, sly" (53). Potter's own slyness is increasing by leaps and bounds, but he will never be a match for the ambitious and manipulative figures like Franklin who always come out on top.

Soon "a very rude gentleman" is introduced, a character with Potter's common touch yet something like Franklin's sagacity: this is John Paul Jones, the half-savage, half-elegant warrior who reveals his true nature when he laments that, rather than be subject to the counsel of others, he would rather be "a Czar" (55, 57). Later Melville will observe explicitly that the unsung Potter was every bit as valiant as the celebrated Jones, but even at this point it is clear that our temperate, industrious, clever, and deserving hero is only a bit player in a world dominated by mad kings, hypocritical statesmen, and rabid military leaders. Melville's other fictional orphans take imperious, brutal sea captains as surrogate fathers. In *Israel Potter* the idea of malign paternity is extended beyond the personal level to the political; our fathers are hopelessly flawed, and the Fathers of Our Country are no better.

But it is just as clear that, without the protection of one or another of these highly anomalous father figures, Israel Potter will hardly have a life at all; his choices seem to be limited to servitude or annihilation. The next few chapters chronicle a series of misadventures ranging from the almost tragic to the highly comical; in short order he returns to England with more secret messages, almost starves when he is trapped in a chimney where one of the pro-American conspirators hides him, swaps clothes with a scarecrow but is then pursued by the scarecrow's maker, is unable to locate his English contacts yet is kept from returning to Franklin in France when cross-Channel travel is suspended by the authorities. An ironic peak is reached when Potter is taken by a Dover press gang and unwillingly becomes a sailor again, this time for the enemy.

If other Melville books have seemed long on philosophy and short on action, *Israel Potter* often reads as though it were his attempt to redress the imbalance in a single volume, as, for example, in chapter 14, titled "In Which Israel Is Sailor under Two Flags, and in Three Ships, and All in One Night" (85). Potter is transferred from a man-of-war to a revenue cutter, which encounters a ship captained by John Paul Jones; when he hears Jones railing against the English vessel, Potter recognizes his voice and mutinies, taking command of the revenue cutter and delivering it to the American captain. In a daring raid, the Americans quietly spike the cannons of the forts at the town of Whitehaven and then burn a British fleet of three hundred ships with a light that the enterprising Potter borrowed from an unsuspecting English householder under the pretext of lighting his pipe.

Other adventures ensue, including the defeat of the *Drake,* an English ship far larger than the American *Ranger,* with predictable glory for John Paul Jones and, by now, predictable obscurity for Israel Potter. "This cruise made loud fame for Paul, especially at the court of France, whose king sent Paul a sword and a medal. But poor Israel, who also had conquered a craft, and all unaided too — what had he?" (113) Called "Yellow-mane" and "my lion" by Jones, Potter may be leonine in battle, but he is acquiescent otherwise, as befits his dependent status.

The epic meeting of the *Bon Homme Richard* and the *Serapis* follows; this is the encounter during which the captain of the *Serapis* asks the captain of the sinking American ship if he is ready to surrender, to which Jones replies, "I have not yet begun to fight." At the end of the conflict, with the *Richard* sunk and the victorious Americans now aboard the English ship, the narrator reflects on the enormous loss of life (about half of the combatants had been either wounded or killed) and asks, "In view of this battle one may well ask — What separates the enlightened man from the savage? Is civilization a thing distinct, or is it an advanced stage of barbarism?" (130). The human-scale Israel Potter is not quite shut of the larger-than-life John Paul Jones; "across the otherwise blue-jean career of Israel," says the narrator, "Paul Jones flits and re-flits like a crimson thread" (131). But each of their adventures has a sameness to it after a while. In each, some civilized act of barbarism is carried out by Potter and a crew of equally adept, obedient cohorts at the behest of the inspired, quasi-maniacal Jones.

The contrast here recalls the contrast between the dreamy, philosophical Ishmael and the obsessive Ahab, even though Potter and Jones are closer to each other on the spectrum of personality types and farther from the extremes represented by the principals of *Moby-Dick*. Utterly dependent on coincidence and chance encounter, the action of *Israel Potter* is more incredible than that of Melville's masterpiece, but the character interactions are more realistic versions of a fundamental Melvillean notion of class. Whereas Melville's stirring paean to democracy in chapter 26 of *Moby-Dick* (see discussion in chapter 3, above) avers that the greatest leaders are drawn from the common ranks, *Israel Potter* makes it clear that other worthy commoners — such as our hero himself — will go unrewarded because they are friendless, luckless, and penniless, which is to say, in America, classless. Whereas class in England is determined by birth, in America it is determined more by money and by fortunate circumstance, and Potter has neither. Again, it is hard not to think that Melville's empathy for his hapless protagonist is based on a sense of his own life being similarly straitened.

Another of Potter's misadventures leads to a scene of quintessential Melvillean isolation. Aboard the *Ariel* now, Jones closes with a frigatelike craft that turns out to be English; an overeager Potter leaps on the deck of the frigate but finds himself alone there when the two ships separate. Taken for an English sailor, Potter is ordered to his post by an officer, but none of the watches will have him; the men at the maintop send him to the forecastle, and so on. Other Melville orphans find substitute families at sea, but not Potter. When at last he is apprehended by the frigate's suspicious officers, Potter falls back on a subterfuge familiar to Melville readers and changes his name. (See the discussion of the significance of name changing in the *Typee* section of chapter 2, above.) Reborn again as "Peter Perkins" and claiming to have been drunk or ill during crucial moments of the voyage, Potter survives the officers' interrogation and once again escapes punishment.

When the frigate docks at Falmouth, Potter meets a final Revolutionary hero, the imprisoned Ethan Allen, a savage giant who shares an epic grotesquery with George III, Benjamin Franklin, and John Paul Jones; the chapter in which Allen is introduced is titled "Samson among the Philistines." Potter seems trivial and hapless in contrast to the heroic Allen, who is noble even in captivity, and when an American prisoner unthinkingly hails him, Potter is seized yet again; however, with the characteristic cunning and eloquence that are the powerless person's strongest weapons, he manages to convince his captors that he is the victim of a mistaken identification.

The final years of Potter's life are highly compressed. Seeking refuge in the London throngs, he becomes a mender of old chairs, a husband, and the father of eleven children, ten of whom die. Accompanied by his surviving son, Potter, now in his eighties and a widower, makes his way back to America in 1826, fifty years after he had left. He visits the farm where he grew up, but all of his old neighbors have moved west, and even the roads are grown over. Forgotten, obscure, unable to get a pension or even a medal for his war service, Potter dictates "a little book" that fades out of print; he himself dies on the same day that the "oldest oak on his native hills" is blown down (169).

This, then, is the end of the war hero. Carolyn L. Karcher observes that, as with *Pierre,* Melville tried to write a conventional story but came to see in this case that "the chief outcome of the American Revolution" was "the enslavement of the white working class to the native American overlords who had replaced the British" (108). Potter seems more like one who is utterly ignored, however, rather than enslaved. Like other Melville protagonists, it is not that the Fates conspire against him; rather, it is as though they are not even aware of his existence.

Throughout his history, Israel Potter has been the type of character described in *White-Jacket* as an unmanageable piece in a Chinese puzzle, for "as, in a Chinese puzzle, many pieces are hard to place, so there are some unfortunate fellows who can never slip into their proper angles, and thus the whole puzzle becomes a puzzle indeed, which is the precise condition of the greatest puzzle in the world — this man-of-war world itself."[11] In *Moby-Dick,* as we have seen, the pieces of the world-puzzle harmoniously dovetail occasionally in such chapters as "The Monkey-rope," "A Squeeze of the Hand," and "The Symphony," even if the puzzle shatters into its constituent pieces at story's end. In this context, *Israel Potter* reads as a further testing of the puzzle idea that finds it wanting. The novel is thus a kind of *Dark-Jacket,* the biography of a puzzle piece himself, the eponymous man-of-war's man who finds no place for himself in the world.

After all of his attempts to fit in somewhere, on land or on sea, in

England or in America, Potter finds a coherence in things only at the conclusion of his life when he revisits the place where he was born. "The ends meet," he says, and then dies (169). As we have seen, Melville's Chinese-puzzle references not only make connections between constructions of all kinds (man, ship, world, and so on) but also refer explicitly to the act of literary construction, and the conclusion of *Israel Potter* is no exception, though in an obliterating rather than an affirming manner: Israel Potter, his book, and the tree of his youth all die together.

The Confidence-Man

But Melville was not entirely done with his Chinese-puzzle idea; having searched for coherence in his other works, in his final novel he creates a coherence of his own, though a decidedly perverse one. The action of *The Confidence-Man* is set entirely aboard a single riverboat that is not only microcosmic but also reminiscent of the Chinese-puzzle passage in *White-Jacket* that is echoed in *Moby-Dick* and *Israel Potter,* for the *Fidèle* is a whole made of parts that seem otherwise unrelated: "fine promenades, domed saloons, long galleries, sunny balconies, confidential passages, bridal chambers, state-rooms plenty as pigeon-holes, and out-of-the-way retreats like secret drawers in an escritoire."[12] Sunny passages, shady ones, public and private places: the *Fidèle* is a ship, of course, but it is also a congeries of unexpectedly linked opposites. It is also "some whitewashed fort on a floating isle" and, because its passengers "buzz on her decks" while "a murmur as of bees in the comb" comes from below deck, a hive. Fort, beehive, and "escritoire" as well: as in other instances of the Chinese-puzzle passage, here Melville is not only describing the individual ship but also, by likening the *Fidèle* to an escritoire or writing desk, alluding to the act of writing itself and thus reminding the reader that this Chinese-puzzle structure is fundamental to all human endeavor, including literary creation. As will be seen below, Melville stops his story at intervals to comment directly on the act of writing; in *Moby-Dick,* too, the reader has observed Melville simultaneously describing the extant world as he sees it and the imagined world as he creates it.

Too, the *Fidèle,* like the *Pequod,* is populated by "an Anacharsis Cloots congress" of crew and passengers (9). But whereas the sailors in *Moby-Dick* represent the full range of humanity and are

probably even more benign in character than their real-life counterparts would have been, the passengers on the *Fidèle* are a cynical
lot whose activities bespeak a fallen world. Early in the novel, they
are depicted as buying and selling money belts to each other; the
first of a variety of analogous transactions, the sale of a money belt
will have a resonant significance in the novel's final chapter as well.
Other salesmen aboard the *Fidèle* are hawking biographies of dead
outlaws who are nonetheless precursors of villains equally bad. For
"Meason, the bandit of Ohio, Murrel, the pirate of the Mississippi,
and the brothers Harpe, the Thugs of the Green River country, in
Kentucky" were "creatures, with others of the sort, one and all
exterminated at the time, and for the most part, like the hunted generations of wolves in the same regions, leaving comparatively few
successors," a fact "which would seem cause for unalloyed gratula-
tion, and is such to all except those who think that in new countries,
where the wolves are killed off, the foxes increase" (4).

In the midst of these desperadoes comes a wondrous white figure,
"a man in cream-colors" whose "cheek was fair, his chin downy,
his hair flaxen, his hat a white fur one." This apparition is also
one of the most solitary of Melville's creations. Even the celebrated
Bartleby, of whom more below, is offered the friendship of his well-
meaning employer, but this lamblike man has "neither trunk, valise,
carpet-bag, nor parcel. No porter followed him. He was unaccom-
panied by friends. From the shrugged shoulders, titters, whispers,
wonderings of the crowd, it was plain that he was, in the extremest
sense of the word, a stranger" (3). To the bafflement of the other
passengers, the newcomer produces a slate and begins to write the
passage celebrating charity from St. Paul's First Letter to the Corin-
thians ("Charity suffereth long, and is kind," etc.), sentiments that
contrast sharply with those expressed on the sign hung out by the
boat's barber and that seem more representative of the community
viewpoint aboard the *Fidèle:* "NO TRUST" (5). Since this lamblike
man's slate is small, he must erase his words each time — a necessity, of course, yet an ironic one in light of the narrative that will
ensue, for the one who is urging charity has none himself.

The other passengers tease and browbeat the newcomer, who is
oblivious to their contempt, in part because he turns out to be a
deaf-mute. But while they deride this interloper, they find that they
cannot dismiss him, and so the deaf-mute becomes the center of a
controversy regarding his identity:

"Odd fish!"
"Poor fellow!"
"Who can he be?"
"Casper Hauser."
"Bless my soul!"
"Uncommon countenance."
"Green prophet from Utah."
"Humbug!"
"Singular innocence."
"Means something."
"Spirit-rapper."
"Moon-calf."
"Piteous."
"Trying to enlist interest."
"Beware of him."
"Fast asleep here, and, doubtless, pick-pockets on board."
"Kind of daylight Endymion."
"Escaped convict, worn out with dodging."
"Jacob dreaming at Luz." (7)

Here the newcomer is associated with a host of figures associated
with trickery or dubious provenance: Kaspar Hauser, the foundling
who appeared mysteriously in Nuremberg in 1828 and who was
rumored to be the son of a nobleman; a member of the Mormon
Church ("green prophet from Utah"), which, as a still-new religion in America, would have been regarded with mistrust by most
nonbelievers; a phony medium ("spirit-rapper"); an "escaped convict"; and, finally, Jacob, father of the twelve tribes of Israel but best
known for having cheated his brother Esau out of his birthright.
But in contrast to this laundry list of confidence men, there is also
a series of tags that describe the newcomer as innocent, piteous,
vulnerable, and perhaps even, like Endymion, the youth given immortality by Zeus yet also condemned to sleep forever, oblivious.
In a succinct manner, then, the unknowing passengers announce
what the rest of the novel will elaborate in detail — that the Confidence Man will be someone different to everyone and will end as he
begins, an insoluble mystery.

He has appeared, as the first sentence of *The Confidence-Man*
tells us, "suddenly as Manco Capac at the lake Titicaca" (3). If he is
not the god of the Incas, exactly, at least the newcomer is described
by the other passengers as having the dazzling, enigmatic qualities

that one might associate with a deity suddenly made manifest. Yet the first sentence of the novel also tells us that the newcomer appears on April 1, so that if he is a god, then he is the God of Fools. These two brief passages, the Confidence Man's miraculous appearance in the book's first sentence and then the list of tags applied to him by his fellow passengers, are the bolt from which the fabric of the novel will unroll. Together, these establish the Confidence Man as a cunning and deceptive shape-shifter beneath whose dazzling surfaces, it is hinted, lies a considerable menace, a menace that will be borne out in the novel's final paragraphs. Indeed, in the end, pure menace may be all that there is to this baffling character; the reader's most frightful realization is liable to be that, as Michael Paul Rogin writes, "there is no self under the confidence man's disguises" (224).

As the God of Fools, it is the newcomer's job to make dunces of his fellows, most of whom regard themselves as too shrewd to be deceived by anyone else. But no one aboard the *Fidèle* is a match for the Confidence Man, who quickly drops his deaf-mute guise and reappears as a "grotesque negro cripple" who introduces the series of incarnations he will assume thereafter — challenged to prove that he is not a fraud himself, the cripple promises that his bona fides can be vouched for by a number of passengers, "a werry nice, good ge'mman wid a weed, and a ge'mman in a gray coat and white tie, what knows all about me; and a ge'mman wid a big book, too; and a yarb-doctor; and a ge'mman in a yaller west; and a ge'mman wid a brass plate; and a ge'mman in a wiolet robe; and a ge'mman as is a sodjer; and ever so many good, kind, honest ge'mman more aboard what knows me and will speak for me" (13). In succession these gentlemen appear: a man in mourning with a crape weed on his hat; the man in gray, who represents the Seminole Widow and Orphan Asylum; the man with the ledger under his arm, who is the agent for the Black Rapids Coal Company; the herb doctor who peddles Omni-Balsamic Reinvigorator and Samaritan Pain Dissuader; a man wearing a brass plate bearing the initial of the Philosophical Intelligence Office; and the violet-robed Cosmopolitan, who becomes the most developed embodiment of the Confidence Man.

The metamorphosis of this central figure from one avatar to the next can, depending on the reader, be amusing, confusing, and irritating. But as Gary Lindberg writes in his exhaustive analysis of the confidence-man figure in American literature, "from his appearance as a lamb-like mute onwards, [Melville's] Confidence-Man serves rather to bring out the qualities of surrounding characters than to interest us in his own inward nature or development."[13] As these surrounding characters are constantly changing, however, the result is an unprecedented set of problems for the reader used to conventional mid-nineteenth-century fiction. The difficulties, as Lindberg says, "are severe. There is extensive critical disagreement not only about the larger value and meaning of the book but even about what is going on and how to make sense of the narrative. The problem begins with the source of information and judgment. This narrator is not trustworthy in the sense, say, of Austen's tellers, but then again he isn't unreliable either"; that is, he is clearly deceiving the other characters he meets, but there is no reason to think that he is deceiving the reader, who, after all, is "in" on the deception of the others. It's just that, "like the world he presents to us," this narrator "simply lacks authority" (19). Clearly, much of import is being disclosed to the reader of this novel, but what? The characters talk endlessly of human nature, but less is revealed *in* the dialogue than *by* the dialogue; that is, ultimately the world seems made of language, and language itself becomes increasingly temporary.

Ultimately, this brilliant, eccentric book, like most of Melville's creations, offers a comprehensive view of the extant world as well as a running commentary on the making of this particular world. As always, the two aspects are inseparable; as an earlier passage told us, the *Fidèle* is a riverboat but an escritoire as well. For example, Melville's handling of character depicts both his view of human nature and his idea of what a novel is like; often, his views on fiction seem more original than his views on human nature. As Lindberg says, "there is little continuity in the characters [in *The Confidence-Man*] and therefore little basis for a 'story' in the familiar sense. Characters . . . are created for the nonce; their existence is explicitly hypothetical — if such a man there be, here is what follows"; the result is a "gambit" rather than a conventional plot (22, 25).

The result of this gambit is "a strange and demanding novel" in which "it is not Melville's larger plot that reveals his point but rather the local transactions" (19). And what is Melville's point? To Lindberg, the point is revealed not only by the characters' patterned interactions but the nature of the characters themselves, who represent a variety of American figures who are historical, literary, and even criminal in nature, from the Indian-hating Colonel John Moredock to Mark Winsome, the character whose Emersonian optimism is yet one more confidence game that the increasingly sardonic Melville found impossible to stomach. Behind this entire "Anacharsis Cloots congress" of villains and shysters stands the original "confidence man," the William Thompson whose exploits had been widely reported in the press in 1849 and who, though not physically present in the novel, stands behind both Melville's central figure and the larger atmosphere of mistrust and deception aboard the *Fidèle*.[14] In his own way, Melville seems even more interested in character here than in *Pierre,* his "psychological" novel that tried to plumb the interior world of the human psyche the way *Moby-Dick* tried to plumb the exterior world of the known universe and, if possible, beyond. *Pierre* is an attempt to get at certain human universals; *The Confidence-Man* has that as a secondary goal, but its specific grounding in the rich culture of its times suggests that Melville was less interested in timeless truths than in the specifically American character of his own day.

Three curious chapters, chapters 14, 33, and 44, illuminate Melville's thinking about the significance of fictional characters and also make clear his attitude toward the America he describes by means of this single representative figure. Each of these chapters is a complete essay in itself. Melville stops the action, addresses an objection that might have been raised by a hypothetical reader, argues his point to its conclusion, and then returns to the story. Some chapters later, he repeats the process, as though the same reader, who has been pondering Melville's argument as he listens to the story, has now sprung to his feet with some new objection; this method of arguing is cumbersome, but by chapter 44, Melville seems to be writing definitively not only about the aesthetics of fiction but also about fiction's ability to tell the truth.

In chapter 14, Melville imagines that there have been objections to the inconsistency of one of his characters, yet he defends himself by arguing that real people *are* inconsistent; there are anomalies in humans just as there are in more primitive forms, which is why, "when the duck-billed beaver of Australia was first brought stuffed to England, the naturalists, appealing to their classifications, maintained that there was, in reality, no such creature." Indeed, and the myopia of scientists notwithstanding, Melville sees inconsistency as a point of connection between the lowest and the highest of forms, with humankind somewhere in the middle, so that the correct view is taken by the person who, "in view of its inconsistencies, says of human nature the same that, in view of its contrasts, is said of the divine nature, that it is past finding out." Just as platypuses and deities are inconsistent, then, so is the human who stands somewhere between them, and the observer who admits this "evinces a better appreciation of it than he who, by always representing it in a clear light, leaves it to be inferred that he clearly knows all about it" (70). In fact, the know-it-all approach to human nature is not only wrong but possibly injurious, since, "after poring over the best novels professing to portray human nature, the studious youth will still run the risk of being too often at fault upon actually entering the world; whereas, had he been furnished with a true delineation, it ought to fare with him something as with a stranger entering, map in hand, Boston town; the streets may be very crooked, he may often pause; but, thanks to his true map, he does not hopelessly lose his way" (71). Thus Melville's first essay on character concludes with a strong endorsement of the "true map" approach and an appeal to the reader's love of verisimilitude.

His second essay, chapter 33, takes virtually the opposite tack by appealing, not to the general reader, but to the sophisticated reader with a greater interest in aesthetics than in fiction's ability to reproduce life faithfully; it is as though, more than halfway through his narrative, Melville has suddenly realized who his true audience is. Essentially, the hypothetical objection is the same — that the characters in *The Confidence-Man* are inconsistent. This time, however, Melville is shocked that "this severe fidelity to real life should be exacted by any one, who, taking up such a work, sufficiently shows that he is not unwilling to drop real life, and turn, for a time, to something different." Whereas previously he had made it clear that he was giving the reader the most verisimilitudinous depiction possible, now he expresses surprise that anyone who "finds real life dull" should demand that the novelist "be true to that dullness." Instead of regarding the novel as though it were a map of Boston, the reader should treat it as though it were a play, in which the characters are based on nature "but nature unfettered, exhilarated, in effect transformed," so that "the people in a fiction, like the people in a play, must dress as nobody exactly dresses, talk as nobody exactly talks, act as nobody exactly acts. It is with fiction as with religion; it should present another world, and yet one to which we feel the tie" (182–83). Whereas the appeal in the previous essay was to verisimilitude, the appeal here is to aesthetics. And an inconsistent character in a novel is admirable because of its resemblance not to a natural creature such as the duck-billed platypus but to a wholly artificial one such as Lear or Lady Macbeth.

Chapter 44, the final essay on character in *The Confidence-Man,* not only combines these two opposing appeals to verisimilitude and aesthetics but transcends them; in doing so, Melville takes what has appeared to be a quirky, personal, uncertain tendency to digress and makes a central statement about art and about America as well. Chapter 44 addresses itself to the sophisticated reader once again, to "the old, or the well-read, or the man who has made the grand tour" rather than "the young, or the unlearned, or the untraveled." This well-read person will recognize that the character who is "original" (the term Melville uses here in place of the pejorative "inconsistent") is lifelike because he or she represents a specific time and place. Thus does Melville bring his two arguments together: verisimilitude (praised in chapter 14) appeals to the sophisticated reader (the true audience identified in chapter 33) not because it is a precise representation, like a map of Boston, but because of a new reason — because the verisimilitudinous character embodies the spirit of the novel's setting. Thus "in nearly all the original characters, loosely accounted such in works of invention, there is discernible something prevailingly local, or of the age." This is because these seemingly original characters are not at all original (in the sense of being created out of thin air) but are based on the novelist's penetrating observations of both person and locale. "Where does any novelist pick up any character?" asks Melville. "For the most part, in town, to be sure. Every great town is a kind of manshow, where the novelist goes for his stock, just as the agriculturist goes to the cattle-show for his" (238). No matter how "inconsistent" or "original" the Confidence Man appears, then, his value lies not in his similarity to other figures the reader has known in real life or in books but in his figuring almost as a kind of nineteenth-century American god, a national exhalation, a genie of the time and place. In his final full-length fiction, a novel about lying, Melville uses an "inconsistent" or "original" character as a means of telling the truth about the country he had come to judge so harshly.

The Confidence Man is not a single, easily visualized character along the lines of Hamlet or Don Quixote or Milton's Satan, to mention three examples of "original" characters cited by Melville in chapter 44 (or an Ahab, for that matter). Because his initial appearance is brief, his motivation unexamined, and his subsequent changes fairly rapid (at least until the point that he becomes the Cosmopolitan, who presides over the last part of the novel), the Confidence Man does indeed seem like more than one character; this is part of the baffling, amusing tone that makes the book challenging. And because he not only stands for himself and the rest of the sharpers aboard the *Fidèle* but also that broad pattern of generally dishonest nature Melville descries in American life, finally the Confidence Man's name is legion and he becomes many characters in the putative guise of one. Earlier it was observed that, according to Gary Lindberg, the specific and repetitive transactions between characters reveal more than any large plot line; these transactions show how "a group of people in some proximity have tacitly agreed to get along with each other and to discover common values." Yet the characters "do not succeed in manufacturing a social order; quite the opposite. During the flow of talk, characters are being made and unmade; identities are forged, tested, and eradicated. Strangers to each other, the characters are also strangers to themselves. They must project and make credible not what they know but what they believe themselves to be." Thus "Melville's hypothesis . . . is that American social activity is a confidence game. Cut off from mutually accepted authority, his characters play upon each other's credulity to find what can be made credible. . . . In one sense, the characters seem accustomed to this game playing, for they are shrewd and cautious in watching each other's maneuvers." But "as the Confidence-Man, with his dazzling verbal obfuscations, erases the predicates that order his victims' worlds, they find their very identities slipping" (44–45). In chapter 1 of this study, the point was made that the Melvillean narrator tended to pause in *Typee* and the other Polynesian novels and make anthropological observations that stood outside of the plot proper. An analogous point might be made here, although in the case of *The Confidence-Man* the observations are of interiors rather than exteriors. And ultimately, the human soul turns out to be empty.

There is an increasingly bitter, vengeful tone to *The Confidence-Man*. The reader who assumes that the gaming will have some benign end or will turn out to be satirical of a limited number of American character types learns that no one is spared, that Americans as a group are gullible and foolish, self-deceiving and easily deceived by others. But the ending of the book contains even darker ideas. The Confidence Man's final victim is a venerable old man who is likened to the Simeon who greets the Messiah for whom he has been patiently waiting when Joseph and Mary bring the Christ child to the temple in Jerusalem; he is seen sitting beneath a lamp whose glass shade bears "the image of a horned altar" and whose flames reveal "the figure of a robed man, his head encircled by a halo" (240). Carolyn L. Karcher points out that at least some nineteenth-century Americans anticipated the physical return of Jesus Christ to the Mississippi Valley and that "one contemporary sect, the Mormons [alluded to in chapter 2 of *The Confidence-Man,* as discussed above], incorporated this belief into a new Bible that specifically envisioned Christ as coming in person to inaugurate the millennium in America." But Melville rebukes "his country's presumptuous millennial expectations" by sending, not Christ, but a Confidence Man who brings "not light, but darkness" (188, 192).

While the Confidence Man and the old gentleman are discussing whether or not humans in general are to be trusted, a boy comes along to sell the latter a traveler's lock to keep thieves out of his stateroom and, in an echo of the first chapter, a money belt. The old man also receives a counterfeit bill detector as a bonus for buying the other items and begins to test his money with it, even though the Confidence Man advises him to throw the device away. Secure in the possession of these articles as well as the stool the Confidence Man has given him to use as a life preserver, the old man begins to make his way confusedly toward his stateroom. The Confidence Man offers to show him the way, but not before extinguishing the lamp with the unusual shade: "The next moment, the waning light expired, and with it the waning flames of the horned altar, and the waning halo round the robed man's brow; while in the darkness which ensued, the cosmopolitan kindly led the old man away." Is the light all that "expires" at the end of this darkest of novels? When a bitter, powerful figure offers false security to a trusting, weaker one and then leads him out into the night, one need not have an overactive imagination to think that the next crime to be committed will be the gravest crime of all. The last words of *The Confidence-Man* are, "Something further may follow of this masquerade" (251). That something may simply be more confidence games, but the words that precede this final conundrum suggest that the book is ending, not only in deceit, but in murder.

Then, of course, there is nothing specific to suggest murder at all, only veiled hints and a sinister setting. Melville insisted on a sophisticated readership, as chapter 44 suggests, and in the end the sophisticated reader will continue the game long after the gamester has disappeared. *The Confidence-Man* is Melville's final version of the Chinese-puzzle idea, here revealed as a fraud and a deception, for if the world is to cohere and make sense, it will do so only as a cruel and highly artificial hoax.

The Confidence-Man also is a kind of negative *Tempest,* the Confidence Man an anti-Prospero of sorts. For just as Prospero renounces his magic in a way that signals Shakespeare's retirement from the London stage and his removal to Stratford, so the Confidence Man, clearly a powerful, shape-changing magician himself, turns his back on the world as Melville ceases his futile attempts at fictional bestsellerdom and seeks refuge in the more private domain of poetry.

5

Tales and Poems

The Piazza Tales

In 1851, then living at Arrowhead, his farm near Pittsfield in the Berkshire region of Massachusetts, Melville borrowed $2,050 from his friend Tertullus D. Stewart to make certain improvements, described by him as "building the new kitchen, wood-house, piazza, making alterations, painting."[1] The piazza that was underwritten by this loan became a symbol both for Melville's remove from a contentious public world and his even deeper immersion in the private world of art. Paradoxically, the piazza is described as offering a view, not of a natural world whose healing forces are sufficient in themselves to renew the human spirit, but a natural world that is curative because it has been transformed into art by the viewer: "for what but picture-galleries are the marble halls of these same limestone hills?" asks the narrator — "galleries hung, month after month anew, with pictures ever fading into pictures ever fresh" (2). His piazza completed, the narrator goes in search of love, but it is a mock-heroic search, as is made clear by the frequent ironic echoes of epical works on that subject.

For example, he alludes to Spenser's extended treatment of courtly romance in *The Faerie Queene* when he says, "How to get to fairy-land, by what road, I did not know; nor could any one inform me; not even Edmund Spenser, who had been there — so he wrote me" (6). Later, he encounters the fair Marianna, who "shyly started, like some Tahiti girl, secreted for a sacrifice, first catching sight, through palms, of Captain Cook," though the narrator knows in his heart that he is less like that doughty explorer and more like the failed romancer "Don Quixote, that sagest sage that ever lived" (9, 6). Thus, and though he is "haunted by Marianna's face," the narrator withdraws from the world like the vanquished Don who became a shepherd and took up the pastoral life (12). Neither story proper nor true introduction, "The Piazza" has puzzled more than one reader who has wondered about its intent. But R. Bruce Bickley notes that "Melville did not intend 'The Piazza' to recapitulate or formally survey the five . . . tales included in the volume. It is more likely that he saw his introductory sketch as Hawthorne had viewed 'The Old Manse,' preface to the *Mosses:* as a portrait of the author looking out over the landscape of his own art and pondering, whimsically and seriously, the complex relationships between art and knowledge."[2]

The Piazza Tales appeared in 1856, the year before the appearance of *The Confidence-Man*, Melville's final full-length work of fiction. Of the five tales collected in this volume, "Bartleby the Scrivener" and "Benito Cereno" are among the three best-known short works by Melville (the third, the posthumously published "Billy Budd," is discussed at the end of this chapter).

The first voice the reader hears in "Bartleby the Scrivener: A Story of Wall-Street" is the smug, self-satisfied, yet eminently winning voice of the Master of Chancery, a lawyer and political appointee whose task it is to settle estates and the like. The Master of Chancery is one of those creatures filled with a kind of self-love so great that it extends to all other creatures; his personal splendor touches everything around him, and thus everyone else is as splendid as he is. Such bonhomie leads to a kind of moral blindness, however, and before long it becomes evident that the Mastery of Chancery is one of a long line of similar figures in Melville. From the "mickonarees" of *Omoo* to Captain Vere of "Billy Budd," Melville's work is populated with well-meaning, even likable characters who become accomplices in some tragedy they seem unable to avoid or even understand. In this case, "Bartleby the Scrivener" makes a withering statement, not about missionary activities or maritime justice, but about something more familiar yet, to Melville, in many ways just as insidious as these other topics. The focus in "Bartleby" is on work: not the dangerous or unethical variety, just ordinary, mind-numbing, soul-destroying work.

Concerning his own duties, the Mastery of Chancery reports, "it was not as very arduous office, but very pleasantly remunerative" (14). Thus it is for most employers in positions similar to his. But the work of his employees is quite different, and it af-

fects their characters accordingly. In the story's opening pages, the
two copyists Turkey and Nippers and the office boy Ginger Nut
are described with some thoroughness. If they nonetheless emerge
as one-dimensional figures, it is because the work they perform
has reduced them to mere ciphers; it is as though Melville delays
Bartleby's entrance as he takes pains to describe the milieu that is
crucial to the point being made about work and its impact on the
workers.

Turkey, the senior copyist, has a "strange, inflamed, flurried,
flighty recklessness of activity about him," though only after lunch,
a largely liquid meal, it would seem (15). The postprandial Turkey
makes a racket with his chair, spills the sand he uses to blot his jot-
tings, splits his pens and throws them angrily to the floor; worse, he
mars the documents he has been assigned. The good-natured Master
of Chancery offers to let Turkey have his afternoons off, but when
the proud copyist insists on putting in a full day, he silently resolves
to give him only less-important documents after lunch.

The junior copyist, Nippers, does not share Turkey's dipsomani-
acal proclivities, and is praised by the Master of Chancery for his
temperance. Yet "nature herself seemed to have been his vintner,
and at birth charged him so thoroughly with an irritable, brandy-
like disposition, that all subsequent potations were needless" and
that therefore "brandy and water were altogether superfluous" for
him (18). Nippers grinds his teeth as he works, hisses maledictions,
and fidgets constantly with his scrivener's table, the height and angle
of which are never satisfactory to him. Fortunately, Nippers's irri-
tability is, according to the Mastery of Chancery, due to indigestion,
so that a hearty (and largely solid) lunch cures it. Thus "the irritabil-
ity and consequent nervousness of Nippers, were mainly observable
in the morning, while in the afternoon he was comparatively mild.
So that Turkey's paroxysms only coming on about twelve o'clock,
I never had to do with their eccentricities at one time. Their fits re-
lieved each other like guards. When Nippers' was on, Turkey's was
off; and *vice versa*. This was a good natural arrangement under the
circumstances" (18).

The third employee, Ginger Nut, is a twelve-year-old who is supposed to be studying the law while carrying out his other duties
and even has a little desk for that purpose, though he is seldom
there, being largely used by Turkey and Nippers to fetch the apples
and ginger cookies that relieve some of the tedium of their work.

Thus the office has evolved into an organism in its own right, with Turkey working calmly in the morning and behaving frenziedly in the afternoon, Nippers doing just the opposite, and Ginger Nut punctuating their activity with his dartlike movements as he charges in and out. In the mind of the good-hearted Master of Chancery, then, the pathology of the workplace is balanced against the good work that gets done, so that ultimately an inherent order establishes itself in his flawed yet productive microcosm.

Seen from a certain remove, the Chancery Office seems like a prison whose inmates, under the eye of a benign warden, produce legal documents instead of license plates. Eventually, Bartleby's arrival will change everything about the office, but at first the pale, sedate copyist has the effect of offering a silent reproof to the delirium of the other employees; indeed, ever hoping for greater efficiency, the Master of Chancery thinks that "a man of so singularly sedate an aspect . . . might operate beneficially upon the flighty temper of Turkey, and the fiery one of Nippers" (19). This is not to say that Bartleby will be largely a passive example; indeed, "at first Bartleby did an extraordinary quantity of writing. As if long famishing for something to copy, he seemed to gorge himself on my documents. There was no pause for digestion." In stark contrast to the other copyists, each of whom is good only for a half-day's work, Bartleby toils around the clock: "He ran a day and night line, copying by sun-light and by candle-light . . . silently, palely, mechanically" (19–20). Though the character of Bartleby is renowned in literature as an image of quietistic withdrawal, it is important to remember that, in the beginning, at least, he is a paragon of industry, working harder than anyone else and betraying none of the dissatisfaction that troubles the others.

Thus it is only after a genuine, thorough, and final testing of the work world that Bartleby embarks on his program of passive resistance. His skill level suggests that he has been employed elsewhere (later we learn that he had been employed by the postal service), yet his decision to find new employment with the Mastery of Chancery suggests dissatisfaction with his previous employment. Or perhaps Bartleby is dissatisfied with *all* employment; his behavior is that of one who has been pushed to the limit of his endurance, decides to see if he can tolerate the intolerable one more time, and then, finding that he cannot, commits himself to a radical, even fatal protest against a world that will not accept him on his own terms.

Though it is easy to make Bartleby out as a classic loser, a defeatist sunk in self-pity, it is just as easy, if unconventional, to make him out as an activist and even a hero. Seen from the conventional American perspective of hard work and of achieving success through a do-or-die attitude, Bartleby is indeed a failure. But a significant body of criticism connects Bartleby to traditions other than this simplistic and deceptive one, traditions that the widely read Melville would have been thoroughly familiar with and with which he would have been inclined to sympathize temperamentally throughout his life and especially in these years when he was experiencing firsthand the falsity of the American dream. A variety of critics have argued that "Bartleby the Scrivener" is best understood from the viewpoint of the religious, philosophical, and political practices variously known as monism and quietism, practices characterized by resistance and withdrawal, and which are best exemplified in Melville's lifetime by the example of his contemporary, Henry David Thoreau.[3] Thoreau's celebrated essay "On Resistance to Civil Government" was published in 1849, or four years before the magazine appearance of "Bartleby." And while it is not possible to say definitively that Melville had Thoreau in mind when he created his scrivener (though certainly some scholars think so), it is clear that Bartleby's program of passive resistance follows Thoreau's scheme quite closely.[4]

Of course, Thoreau's complaint is against, not work, but government (and specifically the government that prosecuted the Mexican War, mistreated Native Americans, and condoned slavery), yet his arguments are the same as the ones that underlie Bartleby's actions. To cooperate with the government is to condone and participate in its actions, so that an honest person has no choice but to withdraw from this partnership. Clearly Bartleby is Thoreau's honest man, withdrawing from and in that way protesting against the oppression that surrounds him. The truly moral person, says Thoreau, must "refuse allegiance to the State" and "withdraw and stand aloof from it effectually," which is precisely what Bartleby does every time he utters his familiar refrain of "I would prefer not to" (20). In the Thoreauvian sense, then, Bartleby's actions are not life-hating and futile, which they might be misconstrued as being if viewed from the narrow perspective of the American success myth, but life-affirming and effective.

Indeed, it is the effectiveness of Bartleby's passive resistance that is often overlooked by unsympathetic readers. The very phrase "passive resistance" has a contemporary ring to it and may seem like the interjection of a present-day political slogan into Melville's tale of yesteryear, but in fact these are the Master of Chancery's own words. "Nothing so aggravates an earnest person as passive resistance," he says upon Bartleby's refusing to perform the simplest of tasks. He might have added that nothing so effectively changes the earnest person's own behavior, for

> now and then, in the eagerness of dispatching pressing business, I would inadvertently summon Bartleby, in a short, rapid tone, to put his finger, say, on the incipient tie of a bit of red tape with which I was about compressing some papers. Of course, from behind the screen the usual answer, "I prefer not to," was sure to come.... However, every added repulse of this sort which I received only tended to lessen the probability of my repeating the inadvertence. (27)

Earlier, Bartleby has "strangely disarmed" the Master of Chancery with his gentle manner; later, when Bartleby refuses to let the Master into his own chambers until he has finished whatever it is that he is doing, the Master reports that the scrivener "had such a strange effect upon me, that incontinently I slunk away from my own door, and did as desired" (21, 27). Before long, he is telling Nippers that he "would prefer if [he] would withdraw for the present." Nor is he the only one affected by Bartleby's actions: Turkey tells the Master of Chancery that he thinks Bartleby would be all right were he to "prefer to take a quart of good ale every day," and Nippers wishes to know if the Master would "prefer to have a certain paper copied on blue paper or white" (31). Thus Bartleby's behavior is not only "strange" (a word that, in this context, means inexplicable but, as well, wondrous) but also extremely productive — itself a "strange" word to use to describe someone who appears to be the very antithesis of productivity. In effect, Bartleby trains the other characters by being consistent and by making the most economical use of his resources. It might be said that he uses the methods of the workplace to subvert it.

After he orders Bartleby off the premises, there is a wonderful moment in which the Master of Chancery assumes that all of New York has taken up the scrivener's cause; on his way to see if Bartleby has in fact departed, he mistakes an election-day bettor's offer to make a wager ("I'll take odds he doesn't") for a bet on Bartleby's persistence and replies, "Doesn't go? — done!' said I, 'put up your money" (34). But this momentary illusion that Bartleby is backed by New York's betting public is merely an indication of the Master's obsession with his recalcitrant employee.

The truth is that Bartleby is one more in a long line of Melvillean orphans, unknown and unloved. The Master of Chancery says, "If he could have but named a single relative or friend, I would have written, and urged their taking the poor fellow away to some convenient retreat. But he seemed alone, absolutely alone in the universe. A bit of wreck in the mid Atlantic" (32). This last image is inappropriate to a story set in New York's financial district, but it creates a powerful link between Bartleby and all of the orphan-sailors of Melville's sea writings, from the narrator of *Typee* to the landlocked mariner John Marr that he would describe in the poetry to come.

Since Bartleby's strategy is passive, not active, the only seeming solution to the Master of Chancery's dilemma is for him to move his offices. In a reversal of the cliché, the mountain must move away from Mohammed: "Since he will not quit me, I must quit him" (39). But Bartleby's strength is such that the new tenant cannot dislodge him, either. Nor will Bartleby accept the Master of Chancery's extraordinary offer to share his home; the office is where he abides until the frustrated landlord has him arrested and sent to the prison so aptly named the Tombs. In this prison Bartleby refuses to eat and dies. When the Mastery of Chancery touches Bartleby's body, he reports, "a tingling shiver ran up my arm and down my spine to my feet." Even in death, Bartleby emanates a force that gives the lie to any suggestion that he might be weak or cowardly. He lies "with kings and counsellors," says the Master of Chancery (45). These words echo the lamentation of Job 3:13–14 ("For now should I have lain still and been quiet, / I should have slept: then had I been at rest, / With kings and counsellors of the earth, / Which built desolate places for themselves"). But it is not Bartleby's choice to live in a place that is "desolate," that is, removed, far from life's hurlyburly. The story's last words are the Master's own lamentation: "Ah Bartleby!" he cries, "Ah humanity!" (45). And this is where the scrivener has chosen to make his stand: in the hivelike commercial atmosphere of Wall Street, immersed in humanity, yet utterly alone.

What is it exactly that kills Bartleby's spirit and leads him to give up his life? Much has been made by readers of the fact that, as the Master of Chancery reports in a coda to the story proper, Bartleby had been a clerk in the Dead Letter Office in Washington: "Dead letters!" he expostulates, "does it not sound like dead men?" (45). Certainly the dead-letters reference connects resonantly with what is already known of Melville's life and work, both in the general sense of his absorption with solitude and in the specific one of this phase of his career, during which his writings must have appeared to him to be "dead letters" to an insensible world. But the dead letters, though discouraging, aren't enough in themselves to kill Bartleby, who, it will be remembered, labored mightily in the Chancery Office before "preferring" not to.

The roots of Bartleby's tragedy are suggested in an anecdote tossed off almost casually by the Master of Chancery after Bartleby has tried his patience to the limit. The story is of an employer who quarreled with and then killed his employee; of particular significance to the Master is the fact that the fatal act occurred in an office and, indeed, could not have taken place anywhere else.

I remembered the tragedy of the unfortunate Adams and the still more unfortunate Colt in the solitary office of the latter; and how poor Colt, being dreadfully incensed by Adams, and imprudently permitting himself to get wildly excited, was at unawares hurried into his fatal act — an act which certainly no man could possibly deplore more than the actor himself. Often it had occurred to me in my ponderings upon the subject, that had the altercation taken place in the public street, or at a private residence, it would not have terminated as it did. It was the circumstance of being alone in a solitary office, up stairs, of a building — *entirely unhallowed by humanizing domestic associations* — an uncarpeted office, doubtless, of a dusty, haggard sort of appearance; — this it must have been, which greatly helped to enhance the irritable desperation of the hapless Colt. (36; emphasis mine)

This passage is typical of the thinking of the generous, thoughtful Master of Chancery, he whose premises are presided over by a "pale plaster-of-Paris bust of Cicero," the Roman orator who was the embodiment of equipoise and moderation. It is the Ciceronian spirit of reason and good sense that rules the Chancery Office rather than any "humanizing domestic associations," and thus it should be — from the employer's perspective, that is. And, without a doubt, the Master of Chancery is an exceptional employer.

His only problem is that he, too, like any employer, no matter how exceptional, is incapable of knowing anyone unlike himself.

He, not Bartleby, is the "dead letter" who connects with no one. After all, in this passage in which the Master of Chancery once again exercises that liberal understanding of poor Bartleby of which he is so proud, it is more than a little disheartening to note that his sympathies lie, not with the "unfortunate" murdered Adams, but with the "still more unfortunate" murderer, the "hapless Colt."[5] The Master's cri de coeur at the story's end seems genuine, yet, like almost every other element of the story, it is both a lamentation for Bartleby's perversity and a dramatization of his employer's benevolence.

One of the difficulties in reading "Bartleby the Scrivener" is that it is difficult to tell if the Master of Chancery's self-presentation is serious or ironic. But the test for seriousness versus irony is to try to catch the speaker unawares in a moment of damaging self-revelation, which occurs here when the Master sympathizes with the criminal Colt and shows as little genuine concern for the victim Adams as he does for the victim of his own tale. Like many benevolent people, the Master of Chancery wants to comfort the afflicted, though his main intention is to persuade the afflicted to be just like him, the idea being that anyone as splendid as he is could not possibly be unhappy. So while it is true that the man who tells the story of Bartleby the scrivener sheds real tears over the fate of his protagonist, it must also be recognized that "Bartleby the Scrivener" is, more than anything else, a lawyerly brief for the teller's own Ciceronian virtues.

But at least one may argue, not Bartleby's seeming passivity, but his disciplined resistance to a world gone mad with aggression and acquisition. Even the most metaphorical writers are nonetheless men and women of their times, though some engage in it more fiercely than others. Melville was engagé for his entire life as a writer, and nothing reflects that engagement more surely than Bartleby's eloquent if silent report on the frenzy of Wall Street.

Of all Melville's sea fictions, none is more overtly exciting and adventure filled than "Benito Cereno." This is a blood-and-thunder tale of treachery on the high seas; it is the type of story of which, at one time, lushly-scored black-and-white movies were made starring matinee idols like Errol Flynn and Basil Rathbone, men braving the sword, the lash, and the elemental forces of nature to right wrongs and make their marks on the world. The characteristic moral ambiguities notwithstanding, there is nothing else like it in Melville, no other story so sparely written, so starkly lit, so free of whimsy, lore, and philosophical digression.

The plot, based on a central character's actual account, is a simple one.[6] An American captain boards a Spanish slave ship whose captain and crew are much debilitated by illness and mishap. Don Benito Cereno, the captain of the slaver, is an invalid himself, though he remains capable of command thanks in part to the support he receives from the selfless slave Babo. But as he leaves the slave ship, the American is surprised when Don Benito leaps after him, which is when he learns that there had been a revolt earlier and that the slaves had actually been in charge all along. Following a pitched battle, the slaves are subdued and Babo, who has been their leader all this time, is taken to Lima, tried, and hanged. But the effects of his experience so blight the depressed and inarticulate Benito Cereno that he too soon dies.

But for all the clean delineation of character and scene, the sharp and colorful imagery — the red of blood, the white of bone, the blue of sea and sky at the story's end — the overall tone of "Benito Cereno" is gray. On that day off the coast of Chile in 1799 when Captain Amasa Delano of Duxbury, Massachusetts, learns from his mate that a strange sail has appeared, the reader is told that

The morning was one peculiar to that coast. Everything was mute and calm; everything gray. The sea, though undulated into long roods of swells, seemed fixed, and was sleeked at the surface like waved lead that has cooled and set in the smelter's mould. The sky seemed a gray surtout. Flights of troubled gray fowl, kith and kin with flights of troubled gray vapors among which they were mixed, skimmed low and fitfully over the waters, as swallows over meadows before storms. Shadows present, foreshadowing deeper shadows to come.(46)

The monochrome references to "gray," "lead," "gray surtout" (or overcoat), "gray fowl," "gray vapors," "shadows," and "deeper shadows" paint a seascape as foreboding as Macbeth's heath. Even the sun, the traditional symbol in literature of clarity and reason, appears through the "low, creeping clouds" like "a Lima intriguante's one sinister eye peering across the Plaza" from the folds of her enshrouding garment (47). Moreover, the strange ship "showed no colors," even though that was "the custom among peaceful seamen of all nations" (47). Everything about this ship, too, is gray; though those aboard are black-and-white and seem to have an unambiguous (if highly idiosyncratic) relation to one another, the crew and human cargo of the *San Dominick* are bound together in an equivocal relationship that is only clarified late in the story. And the central ambiguity of "Benito Cereno," the psychological and spiritual condition of the eponymous Don himself, is a permanently gray element in the story, one that remains forever cryptic.

Perceiving that the *San Dominick* is a ship in distress, the good-hearted Captain Delano puts several baskets of fish into his boat, quits the aptly named *Bachelor's Delight,* and approaches the hapless vessel, observing as he goes that the Spanish merchantmen is ill cared for, its shabby condition belying the signs of its owner's obvious nobility: the coat of arms that continues the theme of ambiguity in its representation of two masked figures, one with its foot on the other's neck, and a slogan that has a heraldic ring, even if it is roughly written under the canvas-covered ship's prow: *"Seguid vuestro jefe* (follow your leader)" (49). The personnel aboard the *San Dominick* tell a tale of woe: scurvy and a fever had wiped out many of them, especially the Spaniards, and for days they had drifted, windless, almost entirely out of food and water.

On this gray and already ambiguous day, boarding the ship is like entering "a strange house with strange inmates in a strange land" to Captain Delano, especially since the grotesque *San Dominick* offers such a "contrast with the blank ocean which zones it" and therefore takes on "something of the effect of enchantment." It is as though a pantomime is being acted out: he notices "four elderly grizzled negroes" chanting as they pick oakum (the tarry rope strands used to caulk seams) and six more likewise bearing "the raw aspect of unsophisticated Africans," polishing hatchets and occasionally clashing them together in a sort of barbarous music (50). A more suspicious (or less good-natured) observer might wonder at this highly mannered activity, but Delano characteristically puts it out of mind as he casts about for the ship's commander.

This turns out to be the sickly and dispirited young nobleman Benito Cereno, though it is difficult to think of him as a Melvillean "captain," given the solitary imperiousness that that word suggests. Cereno is no Ahab. Far from it, he is aided and supported — or is he controlled? — by the diminutive Babo, "a black of small stature" who is like "a shepherd's dog" in his sorrowful, affectionate regard for his master (51). This is not the last time that animal imagery will be used to misrepresent the slaves aboard the *San Dominick* as compliant, simple creatures.

Prompted by Babo, Cereno tells the story of his ill-fated voyage and then invites Delano to join him on the poop deck; the American captain feels "an apprehensive twitch in the calves of his legs" as he passes by the sinister hatchet polishers, but this, too, he ignores (59). He cannot keep silent when he sees a slave boy slash a Spaniard's head with a knife, but this act of insubordination is greeted with an indifference on the part of Cereno that is almost contagious; before long, Delano himself seems to be giving in to the pervasive torpor of this enchanted ship.

If Cereno has been unmanned by the *San Dominick's* bad luck, he seems all but annihilated by the loss of his friend Don Alexandro Aranda, who had owned most of the slaves. Delano speculates aloud that it is the loss of his friend's mortal remains that is particularly devastating to Cereno and that he would be less affected had he been able to preserve the body for a proper shore burial, but at this comment the Spanish captain falls into a dead faint. This is one of the many points in the story at which something is clearly amiss, something that neither Delano nor the reader understands. Yet it is clear that Delano's reaction to the mystery is also wrong.

The literary device of dramatic irony succeeds through the reader's participation in a secret known to some characters yet kept from others. But Melville conveys only that something is wrong without telling the reader what; simultaneously, he tightens his dramatic tension by having Delano not only conspicuously in the dark regarding the mystery aboard the *San Dominick* but also willing to go to any lengths to persuade himself that there is, in fact, no mystery at all. Regarding the Spanish captain's fainting fit, he decides that Cereno has fainted because he is afraid of ghosts, an explanation so trivial and inadequate as to convey the sense of there being two kinds of duplicity aboard the *San Dominick*. Clearly a ruse is being performed by the Spaniards and the slaves, yet the trusting American aids them unwittingly with his own extraordinary capacity for self-deception.

As though to test Delano's credulity, a number of characters parade before the American captain and perform actions that may or may not be fraught with meaning; in every case, Delano chooses to ignore these actions or interpret them either benevolently or wrongly. First, the giant Atufal appears in chains before Cereno, who has promised to release the slave once he has begged pardon for some unnamed offense; noting that Cereno wears the key to Atufal's lock on "a slender silken cord" around his neck, Delano remarks, "So, Don Benito — padlock and key — significant symbols, truly" (63). (As in other instances when Delano misinterprets the "significant symbols" he sees, Cereno nearly faints at the American's obtuseness.) Then a young Spanish sailor tries to signal with his eyes that Cereno and Babo are conspiring together, but Delano reflects only on the Spanish captain's rudeness in whispering with his slave in the American's presence; oddly, this sailor seems to be wearing beneath his rough shirt an undergarment of fine linen as well as a sparkling object, possibly a jewel, but this, too, is merely noted and then set aside by Delano.

When another sailor makes "an imperfect gesture" and then vanishes, however, Delano begins to wonder if there is not indeed a plot aboard the *San Dominick,* one in which Cereno and the slaves mean to do a mischief to the American and his crew. This, too, though, Delano talks himself out of: the slaves are really "too stupid" to conspire, and, as far as Cereno goes, "who ever heard of a white so far a renegade as to apostatize from his very species almost, by leaguing in against it with negroes?" The ambiguities are too many for Delano at this point: "These difficulties recalled former ones," and he is left "lost in their mazes" (74–75).

In this befuddled state, the American notices an aged sailor tying a complicated knot and "his mind, by a not uncongenial transition," passes "from its own entanglements to those of the hemp." The sailor speaks to Delano in slow Spanish but then tosses the knot to him and says "Undo it, cut it, quick" in rapid broken English. Delano stands bemused, "knot in hand, and knot in head," until one of the slaves takes the hemp from him and tosses it overboard. By now the signs of something amiss are almost too great for him to ignore, but Delano manages to tamp down a suspicion that he regards as unmanly: "All this is very queer now, thought Captain Delano, with a qualmish sort of emotion; but as one feeling incipient sea-sickness, he strove, by ignoring the symptoms, to get rid of the malady" (76–77). As the portents gather around Delano like storm clouds, he continues to bask in the radiation of his sanguine worldview.

Amasa Delano's tendency to make a gray world into a sunny one has as its basis an exalted and thoroughgoing self-love; as with the Master of Chancery in "Bartleby," the world is good because he is good. Further, he is good because it is good to be an American. Delano accounts for his outlook in a breathy paean to himself and, by extension, to his countrymen as well:

What, I, Amasa Delano — Jack of the Beach, as they called me when a lad — I, Amasa; the same that, duck-satchel in hand, used to paddle along the waterside to the schoolhouse made from the old hulk; — I, little Jack of the Beach, that used to go berrying with cousin Nat and the rest; I to be murdered here at the ends of the earth, on board a haunted pirate-ship by a horrible Spaniard? — Too nonsensical to think of! Who would murder Amasa Delano? His conscience is clean. There is some one above. Fie, fie, Jack of the Beach! you are a child indeed; a child of the second childhood, old boy; you are beginning to dote and drule, I'm afraid. (77)

The black–white racism in "Benito Cereno" is so obvious as to warrant more censure than interpretive comment; indeed, as will be seen, ultimately the black–white racism of this story proves to be beyond comment. A more subtle form of racism is that involving Delano's belief in American moral superiority over Spanish perfidy. His self-description not only suggests that the innocent Jack of the Beach, child of nature, lives on in the adult Amasa Delano, now a prosperous sea captain, but also that Jack/Amasa enjoys the protection of a benign deity ("There is some one above"). In contrast to this naturally good and divinely guarded American, Cereno is a "horrible" murdering Spaniard, but Spanish wiles are no match for an invincibility that suggests Americans are, as the early settlers described themselves, a latter-day version of the Chosen People.

Besides, Delano's suspicions are always short-lived, and as soon as Babo appears to present Don Benito's compliments, the American thinks, "What a donkey I was. This kind gentleman who here sends me his kind compliments, he, but ten minutes ago, dark-lantern in hand, was dodging round some old grind-stone in the hold, sharpening a hatchet for me, I thought" (77). It is not as though he is incapable of entertaining negative feelings, yet whatever unpleasant thoughts he has are succeeded swiftly by cheerful ones, so that he is capable of thinking, "But as a nation...these Spaniards are all an odd set; the very word Spaniard has a curious, conspirator, Guy-Fawkish twang to it" and then answering himself, in the very next sentence, with "and yet, I dare say, Spaniards in the main are as good folks as any in Duxbury, Massachusetts" (79).

As opposed to his on-again-off-again feelings for Spaniards in general and Benito Cereno in particular, Delano's attitudes toward the slaves aboard the *San Dominick* are quite uniform. He describes them as creatures of nature, compares them to animals (dogs, bats, deer), and, on the whole, deems them rightly destined for lives of cheerful servitude; indeed, since apparently "God had set the whole negro to some pleasant tune," blacks were meant to serve uncomplainingly as much as Delano and others of his ilk were fated divinely for the governance of what he considers an inferior race. Cereno's steward, Francesco, "a tall, rajah-looking mulatto," is praised by Delano for having European features "more regular than King George's of England" (89), but the full-blooded blacks are merely happy animals to him. Delano's partially suspicious attitude toward Spaniards and wholly condescending attitude toward the slaves blinds him to the true nature of the drama being acted out aboard the *San Dominick;* it occurs to him that there may be something amiss, but any harm can only come from the Guy Fawkish Spaniards, not the docile, eager-to-please Africans.

However, the marvelous thing is that it is precisely Amasa Delano's thickheadedness that saves him. A shrewder, more cunning captain would have guessed the facts of the matter instantly — and been put to death by Babo and his minions. Instead, the truth comes to Delano late and in the form of a revelation for which nothing has prepared him. As Delano prepares to return to the *Bachelor's Delight,* Cereno leaps into the boat after him; initially Delano thinks that the Spanish captain means to give his crew the impression that the Americans have kidnapped him but changes his mind when Babo leaps after his erstwhile master and tries to stab him. The bright, hot clarity of the truth strikes Delano like lightning: "All this, with what preceded, and what followed, occurred with such involutions of rapidity, that past, present, and future seemed one.... That moment, across the long-benighted mind of Captain Delano, a flash of revelation swept, illuminating in unanticipated clearness his host's whole mysterious demeanor, with every enigmatic event of the day, as well as the entire past voyage of the San Dominick" (99). The gray fog of incomprehension lifts, at least for a moment.

In the trial that follows the taking of the Spanish ship and the delivery of the rebellious slaves to the authorities in Lima, Benito Cereno's verbatim account of his misadventures is presented as a final and definitive attempt at clarifying the mystery of the *San Dominick;* Delano observes that "if the Deposition have [*sic*] served as the key to fit into the lock of the complications which precede it, then as a vault whose door has been flung back, the San Dominick's hull lies open today" (114). Don Benito's deposition, which follows closely the deposition of the actual Benito Cereno, does provide new detail especially regarding the period following the slave revolt and preceding the arrival of Delano on board the *San Dominick.* Reaction to this startlingly Modernist technique of violating temporal unity by telling and then retelling the same story has not always been favorable, but one effect of this use of multiple points of view is to make doubly troubling the central mystery of "Benito Cereno," namely, the blighted psychological and spiritual condition of Don Benito himself, long after he has been rescued and his tormentors punished.[7] Listening to the Don speak mournfully of his diseased state of mind, Captain Delano replies, beginning with colorful images that contrast sharply with the gray of the story's beginning:

"You generalize, Don Benito; and mournfully enough. But the past is passed; why moralize upon it? Forget it. See, yon bright sun has forgotten it all, and the blue sea, and the blue sky; these have turned over new leaves."
"Because they have no memory," he dejectedly replied; "because they are not human."
"But these mild trades that now fan your cheek, do they not come with a human-like healing to you? Warm friends, steadfast friends are the trades."
"With their steadfastness they but waft me to my tomb, señor," was the foreboding response.
"You are saved," cried Captain Delano, more and more astonished and pained; "you are saved; what has cast such a shadow upon you?"
"The negro."
There was silence, while the moody man sat, slowly and unconsciously gathering his mantle about him, as if it were a pall. (116)

Benito Cereno's two-word reply to Amasa Delano's question, which comes at the end of an interrogatory of a psychological and spiritual nature that parallels yet ultimately fails to supplement the strictly legalistic deposition that precedes it, remains one of the great enigmas of nineteenth-century American fiction. A bonanza for critics, the Don's laconic response can be interpreted in an infinite number of ways.

In attempting to understand what Cereno means, one might begin by asking why he speaks so brusquely — "The negro" are his only words — and then refuses to elaborate. It is not as though he is tongue-tied; his remarks in earlier paragraphs suggest that the Spaniard is, if no orator, capable of ordinary expression. Obviously, then, he does not go on because he knows that no one will understand him, and certainly not the American captain with whom he has shared so much harrowing experience yet who is so fundamentally different from him in nature. Clearly, the educated and noble Don can explain himself but will not. The question then becomes, why is Don Benito certain that no one will understand him?

To answer this question, it is essential to look at several clusters of complex, dreamy, and, on the surface, inappropriate images that both help to make "Benito Cereno" one of the most successful of Melville's fictions and provide essential clues to Don Benito's enigmatic nature. The images are all of a decaying Europe, a cruel, undemocratic, strife-torn, Catholic continent that is represented by the Spanish slavers and that is anathema to the New England Protestant viewpoint represented by the American. These image clusters appear in swift succession at the beginning of the story and are echoed regularly thereafter, as though to establish solidly and then maintain consistently a specific context for the events.

1. As he approaches the *San Dominick,* Delano thinks it "a white-washed monastery . . . perched upon some dun cliff among the Pyrenees." And aboard is "a ship-load of monks . . . throngs of dark cowls . . . Black Friars pacing the cloisters." Later Cereno will appear to him as a "hypochondriac abbot" and Babo as a "begging friar of St. Francis" (48, 52, 57).

2. Upon drawing even closer, Delano remarks that "the castellated forecastle seemed some ancient turret, long ago taken by assault, and then left to decay." Two galleries become "tenantless balconies [that] hung over the sea as if it were the grand Venetian canal." And Cereno's manner suggests that of Charles V, sixteenth-century king of Spain and then Holy Roman Emperor (48, 53).

3. An actual emblem of decaying European culture is the ship's stern-piece, a "relic of faded grandeur . . . intricately carved with the arms of Castile and Leno, medallioned about by groups of mytho-

logical or symbolical devices; uppermost and central of which was a dark satyr in a mask, holding his foot on the prostrate neck of a writhing figure, likewise masked." This image will undergo a significant reversal later in the story when all the players aboard the *San Dominick* drop their masks and Delano grinds the struggling Babo beneath his foot in the battle that ensues; an image of aristocratic oppression becomes one of New World domination (49, 99).

4. The "effect of enchantment" experienced by Delano once he boards this "unreal" ship, which is like "a strange house...in a strange land," becomes more pronounced the longer he remains on board. Leaning against a balustrade, he fancies himself gazing, not into the sea, but into a garden with a "border of green box" and "parterres" and "long formal alleys," with the balustrade itself suggesting "the charred ruin of some summer-house in a grand garden long running to waste" (50).

5. Later this image of a fine house gone to ruin is combined with some especially sinister Catholic imagery. One of the cabins recalls the "wide, cluttered hall of some eccentric bachelor-squire in the country," but the clutter includes some rigging that is like a "poor friar's girdles," settees like "inquisitors' racks," and a chair like "some grotesque, middle-age engine of torment" (74, 82–83).

6. As Babo shaves Don Benito, Delano thinks that "in the black he saw a headsman, and in the white, a man at the block." Later he thinks the sound of the ship's bell is "as of a tolling for execution in some jail-yard" (85, 95–96).

In effect, the democratic American captain is having visited upon him the foulness and corruption of a hierarchical European system that is predicated on the vilest tyranny possible, the subjugation of other human beings. Dead in spirit, the European system is to die literally in the century to come; this death-in-life is dramatized horrifically in the skeleton of Aranda, Cereno's friend and business partner, which has been lashed to the prow of the ship in a sinister illustration of the Spanish motto that reads, in English, *"Follow your leader."* The phrase recurs twice, with resonant meaning each time: once when the mate of the *Bachelor's Delight* sounds the unambiguous version of the phrase, crying, "Follow your leader!" as he leads a charge against the enemy, and again in the final words of the story, when the mortally sick Don Benito, "borne on the bier, did, indeed, follow his leader" (99, 102, 117). There is no escape from the deadly virus of slavery, which kills masters, too.

Benito Cereno has had the unenviable experience of being the only member of the slave-owning class in the story to have actually been a slave. As such, he understands that slaves are human and not dogs or deer, as Amasa Delano thinks. But why does he not speak? A less-reticent character in another nineteenth-century novel, and a character with a less-equivocal view of slavery than Benito Cereno, does articulate the experiential reality of slavery; in Mark Twain's *A Connecticut Yankee in King Arthur's Court,* after he has been seized as a slave, manacled and lettered and sold at auction, Hank Morgan reflects that "freemen had been sold into life-long slavery, without the circumstance making any particular impression upon me; but the minute law and the auction block came into my personal experience, a thing which had been merely improper before, became suddenly hellish."[8] But whereas Hank Morgan is in the company of other protesting freemen-made-slaves and is ostensibly addressing an antislavery post–Civil War readership, Benito Cereno has no one to talk to and therefore he does not talk at all. Hank Morgan is in hell with plenty of company; Benito Cereno burns alone. At the end of his story, Benito Cereno's attitude toward living is the same as Bartleby's at the end of his: he prefers not to.

Similarly, Amasa Delano, like the Master of Chancery in "Bartleby," emerges as one of the happy types who come out ahead in Melville's world, a well-meaning though in many ways blind individual who succeeds through a good fortune denied to others. Many of Melville's protagonists are bachelors, including the captain of the *Bachelor's Delight;* in a sketch entitled "The Paradise of Bachelors and the Tartarus of Maids," a narrator observes, "The thing called pain, the bugbear styled trouble — these two legends seemed preposterous to... bachelor imaginations."[9] (This sketch contrasts bachelor optimism with another nineteenth-century evil: the numbing factory labor practiced by the zombielike "maids.") Delano thinks well of himself for thinking well of the slaves, just as the Master prides himself on his liberal attitudes toward his employees. Yet neither is capable of understanding the dark figure at the center of his story. And in Delano's case, his lack of perception is a boon: as Cereno points out, had he shown any sign of understanding the truth of the drama being acted out aboard the *San Dominick,* the rebellious slaves would have slain him instantly.

At the end of both stories, the Master and Captain Delano have become more knowledgeable, though their core selves seem little changed. Both, in fact, seem hale and hearty and destined for long lives — even immortality, considering that they are still living when their fictions end. In Melville's world, the most successful people are the smart ones who are nonetheless not too smart. Bartleby and Benito Cereno know so much that they die, the Master of Chancery and Amasa Delano so little that they live forever.

"The Lightning-Rod Man," the third of the five *Piazza Tales,* is a curious centerpiece, since it offers a lighthearted contrast to the portentousness that haunts the other stories. Based on a visit from a real lightning-rod salesman as well as encounters with religious preachings that threatened God's wrath, this brief sketch concludes with a prospect telling the lightning-rod man to peddle his wares — and his fears — elsewhere.[10]

But the remaining stories in *The Piazza Tales* partake of the doom-laden atmosphere and sense of woe that characterize "Bartleby the Scrivener" and "Benito Cereno." "The Encantadas" consists of ten sketches based on Melville's visit to the Galápagos Archipelago lying some six hundred miles off the Ecuadorian coast when he was aboard the *Acushnet* (later he passed near the islands again while aboard the *Charles and Henry* and the *United States);* as usual, he added material from other accounts to his own recollections.[11] Volcanically formed, these "enchanted isles" are picturesque though desolate; the last sketch is aptly titled "RUN-AWAYS, CASTAWAYS, SOLITARIES, GRAVESTONES, ETC." (170). As opposed to the rigid social systems in "Bartleby" and "Benito Cereno," life on these desert isles permits and perhaps even encourages the protean ways of such travelers as the deserter/mutineer/author Herman Melville; noticing some pirate relics on one of the isles, a "sentimental voyager" asks himself, "Could it be possible, that they robbed and murdered one day, revelled the next, and rested themselves by turning meditative philosophers, rural poets, and seat-builders the third? Not very improbable, after all. For consider the vacillations of a man" (146). In this cosmos one is either a doomed partaker in a blighted social system or else a solitary seeker destined to vacillate eternally.

The last of *The Piazza Tales,* "The Bell-Tower," is an explicit tribute to Nathaniel Hawthorne. The story's protagonist, Bannadonna, is, like many of Melville's central characters, an "unblest foundling" (174). But he also recalls the protagonists of "Dr. Heidegger's

Experiment," "Rappaccini's Daughter," and the other stories in *Twice-told Tales* and *Mosses from an Old Manse* in which scientists make the Faustian bargains for which they must eventually pay some enormous price. Melville had reviewed *Mosses from an Old Manse* in 1850, five years before he wrote "The Bell-Tower"; R. Bruce Bickley calls this story "Melville's most overt attempt at allegory in the Hawthornean manner."[12] Bannadonna is the victim of an overly complex system of his own creation. He kills one of his workers while constructing a bell tower and is himself killed by a bell-ringing automaton he has devised; the belfry itself collapses at the end of the story. Contrasted with the other *Piazza Tales*, "The Bell-Tower" recalls *The Confidence-Man*, Melville's final novel and the one in which, after a complex series of novels that examine the individual's failure to find a place in the existing "world-puzzle" (see the commentary on *White-Jacket* in chapter 2 of this study), Melville invents his own world, a dark and treacherous place. Bartleby and Benito Cereno are defeated by the social systems in which they live; Bannadonna tries to transcend his surroundings by attempting not to fathom nature but "to rival her, outstrip her, and rule her" (184). He makes his own world; it destroys him and itself.

Poems

Following the publication of *The Confidence-Man,* the last work of fiction he would see published in his lifetime, and a stint as an ineffectual lecturer, Melville turned to the writing of poetry. His poetic works include *Battle-Pieces and Aspects of the War* (1866), a collection of Civil War poems; *Clarel: A Poem and Pilgrimage in the Holy Land* (1876), a lengthy philosophical quest poem dealing with faith and doubt; *John Marr and Other Sailors* (1888), a largely nostalgic prose-poetry treatment of a sailor's memories; *Timoleon* (1891), poems mainly inspired by the author's Mediterranean travels in 1857; and *Weeds and Wildings,* an unfinished manuscript of poems for Elizabeth Shaw Melville that recalls happier days at Arrowhead.

Battle-Pieces represents an unusual departure from traditional Melvillean themes and personae; reading it, one cannot but think of the Emersonian dictum that all arts end in the art of war. After Appomattox, Melville returned to his lifelong interest in philosophy, travel, and the quest motif that combines them, but for the moment his concerns were uncharacteristically topical, with the majority of the poems in *Battle-Pieces* either portraits of warriors or polemics on the horror, pathos, and necessity of war. Almost all of the portraits laud the bravery of the combatants, even those on the Southern side. "Stonewall Jackson" is a paean to a general who, if he was wrong to fight against the eventually triumphant North, was at least bravely and aggressively wrong; as one who was himself a pariah because of differences with convention, Melville clearly sympathized with this defeated hero. One of the polemical poems, "Malvern Hill," reveals the murderous inanity of war in the larger scheme of things; here the trees describe how spring will come each year no matter how many die in battle.

Battle-Pieces is good war poetry, if not the best Melville. Paul Fussell writes that these poems "occasion the shock one always experiences upon seeing how badly a great writer can write."[13] This is excessive, surely, but not by much. Suffice it to say that Melville treated the Civil War better than it treated him. In *Battle-Pieces,* he was less himself and, for what it is worth, more a man of his times. In a supplementary essay that concludes the volume, he argues for generosity toward the South during the Reconstruction period, even though he inveighs against the degradation of slavery as only the author of "Benito Cereno" could.

Melville took up his old pen after the war, and his subsequent writings reveal familiar facets of his persona: in *Clarel,* the seeker after philosophical-religious truth; in *John Marr,* the mariner; in *Timoleon,* the lover of learning and antiquity.[14] *Clarel,* his other major poetic work beside *Battle-Pieces,* has the same essential structure as *Mardi, Israel Potter,* and *The Confidence-Man;* in all of these works, a single traveler encounters others in a way that suggests the actual and intellectual voyaging of Melville himself. The eponymous hero of the poem is an American theological student who travels the Holy Land in the company of various pilgrims. In Jerusalem, Clarel falls in love with Ruth, whose father has just died; forbidden by custom to court his beloved at such a time, he travels from one biblical site to another, discussing faith, doubt, science, and related matters with other travelers who represent a spectrum of ideas and attitudes. On returning to Jerusalem, he finds Ruth, whom the reader may have well forgotten by this time, dead. Clarel reflects bitterly that although Christ rose from the dead, Ruth will not.

Yet the despair that marks so much of Melville's writing is absent here. In a paper aptly entitled "Poetry and Belief: *Clarel* as a Response to Modern Skepticism," Warren Rosenberg notes that "in *Clarel* Melville says *no* to myth, but *yes* to poetry itself. Traditional narratives and heroes cannot be believed; even the Christ myth offers little more than frustration to humanity. But poetry, in its most radical form, as poetic vision ... does offer humanity hope, if not certitude. . . . *Clarel*, then, and even the turn to poetry itself after the rejection of 'false' prose worlds in *The Confidence-Man*, can be interpreted as Melville's personal solution to the problem of belief."[15]

Having examined the various permutations of religious faith, Clarel is advised by the poem's narrator to keep hope in his heart. The questionings of nineteenth-century science have cast more light into the world, according to the poem's final lines, yet in that way they have created more shadows. Institutionalized religion leads to zealotry and bloodshed, but it is better to resign oneself, to accept what one can and believe the best is yet to come than to give in to either sterile science or superstitious faith. *Clarel* represents a viewpoint that is aged, learned, and much-traveled. Melville had ranged the globe as well as the peaks and valleys of his own thoughts and feelings; too, he had plumbed the literatures of more than one culture. The search had been both broad and deep, but near the end he found himself not all that far from the place where he began. The venerable author of *Clarel*, like the callow sailor aboard the *Acushnet*, was still curious, still skeptical. More than ever, though, he was convinced that the true path is the solitary one.

"Billy Budd"

In the decades following the publication of *The Confidence-Man*, Melville went about his duties as customs inspector with sedulous application if not fervor; by all reports, he was a regular, hardworking, and efficient employee. In the meantime, he composed the poems he published himself, more in the manner of a die-hard hobbyist than a professional author. He resigned his position at the customs house on December 31, 1885, and devoted much of his attention to *John Marr and Other Sailors,* a book that, with its emphatic nostalgia and its mixture of genres and of both high rhetorical and low colloquial styles, seems simultaneously behind and ahead of its times. The title work consists of a lengthy prose headnote (discussed in chapter 1 of this study) and a brief poem; for a while, this was also the form of "Billy Budd," initially a headnote and then a poem about a sailor waiting to be hanged for mutiny. But in the June 1888 issue of the *American Magazine* there appeared an article about the *Somers* affair (also discussed in chapter 1), an actual case involving mutiny and execution in which Melville's cousin Guert Gansevoort was involved.[16] This reexamination of the case may have led Melville to revise his conception of "Billy Budd"; in any case, the headnote began to grow, and before long, Melville found himself taking up again a pen he had not touched for decades, the pen of the sailor-turned-storyteller who found in the facts of maritime life the tragedies, beauties, and ironies of all life.

As with "Bartleby the Scrivener" and "Benito Cereno," "Billy Budd" is the story of two men, an open and articulate character who means well yet is helpless to save an enigmatic and voiceless antihero who seems innocent and uncomprehending. It is hardly surprising that a fictionist should take up where he left off, even when the temporal lapse between old work and new is, as in the extraordinary case of "Billy Budd," more than thirty years. Indeed, the Captain Vere who presides over Billy's fate is strongly reminiscent of both the Master of Chancery and Amasa Delano. And while Billy Budd is younger and less experienced than Bartleby and Benito Cereno, he shares more with them than a name beginning with the letter *B*. For Billy too is one of Melville's picaros, an orphan and outcast. Whether or not he is too good for this world, he, like his predecessors, is at one remove from ordinary life throughout his story. And when that story ends, so does his life, like theirs.

One significant difference between "Billy Budd" and the earlier tales is that here there is a third, fully drawn character who catalyzes the relationship between the good if insensitive master and his doomed underling. Babo comes close to playing this role in "Benito Cereno," yet his character is largely a two-dimensional representation of pure (if justifiable) malice. But there is no other character in Melville's fiction quite like the serpentine John Claggart, the master of arms who despises in Billy the very qualities that the sailors and the other officers treasure. In such autobiographically based fictions as *Typee, Redburn,* and *White-Jacket,* Melville depicted the casual viciousness of some of the officers he encountered during his years at sea. In Claggart, this seemingly baseless malevolence is gathered, heightened, focused, and directed with such force that Billy, who is at least as good as Claggart is evil, is helpless against it.

Harrison Hayford and Merton M. Sealts, Jr., have not only produced the definitive edition of the "Billy Budd" that was unfinished at Melville's death but also traced the story's development from its earliest stages.[17] Their genetic study of the relevant materials reveals that "the manuscript of *Billy Budd* as Melville left it at his death in 1891 may be most accurately described as a semi-final draft, not a final fair copy ready for publication" (1). Initially, Billy Budd was a mutinous (and evidently guilty) sailor who is the subject of a poem intended for *John Marr and Other Sailors;* Melville expanded the prose headnote that was to accompany the poem so that, by 1888, he had more than 150 manuscript pages. It was during this phase that the character of Claggart was introduced, complicating the issue of Billy's guilt. The manuscript grew to 351 pages during its third and final phase, which occupied Melville until the end of his life. Here he expanded the character of Captain Vere, a minor figure in the story's earlier phases, and thus complicated even more the matter of Billy's guilt or innocence as well as the rightness or wrongness of the decision to hang him.

The resulting text is an apt conclusion to a career marked by occasional successes and frequent failures, a career in which Melville devoted himself to an unflinching examination of "the ambiguities," to borrow the subtitle of *Pierre,* even if it meant foregoing a popular audience. As with the poetry, Melville was writing for himself when he composed "Billy Budd." But his own standards were higher than those of any readership, and thus his final work ranks with his best. "Billy Budd" is as exciting a tale of sea life as *Israel Potter* or "Benito Cereno," as profound a look at good and evil as *White-Jacket* or *The Confidence-Man.* Not since *Moby-Dick* had Melville combined adventure and introspection so subtly yet engagingly. Those who do not know Melville for his whale story encounter him at his best in his last and most focused study of his single most enduring character type. For Billy Budd, like Tommo, Typee, Redburn, White Jacket, Ishmael, Israel, and the rest, is a solitary, one of God's orphans.

"Billy Budd" begins with a tribute to the concept of the Handsome Sailor, a fellow of strength and beauty tempered by an equally well-developed moral nature and thus the idol of his shipmates. Such a one is Billy Budd, described in his initial appearance as

"welkin-eyed," that is, blue-eyed, from a chiefly literary term meaning "sky" or, more properly, "vault of heaven." Also known as Baby
Budd, Billy is a foretopman serving in the British Navy at "the close
of the last decade of the eighteenth century" (44); later, the date of
the events in the story is given as 1797. Just before the narrative begins, Billy was impressed into service from an English merchantman
bound for home to the ominously named HMS *Bellipotent* (war-
powerful). A civilian, an infant, even, Baby Budd accepts his fate
uncomplainingly, stepping carelessly from one sort of life at sea to
its complete opposite. (It is hard to read about this portentous transition and not imagine the aged author thinking of his youthful self
plunging into the rigors of life aboard the naval vessel *United States*
after his comparatively easy time on civilian ships; see chapter 1 of
this study for details.)

The merchantmen's shipmaster complains of the loss; such a
Handsome Sailor as Billy has not only been, by example, a peace-
maker among his cantankerous crew but has even turned the men
into a "happy family" (47). In his innocence, Billy not only calls
farewell to his friends but breaches naval decorum when he cries
out to the merchantman itself, it, too, bearing a significant name.
"And good-bye to you too, old *Rights-of-Man*," cries Billy, and
is instantly admonished by the naval lieutenant, who assumes the
rigor of his rank, "though with difficulty repressing a smile" (49).
Though he has presumably surrendered the rights of man (Thomas
Paine's book by that title is cited as the source of the merchantman's
name), Billy is instantly taken up by the crew of the *Bellipotent* and
soon begins to exert his benevolent influence there as well.

Billy does seem a bit too good to be true, and some readers
have referred to his semidivine nature, particularly his mysterious,
godlike appearance on this earth. After all, Billy was not born
but found, as he says, "in a pretty silk-lined basket hanging one
morning from the knocker of a good man's door in Bristol" (51).
However, to say, on this basis, that his origin is miraculous is to
overlook the presence of the other orphans in Melville, those figures who seem both blessed and cursed by their solitary states. To
Melville, orphanhood functions as a reminder of the essential loneliness of all humanity, but it is also a necessary condition for the
picaresque characters who give most of his fiction its drive. Being alone is not a happy state in Melville, but it is indispensable;
"thought-divers" do not dive in pairs.

In one sense, though, Billy is radically different from the other orphans who populate Melville's pages. Whereas Tommo, Typee, and the others are cunning, shrewd, even mildly criminal in nature, Billy is utterly guileless. He is a perfect, or a near-perfect, creature, yet he is no god. Perhaps Billy is best described as the embodiment of the highest natural qualities; not quite a complete human being, Billy seems more like an allegorical representation of calm, good cheer, physical good looks, and an even, accepting temperament. The other two main characters are representations of other human qualities; together with Billy, as will be argued below, they more or less comprise a single fully-developed person.

So while it would be wrong to view Billy as a literal demigod, it is clear that Melville is writing allegorically, connecting his character to a venerable religious and literary tradition in order to show that his story is an ageless drama rather than an isolated incident at sea. In typically teasing fashion, Melville notes that Billy is "not presented as a conventional hero, but also that the story in which he is the main figure is no romance" (53). As he emphasizes what "Billy Budd" is not, he clearly invites us to say what it is. And among the most obvious possibilities is allegory.

Thus, in describing Billy's single physical flaw, Melville does so in a manner contrived to make the reader think of Genesis (and of his American master Hawthorne as well):

> Though our Handsome Sailor had as much of masculine beauty as one can expect anywhere to see; nevertheless, like the beautiful woman in one of Hawthorne's minor tales ["The Birthmark"], there was just one thing amiss in him. No visible blemish indeed, as with the lady; no, but an occasional liability to a vocal defect. Though in an hour of elemental uproar or peril he was everything that a sailor should be, yet under sudden provocation of strong heart-feeling his voice, otherwise singularly musical, as if expressive of the harmony within, was apt to develop an organic hesitancy, in fact more or less a stutter or even worse. In this particular Billy was a striking instance that the arch interferer, the envious marplot of Eden, still has more or less to do with every human consignment to this planet of Earth. In every case, one way or another he is sure to slip in his little card, as much to remind us — I too have a hand here. (53)

It is shortly after this Eden reference that Melville introduces into the narrative the other main characters, both of whom recall their counterparts in Genesis. Captain the Honorable Edward Fairfax Vere presides over the *Bellipotent*, godlike and distant. He is identified as a scholar, a lover of antiquity, and, like the Master of Chancery and Amasa Delano, a bachelor. If he is the ship's brain, its muscle is John Claggart, the master-at-arms and thus "a sort of chief of police charged among other matters with the duty of preserving order" (64). He is black-haired and pale-skinned; unlike the ordinary seamen, he spends most of his time in the shadows. Like Billy, Claggart too has a mysterious past; it is thought by some that he may not even be an Englishman. When he falsely accuses Billy of conspiracy, his eyes undergo "a phenomenal change, their wonted rich violet color blurring into a muddy purple. Those lights of human intelligence, losing human expression, were gelidly protruding like the alien eyes of certain uncatalogued creatures of the deep. The first mesmeristic glance was one of serpent fascination; the last was as the paralyzing lurch of the torpedo fish" (98). If "welkin-eyed" Billy is associated with the heavens, Claggart is linked with the wet hell of the deepest seas, a realm of finny monsters.

The clash between Claggart and Billy comes as a complete surprise to the latter, whose innocent nature is devoid of the irony and cynicism that come so naturally to the other sailors. Melville observes that Claggart is the embodiment of "Natural Depravity," a condition of insanity that masks itself in the appearance of reason. Unlike other criminal types, the naturally depraved are born that way; they tend to be prideful, ascetic, and intelligent. Indeed, part of Claggart's malign motivation is that he is intelligent enough both to comprehend Billy's goodness and to know that he can never partake of it. It is this biting jealousy that leads Claggart to falsely accuse Billy of conspiracy to mutiny.

Claggart's charge and the events that follow take momentum from the anxious context in which they occur, for already that year there had been two notable mutinies in the British navy. Additionally, there are dissatisfied sailors aboard the *Bellipotent* whose cryptic mutterings only confuse Billy; it is suggested that at least one of them is a "cat's-paw" sent by Claggart to entrap the Handsome Sailor (85). This troubled atmosphere gives weight to Claggart's false accusation of Billy, a charge the fair-minded Vere is inclined to disbelieve. Vere does things by the book, however, and rather than dismiss Claggart out of hand, he has him repeat the charge in front of Billy, who, tongue-tied, strikes his accuser dead. Vere equates Claggart with Ananias, the biblical liar, and says that he has been " 'struck dead by an angel of God! Yet the angel must hang!' " (101). Even before he calls the drumhead court, Vere knows what sentence is mandated by naval regulations.

There are, of course, options: some of the officers urge Vere to refer the matter to the fleet's admiral, and one of them tries to establish Claggart's motive as a possibly mitigating factor. But as captain, Vere feels compelled to make the decision himself and in accordance with maritime law and specifically with the Articles of War that make striking a superior officer a capital crime. He tells the other members of the drumhead court that he must "strive against scruples that may tend to enervate decision. Not, gentlemen, that I hide from myself that the case is an exceptional one. Speculatively regarded, it well might be referred to a jury of casuists. But for us here, acting not as casuists or moralists, it is a case practical, and under martial law practically to be dealt with" (110). He also argues that the officers' allegiance is to the King, not Nature, and tells them that their cool heads must prevail over their warm hearts. When the others argue that they might convict Billy yet mitigate the penalty, Vere argues that they cannot.

Here is the crux of the story, the turning point at which the narrative can continue to proceed inexorably toward Billy's death or reverse itself and let the hapless sailor live. Vere's argument is that the crew of the *Bellipotent* will think mercy a sign of weakness and perhaps make the false mutiny of which Billy was accused a reality. "Your clement sentence they would account pusillanimous," he tells the other members of the court. "They would think that we flinch, that we are afraid of them. . . . I feel as you do for this unfortunate boy. But did he know our hearts, I take him to be of that generous nature that he would feel even for us on whom . . . so heavy a compulsion is laid" (113). Like the biblical Abraham, Vere puts duty before feeling. And Billy's fate is sealed.

Billy's last hours and execution are saturated with religious imagery, Christian and otherwise. The *Bellipotent*'s chaplain, "the minister of Christ though receiving his stipend from Mars," finds Billy in a peaceful, oblivious state, like a "superior *savage,* so called — a Tahitian, say, of Captain Cook's time" (120–21). Convinced that Billy is utterly ignorant of religion yet as sure of Heaven as any of the faithful, the chaplain kisses him on his cheek and withdraws. Just before the hanging, Billy calls out, "God bless Captain Vere"; in the Handsome Sailor's last mortal act, he affects the crew so movingly that they repeat his words (123). The rope is tightened, and "at that moment it chanced that the vapory fleece hanging low in the East was shot through with a soft glory as of the fleece of the Lamb of God seen in mystical vision, and simultaneously therewith, watched by the wedged mass of upturned faces, Billy ascended; and, ascending, took the full rose of the dawn." Interestingly, as the soul of Billy merges with the morning sun as well as the Son of God, Vere is described as standing "erectly rigid as a musket in the ship-armorer's rack" (124). Further miraculous events, or at least "phenomenal" ones (to use the term chosen by the surgeon and purser, who discuss the execution), ensue: Billy's body does not jerk in the death spasm but hangs motionless from the yard end (125).[18] And upon his burial, seafowl fly screaming to the spot where his body disappears beneath the waves; this stands in marked contrast to the disposal of Claggart's remains, which sink unceremoniously.

In this way Melville the literary confidence man seems to be teasing the reader again, here implying that Billy is in fact godlike. Indeed, that might be the reader's logical assumption were the story to end here, as it very well might. But Melville returns the focus to Captain Vere, who is wounded in a sea battle and dies with Billy's name on his lips. By returning to the Abraham-like Vere, Melville reminds us of the allegorical nature of the story. One might say that Billy, Claggart, and Vere are rough pre-Freudian equivalents of the ego, id, and superego. But it would be more appropriate to Melville's own day and to his particular worldview to see Billy as the orphan doomed through no real fault of his own, Claggart as the malign fate who crosses everyone's path sooner or later, and Vere as the benevolent, helpless figure who tries to live rightly and somehow manages to survive despite his good intentions. These elements mark most of Melville's fiction in one way or another. It is simply that, in "Billy Budd," Melville chose to draw on his considerable knowledge of lore to deck his story in the imagery of the oldest story of all, the one that is in the scripture of every culture — the story of the struggle between good and evil.

Besides, in the end, it is clearly Melville the artist who has the final say. The last two chapters of "Billy Budd" contain two additional but very brief accounts of Billy's life and death. The first is a newspaper article that casts Billy as a mutiny ringleader who stabs Claggart to death with his sheath knife. The second is the sentimental poem that was the genesis of the tale, according to Hayford and

Sealts's account; here the wrongly-accused Billy is astonishingly articulate and even punning as he prepares to go to his death. Thus there are three Billy Budd stories: the full narrative, the "false" (and negative) newspaper account, and the "false" (but positive) poem. In its inconclusive anatomy of a baffling and convoluted system of justice, Melville's final work "anticipates the Kafkaesque strand of literary modernism," according to Michael Paul Rogin.[19] But "Billy Budd" also anticipates modernism in its form, its collage of genres, and its open-endedness.

So the reader of Melville's final fiction has a tough choice to make. The longest account, the story proper, establishes its own authenticity through such traditional fictional devices as repetition and elaboration, but the two shorter ones challenge that authenticity by having, as it were, the last word. Which of these three accounts, then, is the reader to accept? Like Babo or Bartleby or any of the other figures who are islands of silence in the ocean of words that is his oeuvre, the Melville who, as Hawthorne said, could "neither believe, nor be comfortable in his unbelief," does not say.

Perhaps it is too much to ask that a last story be a Last Will and Testament, though. Throughout his career, Melville made plenty of references to final things; typically, the most straightforward of these references occur in out-of-the-way places. Thus, in chapters 184–90 of *Mardi*, when Taji visits Serenia, he voices his suspicion that the secrets of Heaven will not be worth knowing. And in an 1851 letter to Hawthorne, Melville wrote: "And perhaps, after all, there is *no* secret. We incline to think that the Problem of the Universe is like the Freemason's mighty secret, so terrible to all children. It turns out, at last, to consist in a triangle, a mallet, and an apron, — nothing more!"[20] Melville says that Billy goes to Heaven yet he leaves his reader, not a triangle, mallet, and apron, but a story, a newspaper article, and a poem — all we know on earth, to paraphrase another poet, and all we need to know. Having perfected an imperfect system of inquiry at the end of *Moby-Dick*, Ishmael embraces a rich and satisfying loneliness, and his final words to the reader are poetry. So it appears to have been at the end of Melville's own life as well.

6

Conclusion

Throughout this book, Melville's life and writing have been examined within three overlapping contexts. Melville has been treated as an uncommon individual, as a citizen of his time and place, and, most importantly, as an artist; the idiosyncrasies of his temperament have been considered as they both engage and defy the exigencies of life in mid-nineteenth-century America as well as the timeless dream of the author's life, which, in Melville's case, took the form of membership in that elite corps of "thought-divers" who included figures as different as Shakespeare and Emerson. Like each of us, Melville sought a standpoint within himself, within his era, and within a specific profession. And if in his struggle with these issues of identity, citizenship, and professionalism he suffered bitter defeats, he also achieved triumphs of a kind known only to a handful of others.

A towering representative of his own time — though not in his own time — Melville is perhaps best understood in comparison to and in contrast with an equivalent figure of the next period of American cultural history such as Henry James. Where Melville scrambled for economic stability in a developing America, working alternately as sailor, schoolmaster, and even pinsetter in a bowling alley, James lived in a more affluent time; he was the inheritor of a fortune made by his grandfather and thereafter enjoyed the fruits of an independent if not opulent life. Melville took serious issue with many of the social and political developments of his day, whereas James largely ignored such matters, at least on the surface of his work, and decamped for Europe, eventually settling in England. And whereas Melville finally surrendered his dream of becoming a full-time man of letters for a day job much like any other, James made himself into the consummate artist who in late life was called by his disciples "the Master." Melville was a solitary, a rebellious patriot, and, by the end of his life, a mere amateur; James a bon vivant, a cosmopolitan, and a professional writer par excellence.

The difference between the lives and careers of these two writers can in part be attributed to their very different temperaments and in part to sheer luck (or its lack), but many of these differences are generational as well. Looking at these two significant figures in our cultural past helps us see where we are today and also where we came from, for if the affluent world-citizen James seems like the first of the moderns, the struggling nationalist Melville seems like the last representative of an earlier order.

Melville's attempts to define himself as individual, citizen, and professional are closely interrelated, of course, and related as well to the contexts in which they took place. Again, a glance at James's life is instructive. A superb essay by Stuart Culver on James's self-definition shows the later author constructing a concept of himself that is based on the language of financial management as well as references to such professions as civil engineering.[1] Not accidentally, both authors and engineers were organizing themselves professionally for the first time, with the Society of Authors being founded in 1884 in James's newly adopted England and the American Society of Civil Engineers, founded in 1852, becoming truly active and influential in the last decades of the century; the country settled an identity crisis of its own during the Civil War, and the subsequent technological and commercial expansion encouraged professionalism on all levels.

By contrast, Melville's generation was still solving problems of national identity raised during the Revolutionary Period; the question "What is an American?" must be closely followed by "What kind of American am I?" and then by "What kind of person am I — what do I do, and how does what I do make me what I am?" Since James's time, and thanks in part to his unswerving professionalism, it has been possible for a writer to be thought of as an artisan, a skilled professional working within a recognizable social context. To Melville and most of his contemporaries, that prospect was a lot less likely.

One wonders if Melville's versatility as a writer is not in part a reflection of his professional vicissitudes. After all, most of his significant contemporaries were literary specialists of one kind or another: Hawthorne was known mainly for his four romances, Emerson and Thoreau were essayists more than anything else, Whitman made a career of rewriting *Leaves of Grass*. But Melville's work includes autobiography (*Typee, Omoo, Redburn*), fictionalized history (*Israel Potter,* "Benito Cereno"), polemic (*White-Jacket*), the philosophical novel (*Mardi*), the psychological novel (*Pierre*), satire (*The Confidence-Man*), and the encyclopedic narrative *Moby-Dick* that encompasses each of the above genres; he also wrote lyric poetry, the long poem, short fiction, essays, and gave lectures.

Only Poe had a similar range, if a much shorter period in which to exercise it. Loosely associated with the Transcendentalists Emerson and Thoreau and with the Hawthorne who showed a skepticism toward Transcendental verities exceeded only by his own, Melville might also be thought of as a more robust and long-lived Poe with somewhat (but only somewhat) better skill at making domestic arrangements. In their writing, Melville and Poe test the Founding Fathers' laudable but overly optimistic view of human life as ordered and rational, and their lives as well suggest that chance and dark necessity are inescapable. The difference between the two is that the longer-lived Melville had a greater opportunity for bravery and therefore for riches of a kind denied to Poe. Constantly in debt or scrambling for employment, Melville spent his days accumulating aesthetic capital. He never got as much as he wanted — what artist does? — but his ceaseless quest for this intangible currency suggests that the search itself must have been immensely rewarding.

Melville's search for self on personal, national, and professional levels began early and propitiously. His two "Fragments from a Writing Desk," composed when he was only nineteen, reveal both sides of his nature: the first is highly rhetorical and self-intoxicated, the second linear and carefully plotted. In a sense, the later Melville needed little more than these two styles to compose the books that made him famous: the largely rhetorical Melville wrote most of *Mardi* and much of *Pierre* and *The Confidence-Man;* the largely plotty one wrote *Typee, Omoo,* and *Redburn.* At his best, Melville brought the two styles together, the ambitiously philosophical and the grippingly narrative, and this is the Melville who wrote *Moby-Dick,* "Bartleby," and "Billy Budd," works for which he is celebrated even by those who have not read him.

The questions at the end of this book are the same as they were at the beginning, though some of the answers seem clearer now. While it is helpful, in the course of an attempt to position Herman Melville among his contemporaries, to observe that he was dissimilar to

Henry James in certain respects and then similar to Poe in others, eventually we must come around to the questions that can only be answered by examining his case alone. What did Melville want? Who was he? What did he do? And in the end, did he know what he had done?

The first three of these questions, at least, are answerable, if not easily. In rapid succession, the young Melville was fatherless, an assumer of false names, a deserter and mutineer — an *omoo* or "rover," to use the title of one of his early works, or, as a literary historian would say, a picaro. Frustrated, he did what those of a philosophical and creative bent usually do; that is, if he could not find a place for himself in the scheme of things as they already existed, then he would change the scheme or come up with one of his own.

His writing career represents the long search for that new and better vision. Four books in particular represent important stages in his refinement of a worldview that would actually permit his sense of inclusion and belonging. The first of these is *White-Jacket,* about the crew of which Melville writes, "most of us man-of-war's-men harmoniously dove-tail into each other, and by our very points of opposition, unite in a clever whole, like the parts of a Chinese puzzle. But as, in a Chinese puzzle, many pieces are hard to place, so there are some unfortunate fellows who can never slip into their proper angles, and thus the whole puzzle becomes a puzzle indeed, which is the precise condition of the greatest puzzle in the world — this man-of-war world itself."[2]

The second of these key books is *Moby-Dick,* in which the pieces of the world puzzle harmoniously dovetail occasionally in such chapters as "The Monkey-rope," "A Squeeze of the Hand," and "The Symphony," even if the puzzle shatters into its constituent pieces at story's end. The third book, *Israel Potter,* which I have described earlier as a kind of *Dark-Jacket,* is the biography of a puzzle piece himself, the eponymous man-of-war's man who finds no place for himself in the world. Thus, if *White-Jacket* describes the possibility of inclusion and harmony and *Moby-Dick* verifies that possibility, *Israel Potter* denies it, at least on this earth. In a fourth book, *The Confidence-Man,* Melville creates a harmony of his own, though one that is decidedly cruel and harsh.

For much of his career, Melville speculated that the solace never discovered here below might be found to exist in some version of the afterlife, though not an afterlife described by any of the religions he knew. Even this speculation was undercut by serious doubt, however; as early as *Mardi,* Melville conjectured that the secrets of Heaven might not be worth knowing. And though Hawthorne left an indelible portrait of Melville as the writer who "can neither believe, nor be comfortable in his unbelief," a more accurate picture might be conveyed by the words in which Melville describes Pierre, the philosophical romancer whom he came to identify with, the more he elaborated Pierre's unhappy story: "With the soul of an Atheist, he wrote down the godliest things."[3]

Melville's standpoint, the place from which he viewed (or tried to view) himself as individual, citizen, and author, shifted constantly beneath his feet, so that these descriptions from Hawthorne and from Melville himself are especially apt in their ambivalence. Apt, too, is the passage from the *Inferno* that Melville quotes as a gloss on Pierre's state of mind following the discovery that Isabel is his half sister: "Ah! how thou dost change, / Agnello! See! thou art not double now, / Nor only one!" (p. 119). In Dante's poem, the thief Agnello Brunelleschi is attacked and partially consumed by a fellow thief who has been transformed into a six-legged lizard; the passage preceding Melville's excerpt reads, "They fused like hot wax, and their colors ran / together until neither wretch nor monster / appeared what he had been when he began."[4] This state of being half-consumed by the opposite of what one knows or feels is responsible for some of the most vivid passages in Melville's work, and at times it seems like a necessary condition for his writing at all.

In a late poem entitled "After the Pleasure Party," Melville inveighs against Nature's division of humankind into two sexes: "Why hast thou made us but in halves — / Co-relatives? This makes us slaves. / If these co-relatives never meet / Selfhood itself seems incomplete. / And such the dicing of blind fate / Few matching halves here meet and mate."[5] In one obvious sense, Melville may be inveighing as well against a less-than-perfect domestic life, but this does not detract from the larger meaning of these lines, which is that the single or "complete" self is somehow lacking. Instead, the self that is most real, that lives most intensely, is the doubtful, active, and searching self, the disbelieving self that disbelieves its own disbelief, the atheist self that speaks of God.

It is little wonder that, in his final work, Melville sends Billy Budd to Heaven at the end of his story but cannot resist two addenda that falsify everything the reader has just read, a slanderous newspaper article and a sentimental poem. The reader of "Billy Budd" is thus given an ending that looks back in time to an era of relatively more widespread religious belief and then to two additional endings that look ahead to a science-influenced era of doubt and subjective interpretation. That Melville provides both endings and seems not to choose between them is, perhaps, the ultimate vindication of that search for self that made him more of a spokesman for his time than he himself knew, an advocate for doubt, for a rich, life-giving uncertainty. Melville's ideas are not easily mastered, but they are worth mastering, and his writings are a means to the end to which Ishmael pointed when he said, "Why then do you try to 'enlarge' your mind? Subtilize it."[6]

The final irony of Melville's life is that the doubt and uncertainty that troubled him so during the most active years of his writing career was confirmed by him in later life as the very source of his thought and art. The final tragedy of his life is that it took a generation for readers to realize the importance of his work. Following the publication of *Pierre,* one New York newspaper ran the headline, "HERMAN MELVILLE CRAZY."[7] In the present day, given the richness, subtlety, and balance of Melville's vision, one might say there were few as sane as he was and, given the challenges he faced, as brave.

Notes

Introduction

1. Matteo Guarnaccia, *Taipi* (Milan: Edizioni Ottaviano, 1978).
2. Amy Clampitt, *Westward* (New York: Knopf, 1990), p. 77.
3. These remarks are adapted from David Kirby, "Toys of Fortune: The Picaro in Fiction" (review of Richard Bjornson, *The Picaresque Hero in European Fiction* [Madison: University of Wisconsin, 1977]), *Yale Review,* 65 (1978), pp. 153–56.
4. Pierre-Yves Petillon, "Picaro en Démocratie," *Caliban,* 22 (1983), pp. 61–67; reprinted in *Esprit,* 120 (1986), pp. 71–76. According to Petillon, a genuine nostalgia for the picaresque is likely to manifest itself during periods of social history that are otherwise rather tightly buttoned; Petillon's example is the appearance of Kerouac's *On the Road* during the Eisenhower administration. However, the ambivalence toward the picaresque is expressed in such works as Bellow's *The Adventures of Augie March,* whose protagonist's name combines two warring elements: Augustus, the name of a Roman emperor and embodiment of classical stability and order, and March, a verb whose synonyms include such words as "tramp" and "hike."

Perhaps because the picaro is traditionally an Old World figure, there is comparatively little work on picaresque themes in United States literature in proportion to the number of picaros found therein. A good starting place is Ulrich Wicks, *Picaresque Narrative, Picaresque Fictions: A Theory and Research Guide* (New York: Greenwood, 1989), which studies picaresque fictions from the early Spanish novels through Woody Allen's film *Zelig* and includes a chapter on *The Confidence-Man.* Among studies with a narrower focus, Stanton Garner's "The Picaresque Career of Thomas Melvill, Junior," *Melville Society Extracts,* no. 60 (1984), pp. 1–10, and 62 (1985), pp. 1–10, is a close look at the influence of the charming, devious Melvill on his celebrated nephew. Raymond Hedin's "The American Slave Narrative: The Justification of the Picaro," *American Literature,* 53 (1982), pp. 630–45, describes the picaresque slave narrator in terms that are easily extended to include such Melville characters as Tommo, Typee, and White Jacket. And Patrick W. Shaw's "Huck's Children: The Contemporary American Picaro," *Mark Twain Journal,* 21 (1983), pp. 42–43, which includes novels by such authors as J. D. Salinger, Ralph Ellison, Saul Bellow, and Jack Kerouac, is a useful reminder of both the depth and the breadth of the picaresque tradition.

5. David Kirby, *Grace King* (Boston: Twayne, 1980); *Mark Strand and the Poet's Place in Contemporary Culture* (Columbia: University of Missouri Press, 1990); and *The Portrait of a Lady and The Turn of the Screw: Henry James and Melodrama* (London: Macmillan, 1991).

6. Isaiah Berlin, *The Hedgehog and The Fox: An Essay on Tolstoy's View of History* (New York: Simon & Schuster, 1953), p. 1. The distinction is based on a line among the fragments of the Greek poet Archilochus that says: "The fox knows many things, but the hedgehog knows one big thing." In Berlin's scheme, Dante would be a hedgehog and Shakespeare a fox.

7. John Updike, "Reflections: Melville's Withdrawal," *The New Yorker,* May 10, 1982, pp. 120–47.

8. Leon Howard, *Herman Melville* (Minneapolis: University of Minnesota Press, 1961); John Freeman, *Herman Melville* (London: Macmillan, 1926); Newton Arvin, *Herman Melville* (New York: Viking, 1957). Howard's short pamphlet on Melville is not to be confused with his magisterial *Herman Melville: A Biography* (Berkeley: University of California Press, 1951).

9. Tyrus Hillway, *Herman Melville,* rev. ed. (Boston: Twayne, 1979).

Chapter 1: The Life

1. Eleanor Melville Metcalf, *Herman Melville: Cycle and Epicycle* (Cambridge: Harvard University Press, 1953), p. xvi. Subsequent quotations will be followed within the text by page numbers in parentheses.

2. The facts of Melville's life are drawn largely from Leon Howard, *Herman Melville: A Biography* (Berkeley: University of California Press, 1951) and Edwin Haviland Miller, *Melville* (New York: George Braziller, 1975); subsequent quotations from these books will be followed within the text by page numbers in parentheses. Howard's account is avowedly objective; Miller's is a psychobiography that emphasizes Melville's attempts to replace his dead father. Miller's writing is therefore tendentious — a typical passage (on p. 199) reads, " 'Call me Ishmael!' can also be translated, 'Call me Allan Melvill's son' " — yet often more vivid and pictorial than Howard's, as in his account of the Hawthorne-Melville climbing expedition with which his biography begins. The interpretations of the facts reported by Howard and Miller, as well as those of such larger matters as the social milieu described above, are my own unless otherwise noted.

Other useful biographical volumes include Eleanor Melville Metcalf, *Herman Melville: Cycle and Epicycle* (Cambridge: Harvard University Press, 1953), and Jay Leyda, *The Melville Log: A Documentary Life of Herman Melville, 1819–1891,* 2 vols. (New York: Harcourt, Brace, 1951; rpt. with supplementary chapter, New York: Gordian Press, 1969). Students seeking succinct commentaries on Melville's life and art are advised to consult Hennig Cohen, "Herman Melville," *Antebellum Writers in New York and the South,* ed. Joel Myerson, vol. 3, *Dictionary of Literary Biography* (Detroit: Gale, 1979), 221–45 and Tyrus Hillway, *Herman Melville,* rev. ed. (Boston: Twayne, 1979).

3. "Historical Note," *The Piazza Tales and Other Prose Pieces, 1839–1860,* by Herman Melville, ed. Harrison Hayford et al., vol. 9 of *The Writings of Herman Melville: The Northwestern-Newberry Edition* (Evanston and Chicago: Northwestern University Press and the Newberry Library, 1987), p. 462. Subsequent quotations from this edition will be followed within the text by page numbers in parentheses.

4. Harrison Hayford et al., eds., *Moby-Dick; or, The Whale,* by Herman Melville, vol. 6 of *The Writings of Herman Melville: The Northwestern-Newberry Edition* (Evanston and Chicago: Northwestern University Press and the Newberry Library, 1988), p. 6. Subsequent quotations from this edition will be followed within the text by page numbers in parentheses.

5. Miller, p. 138.

6. Carolyn L. Karcher, *Shadow Over the Promised Land: Slavery, Race, and Violence in Melville's America* (Baton Rouge: Louisiana State University Press, 1980), p. 9.

7. Miller, p. 140.

8. These reviews are quoted in Howard, pp. 131–32.

9. *The Letters of Herman Melville,* ed. Merrell R. Davis and William H. Gilman (New Haven: Yale University Press, 1960), pp. 79, 77. Subsequent quotations from this edition will be followed within the text by page numbers in parentheses.

10. *Letters,* p. 86.

11. *Letters,* p. 93.

12. Howard, p. 141; Miller, 175–76.

13. Geoffrey O'Brien, "Now Voyager: Melville's Heavy Seas" (review-essay on *Journals* by Herman Melville, edited by Howard C. Horsford with Lynn Horth), *Voice Literary Supplement,* April 1990, p. 25.

14. For an excellent discussion of the composition of *Moby-Dick,* see James Barbour, " 'All My Books Are Botches': Melville's Struggle with *The Whale,* " in *Writing the American Classics,* edited by James Barbour and Tom Quirk (Chapel Hill: University of North Carolina Press, 1990), pp. 25–52.

15. Edwin Haviland Miller calls this essay "a love letter" to Hawthorne

(36) — a fair statement, though Miller finds in Melville's affection for Hawthorne a homoeroticism that seems to be defined by a very narrow conception of heterosexuality.

16. "Hawthorne and His Mosses, By a Virginian Spending July in Vermont," *The Piazza Tales,* pp. 244, 245, and 247.

17. Letter to her sister, Elizabeth Peabody, May 7, 1851, quoted in "Historical Note" to the Northwestern-Newberry Edition of *Moby-Dick,* p. 616.

18. Harrison Hayford, Hershel Parker, and G. Thomas Tanselle, "Historical Note" to the Northwestern-Newberry Edition of *Moby-Dick,* p. 617.

19. *Letters,* p. 146.

20. Howard, p. 200.

21. For a thorough and insightful discussion of the Agatha story, see R. Bruce Bickley, Jr., *The Method of Melville's Short Fiction* (Durham: Duke University Press, 1975), pp. 17–21, 115.

22. For more on this part of Melville's life, see the "Historical Note" to *Israel Potter: His Fifty Years of Exile,* by Herman Melville, ed. Harrison Hayford et al., vol. 8 of *The Writings of Herman Melville: The Northwestern-Newberry Edition* (Evanston and Chicago: Northwestern University Press and the Newberry Library, 1982), pp. 173–84.

23. "Hawthorne and His Mosses," pp. 247–48. R. Bruce Bickley, Jr., notes that Melville's story "The Happy Failure" ends with an inventor crying " 'Praise be to God for the failure!' " that has made him a finer man if not a successful scientist; Bickley also mentions other Melville stories in which failure is viewed positively (see *The Method of Melville's Short Fiction* [Durham: Duke University Press, 1975], pp. 123–24).

24. *The House of the Seven Gables* vol. 2, Centenary Edition of the Works of Nathaniel Hawthorne, ed. William Charvat, Roy Harvey Pearce, et al. (Columbus: Ohio State University Press, 1965), p. 1.

25. Nathaniel Hawthorne, *The English Notebooks* (New York: Modern Language Association, 1941), p. 432; quoted in Howard, p. 240.

26. Metcalf, p. 72.

27. Quoted in Miller, p. 294.

28. "Historical Note," *The Piazza Tales,* p. 530.

29. John Updike, "Reflections: Melville's Withdrawal," *The New Yorker,* May 10, 1982, p. 147.

30. Metcalf, p. 235.

31. Robert Penn Warren, ed., *Selected Poems of Herman Melville* (New York: Random House, 1970), p. 282.

32. Jay Leyda, *The Melville Log: A Documentary Life of Herman Melville 1819–1891,* vol. 1 (New York: Harcourt, Brace, 1951), p. 325.

33. Howard, p. 338. Howard notes that "although the mistake was rec-

ognized and everything except the initial 'H' was blurred, the proofreader seems to have been unable to recall his Christian name."

34. Letter, about June 1, 1851; quoted in Miller, p. 186.

Chapter 2: The Early Novels

1. In discussing these three novels, I will call the narrator "the narrator" because he is essentially the same person in all three books, which were meant to be sequential. He is sometimes "Tommo" here; "Typee" (as a result of his stay among the Typees) and then "Paul" in *Omoo;* and finally "Taji" in *Mardi.* But Melville is describing one man having three adventures.

2. Harrison Hayford et al., eds., *Typee: A Peep at Polynesian Life,* by Herman Melville, vol. 1 of *The Writings of Herman Melville: The Northwestern-Newberry Edition* (Evanston and Chicago: Northwestern University Press and the Newberry Library, 1968), p. 20. Subsequent quotations from this edition will be followed within the text by page numbers in parentheses.

3. In *Subversive Genealogy: The Politics and Art of Herman Melville* (New York: Knopf, 1983), one of the most thoroughly researched and stimulating of the New Historicist readings, Michael Paul Rogin observes that Melville's own name was changed for him when his mother added the "e" that would distinguish the surviving Melvilles from the ruined and recently deceased Allan Melvill; thus he joined the several other important nineteenth-century authors who took new names to assert their authorial identities: James *Fenimore* Cooper, *Henry* David Thoreau, Nathaniel Ha*w*thorne, *Margaret* Fuller, and *Mark Twain* (32; subsequent quotations will be followed within the text by page numbers in parentheses).

4. Harrison Hayford et al., eds., *Omoo: A Narrative of Adventures in the South Seas,* by Herman Melville, vol. 2 of *The Writings of Herman Melville: The Northwestern-Newberry Edition* (Evanston and Chicago: Northwestern University Press and the Newberry Library, 1968), pp. 5–6. Subsequent quotations from this edition will be followed within the text by page numbers in parentheses.

5. William Braswell, *Melville's Religious Thought: An Essay in Interpretation* (New York: Pageant, 1959), p. 8.

6. Harrison Hayford et al., eds., *Mardi and a Voyage Thither,* by Herman Melville, vol. 3 of *The Writings of Herman Melville: The Northwestern-Newberry Edition* (Evanston and Chicago: Northwestern University Press and the Newberry Library, 1970), p. xvii. Subsequent quotations from this edition will be followed within the text by page numbers in parentheses.

7. Charles Roberts Anderson, *Melville in the South Seas* (New York:

Columbia University Press, 1939), pp. 199, 343–44. Subsequent quotations will be followed within the text by page numbers in parentheses. Another worthwhile study of the so-called nonfiction narratives is John Samson, *White Lies: Melville's Narrative of Facts* (Ithaca: Cornell University Press, 1989).

8. Harrison Hayford et al., eds., *Redburn: His First Voyage, Being the Sailor-boy Confessions and Reminiscences of the Son-of-a-Gentleman, in the Merchant Service,* by Herman Melville, vol. 4 of *The Writings of Herman Melville: The Northwestern-Newberry Edition* (Evanston and Chicago: Northwestern University Press and the Newberry Library, 1969), p. 5. Subsequent quotations from this edition will be followed within the text by page numbers in parentheses.

9. Willard Thorp, "Historical Note," *White-Jacket; or, The World in a Man-of-War,* by Herman Melville, Harrison Hayford et al., eds., vol. 5 of *The Writings of Herman Melville: The Northwestern-Newberry Edition* (Evanston and Chicago: Northwestern University Press and the Newberry Library, 1970), p. 435. Subsequent quotations from this edition will be followed within the text by page numbers in parentheses.

Chapter 3: Moby-Dick

1. Harrison Hayford et al., eds., *Moby-Dick; or, The Whale,* by Herman Melville, vol. 6 of *The Writings of Herman Melville: The Northwestern-Newberry Edition* (Evanston and Chicago: Northwestern University Press and the Newberry Library, 1988), p. xix. Subsequent quotations from this edition will be followed within the text by page numbers in parentheses. In addition to this standard edition of Melville's text, readers will benefit considerably from the "Explanatory Notes" to the Hendricks House edition of *Moby-Dick* (New York, 1962) edited by Luther S. Mansfield and Howard P. Vincent, notes which explain in detail virtually every allusion in the text and thus, as the authors note, constitute "in some sense a biography of Melville's mind during the years of *Moby-Dick*'s composition" or at least "afford the interested critic a chance to study the borrowing techniques of a genius" (571).

2. *The English Notebooks* (New York: Modern Language Association, 1941), p. 432; quoted in Leon Howard, *Herman Melville: A Biography* (Berkeley: University of California Press, 1951), p. 240.

3. James Barbour, " 'All My Books Are Botches': Melville's Struggle with *The Whale,*" in *Writing the American Classics,* ed. James Barbour and Tom Quirk (Chapel Hill: University of North Carolina Press, 1990), pp. 31–32.

4. Edward Mendelson, "Rainbow Corner," *Times Literary Supplement* (London), June 13, 1975, p. 666.

5. *The Letters of Herman Melville,* ed. Merrell R. Davis and William H. Gilman (New Haven: Yale University Press, 1960), p. 79. Subsequent quotations from this edition will be followed within the text by page numbers in parentheses.

6. Vol. 1, *Collected Writings of Edgar Allan Poe,* ed. Burton Pollin (Boston: Twayne, 1981), p. 57.

7. *Melville* (New York: George Braziller, 1975), p. 51; subsequent quotations will be followed within the text by page numbers in parentheses. On pp. 71–72, Miller points out that Pierre's father dies when Pierre is twelve and that both White Jacket and Ginger Nut (of "Bartleby") are twelve-year-old outcasts.

8. For example, see Gregory H. Singleton, "Ishmael and the Covenant," *Discourse* (1969), 54–67.

9. Carolyn L. Karcher, *Shadow Over the Promised Land: Slavery, Race, and Violence in Melville's America* (Baton Rouge: Louisiana State University Press, 1980), p. 71. Subsequent quotations will be followed within the text by page numbers in parentheses. Karcher cites studies by Newton Arvin, Daniel G. Hoffman, Leslie Fiedler, and Edwin Haviland Miller that discuss homosexual overtones in this passage.

10. *Letters,* p. 127; quoted in Carolyn L. Karcher, *Shadow Over the Promised Land: Slavery, Race, and Violence in Melville's America* (Baton Rouge: Louisiana State University Press, 1980), 11.

11. Ronald T. Takaki, *Iron Cages: Race and Culture in Nineteenth-Century America* (New York: Knopf, 1979). In chapter 12 of this insightful study, Takaki effectively contrasts Whitman and Melville on the subject of cultural expansionism, noting that "while Whitman was America's critic of hope, Melville was the critic of despair" (281). Students of this theme will be interested as well in Wai-Chee Dimock, *Empire for Liberty: Melville and the Poetics of Individualism* (Princeton: Princeton University Press, 1989).

12. Doyle, Sir Arthur Conan, *The Complete Sherlock Holmes,* vol. 1 (Garden City: Doubleday, 1930), p. 7.

13. Bruno Bettelheim, *The Uses of Enchantment: The Meaning and Importance of Fairy Tales* (New York: Vintage, 1977), p. 10.

14. David S. Reynolds, *Beneath the American Renaissance: The Subversive Imagination in the Age of Emerson and Melville* (New York: Knopf, 1988), p. 184. Subsequent quotations will be followed within the text by page numbers in parentheses.

15. Barbour, p. 31.

Chapter 4: The Later Novels

1. *The Letters of Herman Melville,* ed. Merrell R. Davis and William H. Gilman (New Haven: Yale University Press, 1960), p. 143; quoted

in "Historical Note" to *Moby-Dick; or, The Whale,* by Herman Melville, Harrison Hayford et al., eds., vol. 6 of *The Writings of Herman Melville: The Northwestern-Newberry Edition* (Evanston and Chicago: Northwestern University Press and the Newberry Library, 1988), p. 633. Subsequent quotations from this edition will be followed within the text by page numbers in parentheses.

2. Letter to Sophia Hawthorne, in *Letters,* p. 146.

3. "Historical Note" to *Moby-Dick,* pp. 689–90.

4. *Democracy in America,* Phillips Bradley, ed., 2 vols. (New York, 1960 [1835, 1840], II, 77–78, 83; quoted in Michael Paul Rogin, *Subversive Genealogy: The Politics and Art of Herman Melville* (New York: Knopf, 1983), 15, 19; subsequent quotations will be followed within the text by page numbers in parentheses.

5. *Pierre; or, The Ambiguities,* by Herman Melville, Harrison Hayford et al., eds., vol. 7 of *The Writings of Herman Melville: The Northwestern-Newberry Edition* (Evanston and Chicago: Northwestern University Press and the Newberry Library, 1971), pp. 5, 16. Page numbers of subsequent references will be given in parentheses following quotations in the text.

6. Hershel Parker discusses Melville's treatment of actual *Moby-Dick* reviews in the text of *Pierre* in "Why *Pierre* Went Wrong," *Studies in the Novel,* 8 (1976), pp. 7–23.

7. Carolyn L. Karcher, *Shadow Over the Promised Land: Slavery, Race, and Violence in Melville's America* (Baton Rouge: Louisiana State University Press, 1980), p. 71. Subsequent quotations will be followed within the text by page numbers in parentheses.

8. *Letters,* pp. 127–28; quoted in Karcher, p. 19.

9. The "Historical Note" to the Northwestern-Newberry edition of *Israel Potter: His Fifty Years of Exile,* by Herman Melville, Harrison Hayford et al., eds., vol. 8 of *The Writings of Herman Melville: The Northwestern-Newberry Edition* (Evanston and Chicago: Northwestern University Press and the Newberry Library, 1982) deals with other sources used by Melville to enhance the original narrative.

10. The frontispiece is reproduced in *Israel Potter: His Fifty Years of Exile,* by Herman Melville, Harrison Hayford et al., eds., vol. 8 of *The Writings of Herman Melville: The Northwestern-Newberry Edition* (Evanston and Chicago: Northwestern University Press and the Newberry Library, 1982), p. 286. Subsequent quotations from *Israel Potter* will be from this edition and will be followed by page numbers within the text.

11. *White-Jacket; or, The World in a Man-of-War,* by Herman Melville, Harrison Hayford et al., eds., vol. 5 of *The Writings of Herman Melville: The Northwestern-Newberry Edition* (Evanston and Chicago: Northwestern University Press and the Newberry Library, 1970), p. 164.

12. Harrison Hayford et al., eds., *The Confidence-Man: His Masquer-*

ade, by Herman Melville, vol. 10 of *The Writings of Herman Melville: The Northwestern-Newberry Edition* (Evanston and Chicago: Northwestern University Press and the Newberry Library, 1984), p. 8. Subsequent quotations from this edition will be followed within the text by page numbers in parentheses.

13. Gary Lindberg, *The Confidence Man in American Literature* (New York: Oxford University Press, 1982), p. 39. Another excellent study of the same topic is William E. Lenz, *Fast Talk & Flush Times: The Confidence Man as a Literary Convention* (Columbia: University of Missouri Press, 1985). I am grateful to Professor Rip Lhamon for introducing me to these exemplary scholarly books.

14. For more on the novel's factual background, see Johannes D. Bergmann, "The Original Confidence Man," *American Quarterly,* 21 (1969), 560–77.

Chapter 5: Tales and Poems

1. The description is from an 1856 letter to Melville's father-in-law, Lemuel Shaw, in which the author rehearsed now-familiar financial woes; see Patricia Barber, "Two New Melville Letters," *American Literature,* 49 (1977), 418–21, quoted in *The Piazza Tales and Other Prose Pieces, 1839–1860,* by Herman Melville, Harrison Hayford et al., eds., vol. 9 of *The Writings of Herman Melville: The Northwestern-Newberry Edition* (Evanston and Chicago: Northwestern University Press and the Newberry Library, 1987), p. 497. Subsequent quotations from *The Piazza Tales* will be from this edition and will be followed by page numbers within the text.

2. R. Bruce Bickley, Jr., *The Method of Melville's Short Fiction* (Durham: Duke University Press, 1975), p. 125. Bickley also suggests that, as "a study of the artist's ironic quest for the fairyland of art and for the realms of truth, 'The Piazza' seems to represent Melville's whole career as a fiction-maker" (p. 126). Subsequent quotations from Bickley will be from this edition and will be followed within the text by page numbers in parentheses.

3. For Oriental perspectives on "Bartleby," see Saburo Yamaya, "The Stone Image of Melville's Pierre," *Studies in English Literature* (Tokyo), 34 (1957), 38–39, and H. Bruce Franklin, *The Wake of the Gods: Melville's Mythology* (Stanford University Press, 1963), 135ff. For socialist/Marxist readings, see Louis K. Barnett, see "Bartleby as Alienated Worker," *Studies in Short Fiction,* 11 (1974), 379–85, and Neil Ross, "Bartleby, Socialist Reformer," *Extracts: An Occasional Newsletter,* no. 35 (1978), 38–39. For a reading of "Bartleby" within the Western tradition of monism and quietism, see David Kirby, "Bartleby the Scrivener," in *The Sun Rises in*

the Evening: Monism and Quietism in Western Culture (Metuchen, NJ: Scarecrow Press, 1982), pp. 52–63.

4. For more on Thoreau's influence on Melville, see Egbert S. Oliver, "A Second Look at 'Bartleby'," College English, 6 (1945), 431–39; Robert E. Morsberger, " 'I Prefer Not to': Melville and the Theme of Withdrawal," University College Quarterly, 10 (1965), 24–29; and Frederick Busch, "Thoreau and Melville as Cellmates," Modern Fiction Studies, 23 (1977), 239–42.

5. The facts of the Colt-Adams case are set forth in T. H. Giddings, "Melville, the Colt-Adams Murder, and 'Bartleby,' " Studies in American Fiction, 2 (1974), 123–32.

6. The story of Benito Cereno is contained in chapter 18 of Amasa Delano's A Narrative of Voyages and Travels in the Northern and Southern Hemispheres (Boston: Printed by E. G. House, for the Author, 1817). This chapter is reproduced as an appendix in the Northwestern-Newberry edition of The Piazza Tales, pp. 809–47.

7. See p. 581 of the Northwestern-Newberry edition of The Piazza Tales for an unfavorable (yet ultimately yielding) attitude toward the deposition at Putnam's, the journal in which "Benito Cereno" first appeared.

8. Mark Twain, A Connecticut Yankee at King Arthur's Court, ed. Bernard L. Stein (Berkeley: University of California Press, 1984), p. 346.

9. Piazza Tales, p. 322.

10. See the notes on "The Lightning-Rod Man" in the Northwestern-Newberry edition of The Piazza Tales, pp. 597–600. Jay Leyda also proposes that the story is based on an encounter with a real lightning-rod salesman in Pittsfield, noting that, in the fall of 1853, "the Berkshires were enduring an intense lightning-rod sales campaign, with advertisements and warnings on the subject in all the Berkshire papers" (The Complete Stories of Herman Melville [New York: Random House, 1949], p. xxvi, quoted in R. Bruce Bickley, Jr., The Method of Melville's Short Fiction [Durham: Duke University Press, 1975], pp. 67–68.) Bickley notes that critics generally view "The Lightning-Rod Man" as religious allegory that focusses on the falsity of the salesman but then asks: " ...is the narrator's 'rod' any truer or more potent...? Always the skeptic, Melville seems to choose the middle ground between total capitulation to fear, on the one hand, and blithely serene confidence in the efficacy of God's plan, on the other. Working through the humor and repartee of the story, Melville as implied author meditates on the dangers of total commitment to the dark or to the bright" (p. 70). Once again the reader encounters the same Melville that Hawthorne met on the beach in England, the one who could "neither believe, nor be comfortable in his unbelief."

11. A full account of the composition of "The Encantadas" is found

in the notes to the Northwestern-Newberry edition of *The Piazza Tales,* pp. 600–617. R. Bruce Bickley, Jr., notes critics' disagreement over the success of "The Encantadas," with some finding the sketches thematically united and others finding them too casually linked to qualify as high art; Bickley finds that the major tension in the sketches is between the stark reality of the islands and their "baffling unreality and supernatural quality" (pp. 110–11).

12. Bickley, p. 96.

13. Paul Fussell, "Killing, in Verse and Prose," in *Thank God for the Atom Bomb and Other Essays* (New York: Summit, 1988), p. 128. A more sympathetic view is expressed in A. Robert Lee, " 'Eminently adapted for unpopularity'? Melville's Poetry," in *Nineteenth-Century American Poetry,* ed. A. Robert Lee (London: Vision, 1985), pp. 118–45 (the title is Melville's own description of his poetry in an 1884 letter to a British admirer). According to Lee, the poems in *Battle-Pieces* "rarely seek to resolve their typical inversions and oppositions; rather they calibrate and then hover over the knot of tensions which have been the war. The idiom can go wrong, to be sure, bordering at worst on doggerel and infelicities of word and rhyme. But, equally, it can triumph ... " (p. 132).

14. *Timoleon* includes "Monody," an elegy thought by many to be about Hawthorne. The most thorough examination of the "Monody" scholarship (and a model of its kind) is Harrison Hayford, *Melville's 'Monody': Really for Hawthorne?* (Evanston: Northwestern University Press, 1990).

15. Warren Rosenberg, *Melville Society Extracts,* no. 66 (1986), p. 6.

16. For a penetrating analysis of the *Somers* affair and its impact on Melville, see Michael Paul Rogin, *Subversive Genealogy: The Politics and Art of Herman Melville* (New York: Knopf, 1983), 6–7, 80, and 85.

17. Herman Melville, *Billy Budd, Sailor (An Inside Narrative),* ed. Harrison Hayford and Merton M. Sealts, Jr. (Chicago: University of Chicago Press, 1962), 1–3. Subsequent quotations will be from this edition and will be followed by page numbers within the text.

18. Hayford and Sealts point out that here Melville may have drawn on the case of one Samuel Jackson, an American sailor hanged in 1846 for striking an officer who had thrown his shoes overboard. Jackson's body, too, hung motionless, possibly because the sailor had been killed by the concussion of the signal gun that had been fired as he was run up (31).

19. Rogin, p. 296.

20. *The Letters of Herman Melville,* ed. Merrell R. Davis and William H. Gilman (New Haven: Yale University Press, 1960), p. 125.

Chapter 6: Conclusion

1. Stuart Culver, "Representing the Author: Henry James, Intellectual Property and the Work of Writing," in *Henry James: Fiction as History*, edited by Ian F. A. Bell (London: Vision, 1984).

2. *White-Jacket; or, The World in a Man-of-War*, by Herman Melville, Harrison Hayford et al., eds., vol. 5 of *The Writings of Herman Melville: The Northwestern-Newberry Edition* (Evanston and Chicago: Northwestern University Press and the Newberry Library, 1970), p. 164.

3. The Hawthorne quote is from *The English Notebooks* (New York: Modern Language Association, 1941), p. 432, and the *Pierre* quote from *Pierre; or, The Ambiguities*, Harrison Hayford et al., eds., vol. 7 of *The Writings of Herman Melville: The Northwestern-Newberry Edition* (Evanston and Chicago: Northwestern University Press and the Newberry Library, 1971), p. 284.

4. Dante Alighieri, *The Inferno*, translated by John Ciardi (New York: New American Library, 1954), p. 215.

5. *Selected Poems of Herman Melville: A Reader's Edition*, ed. Robert Penn Warren (New York: Random House, 1970), p. 330.

6. Harrison Hayford et al., eds., *Moby-Dick; or, The Whale*, by Herman Melville, vol. 6 of *The Writings of Herman Melville: The Northwestern-Newberry Edition* (Evanston and Chicago: Northwestern University Press and the Newberry Library, 1988), p. 331.

7. Quoted in Watson Branch et al., "Historical Note" to *The Confidence-Man: His Masquerade*, by Herman Melville, vol. 10 of *The Writings of Herman Melville: The Northwestern-Newberry Edition* (Evanston and Chicago: Northwestern University Press and the Newberry Library, 1984), p. 273.

Select Bibliography

This is the first general study of Melville based on the definitive, multivolume, and nearly complete Northwestern-Newberry Edition of Melville's works edited by Harrison Hayford et al. (Evanston and Chicago: Northwestern University Press and the Newberry Library, 1968–).

The two full-length modern biographies of Melville are Leon Howard, *Herman Melville: A Biography* (Berkeley: University of California Press, 1951) and Edwin Haviland Miller, *Melville* (New York: George Braziller, 1975).

The endnotes to each chapter give complete bibliographical information on the most helpful studies of Melville's works. I have found the following especially useful in illuminating the main concerns of this book, i.e., Melville's life, his writings, and the period in which he lived: Charles Roberts Anderson, *Melville in the South Seas* (New York: Columbia University Press, 1939); R. Bruce Bickley, Jr., *The Method of Melville's Short Fiction* (Durham: Duke University Press, 1975); William Braswell, *Melville's Religious Thought: An Essay in Interpretation* (New York: Pageant, 1959); Wai-Chee Dimock, *Empire for Liberty: Melville and the Poetics of Individualism* (Princeton: Princeton University Press, 1989); Tyrus Hillway, *Herman Melville*, rev. ed. (Boston: Twayne, 1979); Carolyn L. Karcher, *Shadow Over the Promised Land: Slavery, Race, and Violence in Melville's America* (Baton Rouge: Louisiana State University, 1980); William E. Lenz, *Fast Talk & Flush Times: The Confidence Man as a Literary Convention* (Columbia: University of Missouri Press, 1985); Gary Lindberg, *The Confidence Man in American Literature* (New York: Oxford University Press, 1982); David S. Reynolds, *Beneath the American Renaissance: The Subversive Imagination in the Age of Emerson and Melville* (New York: Knopf, 1988); Michael Paul Rogin, *Subversive Genealogy: The Politics and Art of*

Herman Melville (New York: Knopf, 1983); John Samson, *White Lies: Melville's Narrative of Facts* (Ithaca: Cornell University Press, 1989); and Ronald T. Takaki, *Iron Cages: Race and Culture in Nineteenth-Century America* (New York: Knopf, 1979).

Index